Jean-Luc Godard's
Hail Mary
WOMEN AND THE
SACRED IN FILM

Edited by Maryel Locke and Charles Warren

With a Foreword by Stanley Cavell

Southern Illinois University Press

Carbondale and Edwardsville

Library of Congress Cataloging-in-Publication Data

Jean-Luc Godard's Hail Mary : women and the sacred in film /
edited by Maryel Locke and Charles Warren ; with a foreword
by Stanley Cavell.
    p.   cm.
Includes a complete shot breakdown of Hail Mary and The
book of Mary by Anne-Marie Miéville, with the English subtitles and the French dialogue.
            Includes filmographies and index.
1. Je vous salue, Marie (Motion picture) 2. Livre de Marie (Motion picture) 3. Mary, Blessed Virgin, Saint, in motion pictures.
I. Locke, Maryel. II. Warren, Charles, 1948– . III. Godard, Jean
Luc, 1930– Je vous salue, Marie. English & French. 1993. IV.
Miéville, Anne-Marie. Livre de Marie. English & French. 1993.
PN1997.J36J4   1993
791.43′72—dc20   92-29569
ISBN 0-8093-1824-5. — ISBN 0-8093-1891-1 (pbk.)   CIP

Contents

Demonstrators protest the screening of *Hail Mary* at the New York Film Festival, Lincoln Center, New York, October, 1985. Courtesy of Richard Koch.

Cartoonist Paul Szep responds to local protests against the screening of *Hail Mary*, November 22, 1985. Reprinted courtesy of *Boston Globe*.

Jean-Luc Godard. Courtesy of *Film Comment*, published by the Film Society of Lincoln Center.

Anne-Marie Miéville. Courtesy of Maryel Locke.

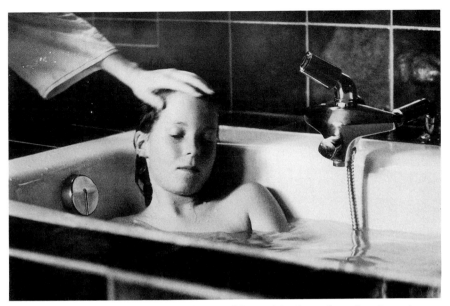

The Book of Mary, shot 51. "Dry your hair well," says Mary's mother after she and Mary have had a bath together. Photo courtesy of New Yorker Films.

The Book of Mary, shot 63. In a discussion of triangles, Mary states, "An angle's like this." Her father replies, "Like this, too." Photo courtesy of New Yorker Films.

The Book of Mary, shot 81. "You must have confidence," says Mary's mother when Mary collapses after dancing to Mahler's Ninth Symphony. Photo courtesy of New Yorker Films.

Hail Mary, shot 51. "What do you want?" Mary asks when Gabriel first visits her at her father's gas station. Photo courtesy of New Yorker Films.

Hail Mary, shot 70. "You should trust me," Mary pleads before Joseph angrily pins her down onto the hood of his taxi. Photo courtesy of New Yorker Films.

Hail Mary, shot 88. "Answer me! Look at me!" insists Joseph as he questions Mary about her future child. Photo courtesy of New Yorker Films.

Hail Mary, shot 150. After undressing completely, Mary puts on her nightgown. "Let the soul be body . . . ," she says. Photo courtesy of New Yorker Films.

Hail Mary, shot 283. "Where's my coffee!" demands Jesus at breakfast with Mary and Joseph. Photo courtesy of New Yorker Films.

Two Catholics protest the opening of *Hail Mary* at the Orson Welles Theater, an independent theater in Cambridge, Massachusetts, November 22, 1985. Boston's main film exhibitor refused to show the film. The Orson Welles Theater later was destroyed in a fire and never reopened. Courtesy of Stephen P. Berczuk.

View of the Orson Welles Theater's marquee announcing the opening of *Hail Mary,* Cambridge, Massachusetts, November 22, 1985. Courtesy of Stephen P. Berczuk.

Preface

THIS BOOK BEGAN at a two-day conference put together by Vlada Petric, curator of the Harvard Film Archive, and held at Harvard University's Carpenter Center for the Visual Arts in April 1987. The conference was an attempt to explore and understand the reason why Jean-Luc Godard's film *Hail Mary* had caught the attention and emotions of so many people on its release in 1985. Godard had made history by creating a film that outraged the Vatican, and protests and defenses of the right to show the film had greeted its exhibition in Europe and the United States. But *Hail Mary* and the film that always accompanies it, *The Book of Mary*, by Godard's colleague Anne-Marie Miéville, are works of art, and the conference was designed also to examine them as such.

We decided to put a book together on *Hail Mary* since Godard is an important figure in cinema whose late work has not been written about much outside France. Several participants in the conference agreed to write formal essays, and we asked a number of other people to contribute. Godard's own point of view is represented by two interviews he gave in 1985. In addition, to facilitate study and provide a record, we present a complete shot breakdown of both films with the English subtitles and the French dialogue.

We believe this book contains a rich spectrum of analysis and opinions. It is interesting to see what people in film studies (some of them filmmakers), philosophy, religious studies, and literary studies have to say about *Hail Mary* and *The Book of Mary*. Issues are raised about the nature of scandal, about women in film, about the nature of film itself, about the significance of the Virgin Mary in the modern world, and about the career and the thinking of Jean-Luc Godard as well as those of Anne-Marie Miéville.

Readers of this book will hear a variety of voices and see a variety of approaches. Some of our contributors sharply disagree with one another about interpretation and even about the value of the films. The areas of agreement are remarkable too, appearing as they do in the work of writers with such different perspectives. We hope readers, especially students of film, will regard this book as a case study, showing the diversity and the range of possibility that can come to life if we set out to think seriously about a film and its place in our world.

WE WANT TO THANK Vlada Petric for giving Maryel Locke the tapes of the conference with background material and suggestions to use as she wished. Charles Warren came on as coeditor a year later, replacing Geraldine Bard, who did not have the time to continue.

We appreciate the goodwill of all the authors who believed in our project and took time to write essays for us.

Inez Hedges, one of the first authors to give us a finished essay, is responsible for our obtaining the dialogue and subtitles from the two film-makers, who are not easy to reach. Inez suggested that we ask Caroline Eades, the *attachée culturelle* of the French consulate in Boston, to write to them: the result was a photocopy of her letter sent back with "OK, *gratuit*" and the signatures of Jean-Luc Godard and Anne-Marie Miéville, along with the French dialogue in the form of the "spotting list" or "réperage cinétitres." We thank Inez and Ms. Eades. Of course we are very grateful to Jean-Luc Godard and Anne-Marie Miéville for their cooperation.

Another of our authors, John Gianvito, must be thanked for taking on the additional task of preparing half of the shot breakdown as well as the filmographies and biographical sketches of Godard and Miéville.

Stanley Cavell was very encouraging about the project all along and has given us advice on many important matters. At the beginning, he expressed the desire to write a foreword, and we are grateful to him for carrying this out. William Rothman, a friend and film scholar at the University of Miami, read the manuscripts and provided invaluable advice on shaping the book. We also want to thank Marian Keane, of the University of Colorado, Boulder, and James Maraniss, of Amherst College, for their comments on the manuscripts.

Joanne Koch, executive director of the Film Society of Lincoln Center, allowed Maryel Locke to interview her on a busy afternoon and xeroxed or loaned vital material from her extensive file. Jay Carr, film critic for *The Boston Globe*, donated printouts of the articles he had written on *Hail Mary*. Pasquale G. Tatò began as our translator and ended as our adviser. Laura Bergamini-Loomis was a resourceful transcriber of our material to disks.

We must mention editors at our press: James Simmons, associate director and film editor, was a supportive and knowledgeable coach. Susan Wilson, managing editor, gave us guidance, and Carol Burns, project editor, patiently saw us through the editorial process.

Maryel Locke wants to thank her husband, Laurence Locke, for his continual support of this project. He spent many hours working with her on the shot breakdown, refusing a byline, and gave advice and help when asked.

Charles Warren wants to thank Katherine Kimball for her help and encouragement all through the working out of this book.

Foreword

Prénom: Marie

Stanley Cavell

> They say miracles are past; and we have our philosophi-
> cal persons to make modern and familiar, things super-
> natural and causeless. Hence is it that we make trifles
> of terrors, ensconcing ourselves into seeming knowl-
> edge when we should submit ourselves to an unknown
> fear.
> —Shakespeare, *All's Well That Ends Well*

AT THAT TIME I was glad for the invitation to prepare an introductory note for the volume Maryel Locke and Charles Warren were proposing to put together on Godard's *Hail Mary*, the idea of which, and now the materializa-tion of which, are both so excellent. But I can only use the occasion of its appearance to congratulate them publicly, together with their coauthors, on the condition that now, in a time not essentially different, however broken it seems, from that in which I agreed to write, I find something worth saying beyond the private salute. I will not date my search beyond noting that today is Friday. Let's see what the weekend brings.

Of course I am at once attracted to the idea of the ordinary, we may say the banal, as scandalous, hence to the fact that *Hail Mary*, in its ordinariness, its smallness, caused a version of the scandal it depicts. (I am thinking of the scandal as tripping up settled ideas of importance, hence of interest and of destruction. Christianity has been a way to this unsettling. Philosophy has had its ways, as in Wittgenstein's *Philosophical Investigations* [sec. 118]: "Where does our investigation get its importance from since it seems only to destroy everything interesting, that is, all that is great and important?") And I am of course attracted at the same time to the interpretation of Mary and of touching Joseph as simultaneously a story of psychic trauma and of skepticism.

I begin by recalling that at the late birth of film into the shared intellectual life, such as it was, of the American 1950s, and then into its unshared political life, such as it may have been, in the second half of the 1960s and the early 1970s, Godard, I suppose more than any other filmmaker, was throughout in attendance. How far from that time was the appearance of the dual films *Prénom: Carmen (First Name: Carmen)* and *Je vous salue, Marie (Hail Mary)* in, respectively, 1983 and 1984? If you were inclined to side with the earlier Godard's politics, so with his apparent enlisting of art in the service of politics, then you are apt to sense a falling off, or backing off, in the later work, and become disappointed or disaffected with its apparent avoidance or evasion of politics. If, contrariwise, you were inclined against Godard's earlier politics, and perhaps sensed his hatred of hateful, exploitative society as a cover for his spiritual coldness and isolation, then you are more apt to feel, and welcome, a redemptive move in the later work, a search for perspective on the individualities of his work that signals an affecting effort to take responsibility for it, for its irresponsibilities that are as necessitated artistically as they ever were politically. But in that case *Hail Mary* will have traveled the familiar route from a totalizing politics to a totalizing religion, and from an apparent quest for a transcendence of the self (if just from one circle or stance to the next) to a self-indulgent transcendentalizing (or philosophizing) of nature or retheologizing of science.

Suppose, though, that *Hail Mary* is not an evasion of politics but a critique of it, of what Godard had at some time named politics. (Can we bear to hear those words of Marx again?: "The critique of religion is the beginning of all critique." But shouldn't the ending, in principle, have been the critique of critique itself, of the claim to have found a position from which to measure the cost of accounting for the costs of other people's ideas, of all but your own? This ending is so easy to postpone.) And suppose that Godard's criticism of his irresponsibilities is a continuation of a mode of criticism there in his work from the beginning—since the later films are recognizably continuous with the earlier, bearing no different signature. Then from what perspective is such an effort at truth to be assessed? Does philosophy provide one?—call it thinking. (We were duly warned in *First Name: Carmen* that something basic, banal, is amiss with our registration of our experience into, for example, a division of politics and poetry. In that film, the line "Beauty is but the beginning of terror," remembered from the *Duino Elegies*, is dangerously tossed into a context invoking terrorism.)

If Godard is thinking, and his thinking is to provoke thought, then he must be thinking about film and about films; about, let's say, the conditions of their possibility. Wasn't he always? But in *Hail Mary* his thinking is not expressed by more or less routine showings of his hand, self-reflections on the fact of a film's making, of the sheer fact that what he has produced is a film. Because the question he is raising at that time is precisely whether this that appears is, or what it means to say that it is, a film—it is unlike other things so called. The question raises others—whether it is comprehensible that those responsible with him for it can want it, as it is; whether it is something to be proud or ashamed of, encouraged or disheartened by, an opening or a closing of further work, of others' work, scandalous or glib.

In this film Godard is thinking whether thinking, say spirit, is representable on film, and in which ways film represents body, say flesh. Is a quick young woman (with organized help, but against opposition), shooting the moon through a basketball hoop, thinking? Are a man called Gabriel and a young girl, having just landed on earth, stopping to retie a shoe using one hand offered by each of them, thinking—stopping to remind themselves, awkwardly—that "one mightier than I cometh, the lachet of whose shoes I am not worthy to unloose" (Luke 3.16)? When a woman asks a man called a professor what's on his mind and he answers, as the woman shows she knows, by quoting late Heidegger, and the man goes on to say, "I think politics today must be the voice of horror," is he in a state of physical revulsion? The woman, called Eva, probes the authenticity of the man's reaction by asking, "The voice, but the way or the word?" This echoes Mary's probing (or postponing) of the earlier, annunciatory "Follow Thy way" by asking, "My Way! But the voice or the word?" Does Eva's invocation of Mary's words receive them as underwriting her voice (as of all women), or as undermining Mary's? Leaving the question open, the man's revulsion from politics is hardly to be understood as an avoidance of it. It is much rather a claim that the victory (in fact and in theory) of what is at that time called politics over religion, over philosophy, over art, was (is) a voiding, unassessed, inexpressibly so, since it leaves nothing to assess itself with. Or does the matter reduce itself to showing that the exciting linking of politics to philosophy and horror was a matter of a sublimated turn of seduction, since the professor goes on to propose, and the woman concedes, that time and space have conjoined for them to expect the advent of sex?

If Godard is observing, in this man and woman, difficulties of thinking politically, the end of the film finds him observing in Gabriel and Mary difficulties of thinking religiously. Gabriel—which man not?—standing beside his car with something on his mind to say to a woman in the street, calls to her and then says, "Nothing. Hail Mary." But now, with her child taken over by the world, having nothing at this interval to do with her ("Jesus sayeth unto her, Woman, what have I to do with thee? mine hour is not yet come" [John 2.4]), she seems to take Gabriel's salute as a sublimated turn of seduction. Is it that she is free now to respond this way, hence free not to? Or is it that she is bound, if despite all she is responsive to a man, to make herself comprehensible to men, hence to renounce, or to rename, the man's way of comprehending her? Either way, her invitation of lipstick poses the question of who is called Gabriel, who assumes, or arrogates, the right to hail Mary, to voice an opening word.

In my imaginary of Godard as touchingly, awkwardly, addressing this question to himself, to his own right of hailing, I accept it as a turn I had missed in his work at that time, a couple of hundred full moons ago, when I wrote of him, with stuffy admiration: "I do not wish to deny Godard's inventiveness, and no one can ignore his facility. But the forms of culture he wishes to hold in contempt are no less inventive and facile. . . . An artist, because a human being, does have a position and does have his reasons for calling his events to our attention. What entitles him to our attention is precisely his responsibility to this condition. . . . One reads the distance from and between his characters [not, as has been claimed, as a Brechtian discovery but] as one does in reality, as the inability to feel; and we attribute our distance from the filmed events, because of their force upon us, to Godard's position toward them" (*The World Viewed*, pp. 99, 98, 97). Now I would like to imagine the maker of *Hail Mary* as genuinely surprised by the scandal his film occasioned, both because, as implied, the Christian project understands itself as scandalous beyond any further complications, and because Godard's film seems to me understandable as before all scandalous to himself: it would no doubt, if it could, constitute a stumbling block to all the dances of death, say to the world's inability to stop and think; but surely before that to his own terrible facility in explaining this inability.

Then what is called Joseph? When he says to Mary that he'll go jump in the lake, she instructs him that he is in effect calling himself by the wrong name: "Ophelia's no role for you." She would have learned this philosophy of naming—that we are called by the names we give ourselves—from Carmen, even Godard's Carmen, who had asked her own Joseph what comes before a name. He had given her the answer *"Prénom,"* what we call a Christian name, or now more usually I expect a given name; in any case, another name. This also smacks of theory, this time of names as radically arbitrary. (That on a certain picture of exiting there is no exit from the store of names does not mean that we have not had to break into the store. Hence perhaps the sense of ourselves as extraterrestrials. Since I and language precede one another, there is no beginning to us.) Carmen rejects this theory, demanding to be called on her own terms. To me this seems a welcome rejection of the current notion according to which (if I understand its implications) declaring one's subject-position is supposed to exhaust one's subjectivity.

How has Mary so called herself? Is she going on her willingness to trust—

and not to trust—her own innocence, to be possessed by no man but by an idea, say a word? Does she put before all her willingness to let something matter, to happen to her unforgettably? But these attributes resemble those Godard's Carmen assigns herself in taking Carmen on. They seem attributes of philosophy. Here the question whether Mary skirts skepticism may come to the fore. Unlike Kleist's Marquise of O—, Godard's Mary seems never to be driven in her unfathomable position to the shore of madness. Yet we see her thrashing on her bed, sheets twisted more or less around her, as if eventually and equally to swaddle or to shroud—as if soul should become body, or abandon body, hence yield the desire to know beyond itself. The Marquise of O— is drawn to madness by her questioning how this pregnancy has happened. Godard's Mary is kept sane by the acknowledgment that it has happened, while shaken by the question why something so disproportionate has happened to her. It may become anybody's question.

The idea of a body "having" a soul is apparently so banal from Mary's perspective that she turns the words into the question of a soul having a body. Her doctor is impatient with her for this confusion, even though he has just verified that she is bodily both virginal and pregnant, which could be explained as her being immersed in the spirit, a state describable not as a spirit possessing the body but perhaps as spirit enveloping the body, so in this way having it— whether as a plan has risks, or a person has premonitions, or as a pond has fish, or the hand has fingers, or as the mind has mountains. Perhaps what the obstetrician lacks is the concept of being born again. Death and departure are as different in the case of the soul as in the case of God. What prevents the announcing of the death of the soul? Or was this Nietzsche's question?

Isn't Mary serious in her speculations? Doesn't her life depend upon them? That Wittgenstein takes the idea of the soul as "having" a body to be philosophically arousing (*Investigations*, sec. 283) is encouraging but not decisive. The body's having a soul suggests that in the array of bodies we encounter, certain among them may not have souls, an idea of the presence of humanoids or other aliens of some other species, zombies, golems, automatons, an inhabitation of eternal death. We do not, not even a Mary among us at this time, I assume, have an analogous idea of our familiarity with an array of souls some of which are fated to be encountered in the presence of bodies. Accordingly, the idea of the soul having a body seems rather my idea of what makes my body mine, and of the change it will suffer at my death, should it survive me. Then, in a word, it would be I who have a soul—or not— something else besides an ego, so to speak. Then self-intimacy seems, paradoxically, to ease my imagination of others, to reach them without attempting to overcome their distance or separation from me—as if knowing others, what-ever men think, is not entering them but bearing them, bearing their annuncia-tions of us, so renunciations.

I used Mary's invocation of Shakespeare to justify my calling, in my epigraph, upon Shakeapeare's words on miracles—all but beaten into banality by fame—from another play of and about the mystery and magic and trick of marriage, and of the irony of human identity, especially of the identity of husbands and sons and kings, and of the defiling of a woman that is no defiling. We would ask, were there time at this time for philosophical patience, what idea of miracles Godard's Mary's Joseph has that backs him in claiming, "Miracles don't exist." To retrieve the picture would take the patience Kierke-gaard exercises, in his book on Adler, in claiming that the church has lost or forgotten the concept of revelation, so that it is religiously in the position, awkward for this church, of knowing that it necessarily cannot recognize anything that happens—however interesting or important or destructive—as a revelation. Yet in a time and place closer perhaps to Kierkegaard's than ours, Ibsen's *A Doll's House* calls marriage "the miracle of miracles," and its heroine's justification for walking away from her sacred duties as wife and mother depends on acknowledging that under that concept she has not been taken in marriage.

If we may still, barely, take Ibsen seriously on such a matter, with or against what grain can we take the moment in Cukor's smallish film *Adam's Rib* in which Eve, I mean Amanda, the wife-attorney (Katharine Hepburn), amazedly asks of a dainty hat given her by her husband-attorney (Spencer Tracy), "Isn't that a miracle?"? The seriousness or banality of that description (of the hat and of its gift) doesn't really come into question until the ending sequence, where the husband and the wife, about to disappear into bed, are both wearing hats, so that a miracle and the echo or contest of a miracle are associated with the possibility of marriage. If, further, we remember Freud's listing the hat, in his *Interpretation of Dreams*, typically a woman's hat, as a symbol for the male genitals, then we may pose for ourselves the following question about our experience of this pair's disappearance into their marriage: Do we experience their joining the struggle between the sexes as a contest over who wears the hat? Or do we instead understand them as joining to contest this concept of the struggle? The scandal in such a (Hollywood) film's accepting marriage as a struggle against so-called marriage took some four decades after the making of such films to recognize, and they still hardly constitute big news. That Godard's small, thoughtful film, with its plain events and its reconceptualizing, or say recalling, of a popular set of names, caused its scandal almost at once, as part of its reception, is, to my mind, glad news.

A parting memory. Of the pieces of Bach called upon for the sound in *Hail Mary*, the choice underscoring the early basketball sequence is the opening Prelude of the first volume of *The Well-Tempered Clavier*. It is—how may we forget it?—the piece appropriated by Gounod to which, on which, to set his *"Ave Maria."* Godard's charming identification here of his work with Gounod's asks us to think of the exploitation of Bach but also of the insight in Gounod's seeing that that piece of Bach's is interpretable as an accompaniment (an accompaniment to *that*, to hailing Mary, which Godard accepts as imperishable, but contests). And, I suppose, asks us to think further that these small insights may blur Bach's insight into smallness, or plainness—that this minimal figuration of C major in the opening Prelude is not fragmentary, not lacking; it is intact and open, virginal and pregnant. (Mary said, "Being a virgin should mean being available, or free. Not being hurt.") Blank of signature, and its dozen accidentals heard to be movingly necessary, the Prelude's indestructibility as a field for generations of child's play (each learning to position herself or himself at that initial, unprotected, middle C) confirms its right to continue into a pair of volumes whose demands and possibilities circle, and again circle, inexhaustibly, the universe of the major and minor keys. Men's insights seem in general not to contain such patience.

Jean-Luc Godard's
Hail Mary

1

A History of the Public Controversy

Maryel Locke

FROM TIME TO TIME, a work of art appears that upsets people. To vent their feelings, they try to ban or damage the work or attack the author. Jean-Luc Godard's film *Hail Mary* was for many people that kind of affront.

Godard was the first, and still is the only, director to base a film on the story of the Virgin Mary, her pregnancy, and her relationship to Joseph and her young child. To emphasize that he was concerned with the traditional Mary, Godard gave his film the title *"Je vous salue, Marie"* in quotation marks (not used afterward in publicity releases or reviews), referring to the famous prayer. As Godard said about the film, "Jesus has appeared often on the screen. But no one has told the story of Mary and Joseph."[1]

The reasons are easy to see. The Bible gives only a bare outline of Mary's life, with a few words spoken by Mary and little mention of Joseph. There is not enough material on which to base a dramatic feature film unless the basic story is embellished with additional fictional details. Therein lies the trap. Since Mary has been the focus of intense worship through the centuries, her followers are likely to be angry at any images and details that seem to detract from their perception of her as a holy person.

Godard decided to make a modern-day version of Mary's story, creating a real Mary in her surroundings. To frame the story with natural signs and symbols, Godard wanted to show certain unusual phenomena of earth, water, and sky. "I used 90,000 meters of film—usually enough for four films. I'm not a religious person, but I'm a faithful person. I believe in images. I have no children, only movies."[2] This attention to detail is impressive, since Godard made the film with his own money: it cost him $600,000, three times as much as he expected. "I had a lot of debts, so I stopped this film in the middle and made another, *Detective*, for money. Then I went back and finished editing *Hail Mary*."[3]

Despite his care in telling Mary's story tenderly, Godard nonetheless challenges the devout. Godard said at the time, "What I remember most from my religious childhood are the gymnastics and soccer games that we played every Sunday close by to the church."[4] Mary plays basketball at high school.

She has a boyfriend named Joseph with whom she refuses to make love, despite his pressure to do so. Gabriel, a ruffian, comes by airplane to tell her about her future. She sees the family doctor, who gives her a gynecological examination, finding that she is a virgin but is pregnant. She has a restless scene alone, naked, in her bedroom, wondering what is happening to her and why. She has a tempestuous scene with Joseph, who reluctantly pledges his loyalty. She uses four-letter words when angry. She gives birth (offscreen) to Jesus, who later is seen as a child naming his friends after the Apostles. In the final scene, Mary is seen in close-up smoking a cigarette and then putting on red lipstick—the last image in the film is her mouth in the shape of a giant O filling the screen.

Godard chose to require that *Hail Mary* always be screened with *The Book of Mary*, a shorter film directed by Anne-Marie Miéville, his companion and often his coworker. The Godard film follows the Miéville with no break, often confusing the first-time viewer. The two directors claim that their films were made separately with no attempt to coordinate, and the films do differ greatly in style and subject. *The Book of Mary* is the poignant story of an eleven-year-old girl named Mary whose parents are discussing separation at the beginning of the film; subsequent scenes show her attempts to avoid, and then come to grips with, her new world. The two films can be seen as connected in various ways, but it was *Hail Mary* alone which provoked the controversy that has made it infamous.

The words *JLG Films 1984* appear with the title of each film, but Gaumont, Inc., Godard's European distributor, states that the official release date was January 23, 1985. *Hail Mary* had some screenings in 1984, so that articles on the film appeared in French magazines and newspapers in late 1984 and early 1985, alerting the public.

Opponents prepared to do battle to protect the Virgin Mary. The first major attempt to suppress the film came in France from two organizations: the National Confederation of Catholic Family Relations and the Alliance against Racism and for the Respect of French and Christian Identity. They petitioned a Paris court to ban the film or to censor certain sequences. On January 28, 1985, M. Pierre Drey, presiding judge of the superior court in Paris, rejected the request for censorship after screening the film in the presence of the attorneys for the opposing sides. He decreed:

> Such a modernist update [of the mystery and of the dogma] made through images of full nudity and speech intentionally devoid of delicacy, apparently provokes opposing reactions and emotions in certain people, although not one scene can qualify the film as pornographic or even obscene. . . . They cannot hold as a grievance against the author,

the producer, and the distributor—barring any offensive publicity—their submission of their work to the criticism and the sanction of a viewer . . . who takes the initiative, by paying for the entrance-ticket, of engaging in a singular dialogue with said work.[5]

There were pickets at various theaters in France but no serious trouble: the film was shown. However, Godard had a difficult time at the Cannes Film Festival on May 10, 1985. A middle-aged man threw a cake topped with shaving cream in Godard's face. Godard's film *Detective* was booed at a crowded press screening. And on the same day, his Italian distributor refused his request to withdraw the theater screening of *Hail Mary* in Rome, a request he had made in response to Vatican reaction to the film.[6]

Other European responses to *Hail Mary* began in a positive way with the Catholic Cinema Office awarding a prize to the film at the Berlin Film Festival. The film was well received in Krakow, Poland. However, in Fulda, West Germany, the film was withdrawn when twenty people protested. In Athens, Greek Orthodox demonstrators forced cancellation of the film in one theater.[7]

On June 19 in Madrid, the day that *Hail Mary* opened in only one theater, at least four hundred people demonstrated in front of another theater where Godard's *Alphaville* was playing, requiring thirty policemen to maintain order. On June 22, Monsignor Angel Suquia invited believers of the diocese of Madrid to organize acts of prayer and reflection in atonement to the Virgin. Spanish resistance seems to have ended peacefully.[8]

The film aroused the greatest opposition and excitement in Italy, with action centered in Rome and the Vatican. Italy was within three weeks of local and regional elections, and feelings ran high. Before its opening, a screening of the original French version of *Hail Mary* (not dubbed into Italian, as is customary in Italy) was held on April 14 for invited guests and the public, sponsored by the Italian Association of Friends of Experimental Film. A professor introduced the film, pointing out its positive themes.[9]

The film was scheduled to open on April 16, but a crowd led by priests and nuns, carrying a statue of the Virgin Mary, gathered in front of the theater and forced postponement; the theater manager decided to have the Italian secretary of entertainment personally sign the screening permit. The film finally opened in its Italian version on April 17 to commotion and the need for police. On April 18, about thirty young people armed with clubs and antipornography posters burst into the theater and beat up the manager. After that, at least two policemen were on duty every day at the theater.

Major Catholic groups sent a message to the deputy cardinal of the diocese of Rome asking for prayers of atonement and to the mayor of Rome asking for "positive action protecting cultural identity" since Rome is the

"Center of Christianity where all religious faith expects respect." On April 20, the Ardent Marial Youth and World Fatima Movement announced a prayer meeting for atonement to be held on April 23 in the Basilica of St. John Lateran. The Vatican showed its solidarity with the prayer meeting through the following message from Pope John Paul II:

> The Sovereign Pontiff joins in the unanimous tribulation of the faithful of the Diocese of Rome concerning the programming of a film that insults and deforms the fundamental tenets of Christian faith, and desecrates the spiritual significance and historic value, and deeply injures the religious feeling of believers and the respect for the sacred and the Virgin Mary, venerated with so much love by Catholics and so dear to Christians. . . . [Through] the spiritual presence with those who assemble for reflection and prayer taking place in the Basilica of Saint John Lateran as a gesture of community atonement towards the Holy Virgin, the Holy Father invokes her maternal mercy for the Church and the world, and bestows his Apostolic Benediction upon the participants of the propitiatory celebration.[10]

The pope's message appeared on the front page of *L'Osservatore Romano*, the official Vatican newspaper, along with a three-column article entitled "The Inviolable Supremacy of That Which Is Sacred," which said:

> It's about the Virgin Mary. Even during a period of secularization, the fatuousness, nudity, and eccentricity of certain sequences desecrate a very high reality of which Godard has understood nothing. . . . Her [the real Mary's] response to the Archangel . . . is not the casual unthought-out reaction of a young woman lacking culture and awareness. . . . It is the response of a pre-destined soul who is prepared and who, in the deepest recesses of her Virginal being, is constantly in touch with God and fully ready for this spiritual offering. . . . It is stupifying that the unthinkable sacrilege of daring to portray . . . [Mary] stark naked and conversing with Joseph . . . could attract support, even if those who do so add that the film is debatable, abstruse and unsettling.[11]

The pope made a second public gesture against the film. On May 2, the Vatican newspaper announced that on May 4 the pope would lead special prayers at his monthly public prayer session, which would be broadcast worldwide. The subject: "to repair the insult" to the Virgin Mary caused by *Hail Mary*.[12] On May 4, under heavy police surveillance, a large number of people, mostly priests and nuns and tourists, gathered in the Vatican courtyard; the count varied from one thousand to four thousand, depending on the newspaper. An illuminated tapestry of the Virgin and Child hung from the balcony where the pope delivered his message and received applause afterward.

This apparently was the first time that a pope had publicly opposed a film, an important acknowledgment of the power of cinema. The manager of the theater screening *Hail Mary* said, "It's the first time that the church has come down so heavily on a film here."[13] Meanwhile, the Vatican newspaper continued to run articles against the film.

The Vatican's campaign against *Hail Mary* was received with mixed feelings in Italy. Press coverage of the prayer sessions was rarely sympathetic and often critical. There was marked opposition to any form of censorship, and there were attempts to look at the film from different perspectives. Alberto Moravia, writer, said, "It's a beautiful film." Sergio Saviane, writer, said, "It's a hyper-Catholic film! I never would have expected this from Godard. . . . It's full of infinite love and gentleness. There's not a stitch of obscenity or blasphemy in it." Agosto Creggi, Christian Democrat delegate noted for his campaign against divorce, said, "The film is worthless and has nothing to say. It's not even blasphemous or obscene. . . . All those people, those priests who demonstrated against the film, should have seen it first. Then they wouldn't have attracted so much attention to it."[14] When a judge in Rimini, Federico Fellini's hometown, ordered the film confiscated temporarily, thirty leaders of the Italian film world signed a petition defending the film's "right to exist and circulate and the right of the public to choose whether to see it or not."[15]

From the time that the film opened in Italy, Godard was besieged by journalists phoning him for interviews at his home in Switzerland. He defended his film, but he also at times tried to tone down its religious aspect. Occasionally he even denied it was about the Virgin Mary, claiming, "It's about a woman named Mary who . . . finds herself part of an exceptional event that she never would have wished for herself."[16]

In deference to the pope, Godard asked his Italian distributor to cancel screenings in Rome. On May 9, Godard sent a letter to a Catholic official; the letter was made public on May 14. His letter deserves to be read in its entirety:

JLG FILMS Neuilly, France

May 9, 1985
Reverend Father di Falco
Sir,
    We have learned through the press, undoubtedly with some inaccuracies, that the opening of our film *The Book of Mary—Hail Mary* at a movie theatre in the Eternal City provoked a strong response in the Vatican community, and that the Holy Father Himself had expressed this blind suffering through gestures of prayer.
    It is our wish, given the generosity of your reception of the film when it was distributed in France, that you have the following message deliv-

ered immediately to the Holy See, along with a copy of the telex sent
this day to the Italian distributor.

The message is as follows:

> "We think that human nature is riddled with so many flaws that it is able
> to resist the strongest interventions of mercy, and this is, most often, the
> case.
>
> "Christ never said the Church would function without sin, or even in an
> intelligent manner, but only that it would not err in its teaching within
> the realm of faith, when it would succeed in expressing itself fully
> through the instrument of the Pope's voice.
>
> "This voice has spoken out a second time about the central subject matter
> of the film and that, neither the producers, the distributors, or the shouts
> of the critics, had made known.
>
> "It was the voice of John Paul II that first spoke out, at the Piazza San
> Pietro, on December 12, 1980. The text of this was published by Paoline
> Publications in the collection, *'Teologia del corpo'* ('Theology of the Body'),
> under the title: *'La pienezza dell'eros nella spontaneità dell'amore umano'*
> ('The Plenitude of Eros in the Spontaneity of Human Love').
>
> "It thus so happens that the Holy Father was one of the screenwriters of
> this film and for us it seems just that he be able to express his pain, de-
> spite the weighty politics involved, concerning this sincere but imperfect
> film."

It was reading passages from Saint Paul ("the plenitude of the image will
be achieved through the Resurrection") and the Catholic writer Flannery
O'Connor that brought us to ask you to transmit this message. At the
same time, we are asking the Italian distributor, although we exercise no
temporal powers over him, to stop the film screenings in and around the
house of the Holy Father.

With respect and friendship,

Jean-Luc Godard[17]

The Vatican did not acknowledge Godard's letter.

Meanwhile, Godard told his Italian distributor that he thought they
would come out of the Italian debacle well once the figures were in and
offered him one of his future films free of charge if the distributor required
reimbursement. Although ultimate control was with Gaumont, Godard's
European distributor, it was announced in late May that screenings of the
film in Rome would stop on June 2.

There were incidents in the rest of Italy. Judges in two towns banned the
film but were forced to reinstate it. The film was discontinued in another
town because of protests. Protestors vandalized the theater where the film
was playing in Turin. In Milan, the cardinal kept his congregation calm by
giving lectures on Mary to large groups of young people and did not attack
the film. In July, the public prosecutor in Bologna tried to ban the film. The
case, similar to one in Lecce, was dismissed by the court with a statement
finding that the film was not obscene and not offensive to religion.

Hail Mary first appeared in the United States at the twenty-third New York Film Festival on October 7, 1985. For weeks before it was shown, there was opposition to the film. However, no attempt was made to seek a court order to ban the film because there was a strong precedent from a prior situation. An Italian film, *The Miracle* (1948), directed by Roberto Rossellini, featuring Anna Magnani and Federico Fellini, told the story of a simple-minded peasant girl who meets a shepherd she thinks is an angel; she conceives and bears a child who she believes is divinely fathered. The New York censorship board ruled the film sacrilegious, but a 1952 appeal overturned the ruling. The U.S. Supreme Court, in *Burstyn v. Wilson*, 343 U.S. 495, stated for the first time that films are "a significant medium for the communication of ideas" warranting First Amendment protection. However, the Court set no guidelines for review boards, and prerelease censorship in the form of licensing of films continued in many states.[18]

According to Joanne Koch, executive director of the Film Society of Lincoln Center, which presents the New York Film Festival, protesters phoned Lincoln Center steadily about *Hail Mary*, tying up telephone lines and interrupting office business for weeks. The society also received hundreds of letters, many with the same message. John Cardinal O'Connor denounced the film from the pulpit of St. Patrick's Cathedral on October 6, 1985, and in a TV interview, calling it "tragic" that any filmmaker would portray Mary as Godard did in *Hail Mary*. He categorized Godard's film as "an act of contempt for our sacred beliefs." He warned that the church would support only peaceful demonstrations, marked by "hatred toward none, only sadness."[19] Mrs. Koch stated the Film Society's viewpoint in a TV interview: "The film is not anti-Catholic. . . . We've hit a taboo here. . . . We don't mean to offend—certainly that was not our intent—but we feel strongly that art has to be respected as art."[20]

On October 7, when *Hail Mary* was first screened at the festival, five thousand demonstrators protested, some wearing blue armbands and carrying blue candles, blue being the color associated with the Virgin Mary. Holy water was sprinkled and rosaries recited. A group of thirty-two seminarians from St. Thomas Aquinas Seminary in Richfield, Connecticut, brought a statue of the Virgin and set up a shrine. The seminary's rector said, "When the bombs fall on Manhattan, one will especially fall on the cinema where this film is being shown. . . . God does not allow His Mother to be insulted with impunity."[21] Ticket holders had to make their way through the mob, who shouted, "Shame." Fewer than one thousand demonstrators appeared for the second night's screening. "Defenders of the film kept observing . . . that like the Pope most of the protesters had not seen *Hail Mary*."[22]

Godard appeared at the festival's press screening and at the press conference about his film, but he did not stay for the public festival screening where
the filmmaker is introduced and honored. When Mrs. Koch pleaded with him
to stay, since the Film Society had stood behind him, he said, "It's only a
movie." She wondered if he had been urged to leave for safety's sake—or
threatened.[23]

It was difficult to get a U.S. distributor for *Hail Mary*. Triumph, a
coventure of Columbia Pictures and Gaumont (Godard's European distributor), was originally to be the distributor. However, according to the executive
director of the greater New York chapter of the Catholic League for Religious
and Civil Rights, members of his group made "lots of calls" protesting the
film to Columbia Pictures executives. Triumph pulled out in late August,
and distribution was taken over by New Yorker Films in conjunction with
Gaumont.[24] As of late 1991, a representative of New Yorker Films stated that
its files contained hundreds of protest letters about *Hail Mary*, "all of them
sounding exactly alike."[25]

After the festival screening on October 7 and 8, the film opened at a New
York theater without incident. It also opened at other theaters throughout
the United States, with some minor protests or demonstrations, or a change
of theater in some cities. *Hail Mary* had run the gauntlet and come out alive.
The film can still be rented or bought at video stores throughout the United
States.

A last gasp of opposition appeared four years later when the film was
shown at Lincoln Center by the Film Society on August 25, 1989. One hundred
pickets from a religious sect in Bayside, Long Island, gave the film one more
protest.[26]

Time magazine ran a cover story on Mary on December 30, 1991. The
picture on the cover was the face of a beautiful contemplative young woman,
Raphael's *Madonna del Granduca,* with the words "The Search for Mary: Was
the most revered woman in history God's handmaid—or the first feminist?"
Inside, the title of the article was "Handmaid or Feminist?" followed by the
subtitle "More and more people around the world are worshipping Mary—
and it's led to a holy struggle over what she really stands for."[27] Once again
it turns out that Godard was a leader on a major subject of our time.

Notes

1. Maria Pia Fusco, interview, *La Repubblica* (Rome), April 25, 1985; "Rome and
Godard, April 14–June 2, 1985: A Chronology," New Yorker Films, Fall 1985, 8 (press
materials).

2. Jay Carr, "A Muted Godard Awaits US Bow of 'Hail Mary,'" *Boston Globe*, October 7, 1985, 28. For details about Godard's images in *Hail Mary*, see "Godard in His 'Fifth Period,'" an interview by Katherine Dieckmann, reprinted in this volume.

3. Carr, "Controversy Follows Wherever Film Goes," *Boston Globe*, November 17, 1985, A8. Both of Carr's articles use material from a private interview with Godard.

4. Fusco, interview.

5. Claude Baignères, "Godard: l'absolution," trans. Pasquale G. Tatò, *Le Figaro* (Paris), January 29, 1985, 28N.

6. Aljean Harmetz, "Godard Has a Bad Day in Cannes," *New York Times*, May 11, 1985, 13.

7. "Europe and Godard," New Yorker Films, Fall 1985, 2 (press materials).

8. "Rome and Godard," 14.

9. "Rome and Godard," 1. All historical facts about *Hail Mary* in Italy not attributed to other sources are from this document.

10. *L'Osservatore Romano* (Rome), April 30, 1985, 1; "Rome and Godard," 5.

11. Raimondo Manzini, "The Inviolable Supremacy of That Which Is Sacred," *L'Osservatore Romano* (Rome), April 30, 1985, 1; "Rome and Godard," 5.

12. "Pope to Lead Prayers over 'Insult' to St. Mary," *New York Times*, May 4, 1985, 16.

13. Carin Romano, "Italy's 'Hail Mary' Headaches: Even the Ticket Sellers Suffered," *Philadelphia Inquirer*, June 16, 1985, 3-G.

14. "Rome and Godard," 2–3.

15. E. J. Dionne, Jr., "And [Godard] Tries to Withdraw 'Hail Mary' in Italy," *New York Times*, May 11, 1985, 13. See note 6.

16. Giuseppina Marin, interview, *Corriere della Sera* (Milan), April 25, 1985; "Rome and Godard," 6–7.

17. "Rome and Godard," 11–12.

18. Wayne Overbeck and Rick D. Pullen, *Major Principles of Media Law* (New York: Harcourt Brace Jovanovich, 1991), 303.

19. Linda Stevens, "O'Connor Launches Attack on Virgin Mary Movie," *New York Post*, October 7, 1985, 3.

20. Videotape of TV interview with Joanne Koch, n.d.

21. Linda Stevens and Fredric Dicker, "4000 Catholics Protest 'Hail Mary' Film," *New York Post*, October 8, 1985, 5.

22. Richard Schickel, "Crying 'Shame' at Lincoln Center," *Time*, October 21, 1985, 81.

23. Joanne Koch, interview by Maryel Locke about reception of film, February 23, 1989.

24. "Gaumont, New Yorker Will Distribute 'Mary' Jointly in the States," *Variety* (New York), September 25, 1985, 5.

25. Audrey Mahler, advertising director, New Yorker Films, conversation with Maryel Locke, October 10, 1991.

26. Richard Peña, program director, Film Society of Lincoln Center, conversation with Maryel Locke, March 16, 1990.

27. Richard N. Ostling, "Handmaid or Feminist," *Time*, December 30, 1991, 62.

2

Whim, God, and the Screen

Charles Warren

GODARD'S *Hail Mary* is a modern story whose characters do not speak of the Bible or the resemblance of their lives to biblical events. Yet the film is about a virgin named Mary who becomes pregnant while remaining a virgin, gives birth to a child, and feels that God is involved in all this. She has problems with her fiancé, Joseph, who eventually marries her. And a character named Gabriel intervenes in their lives, rather bullyingly, to give advice and explanations. Do we have here a presentation in a modern setting of the early phase of the life of Christ? Or is the film a presentation of something else— just a modern story? modern ideas?—using the life of Christ and Mary as a means to its own end?

But what would be the difference? We do not know, do we, exactly what the life of Christ is. A mysterious fact to be faced? Something we have made up (even if inspired by God) that serves as a metaphor for our life, a way of interpreting human life? A way for us to make ourselves change? Godard's film asks us to ponder just what the life of Christ is and what ours is in relation to that.

The film does its work in part by getting us to ponder what is at stake in the act of telling the tale. *Hail Mary* quotes versions of the life of Christ (the Gospels, Bach's *St. Matthew Passion*) and suggests comparisons to others. Godard seems to want to join the rank of tellers of the tale or to supersede them. At any rate he gets us to think: what has the telling of this tale, the occasion and the form or manner that is found to tell the tale, got to reveal of what Christ's life, and ours, is?

Whim is a force commonly felt by tellers of the tale, a force Godard feels and does something with in his own way. Our attitude to these events must be such, it seems, that we feel we half create them. There is the sense that anything might happen, and all will be well. We feel that to yield to the play of these things, coming from within us or from without as it may be, is to realize a deep necessity, a very principle of life—rather in the way specified in the Upanishads, or in Emerson. The speaker in T. S. Eliot's "Journey of the Magi" is at first down to earth, complaining of the camels, the cold, the unfriendly people and high prices on the journey. But he is open to the mood of

> a water-mill beating the darkness,
> And three trees on the low sky,
> And an old white horse galloped away in the meadow.

The man comes at last to witness a birth that is "like Death," and he is left both uneasy and glad.

Hail Mary is a notably whimsical film. And first in a way that is like other Godard films: there is a seeming arbitrariness about images and sounds. Is this film asking us to conclude that the general style of a Godard film is finally specially suited to tell the life of Christ? In Godard we constantly experience shocks, as our attention to the unfolding narrative—to *some* unfolding narrative, so it seems—is interrupted to have us look at a new, at first sight incongruous, image or to have us take in someone's words from outside the present scene or a strange sound or bit of music. Each of these items seems to offer a comment on what has been going on in the film, as if from a heightened, not to say nervous, consciousness on the part of the filmmaker—and from no clearly fixed or summarizable point of view. Is the new item a comment, or an extension of narrative in some sense? Of course, with Godard's best work—perhaps with all of it—the more we attend, or re-view, the more right seems each of the surprising gestures. We think about meaning, and we adjust in ways that are beyond, or below, such thinking, reconciling ourselves to all the facts of the film. Whim seems to prove "more than whim at last" (Emerson).

Now Godard was first a critic and appreciator of film and then a maker of films, as if making the kind of film he already admired or allowing something he had seen in earlier film to come to the fore and be obvious in his own work. This is so for all his revisionism and contentiousness. After Godard, a great deal of film—Hollywood film, Renoir, and other work—looks more like Godard than it did before. There is much of the surprising and thought-provoking and difficult to rationalize in the earlier work if only we will see it. Is film virtually of its nature whim that is more than whim? Is film of its nature suited to deal with the coming of God into life?

Hail Mary is particularly whimsical in eliciting something like the Annunciation and Christmas story from the lives of *these* people, driving their cars around a clean, electrified city; working in a gas station; playing basketball in a spiffy gymnasium. The people seem very much a part of the modern surfaces and ambiences. The lead couple are the familiar Godard sulking adolescents—self-absorbed, fighting over sex and commitment. The film seems just to *declare* that its characters are Mary, Joseph, and Gabriel. And the later part of the film, when the child is born, with shots of blossoming branches and beasts ogling the camera, seems a joke in a way, a ritual going through the steps of the Christmas scenario. There is a willful turn to lightheartedness. The film's early use of Bach on the sound track, which has given way to an obsession through the middle portion with the Dvořák Cello Concerto—a whimsical turn in itself—now comes home with "Jesu, Joy of Man's Desiring" in a piano version.

But Christmas is like this. The most important Christian feast, inspired by the most astonishing of mysteries, Incarnation, has a way of going unaccountable and lighthearted. Romance, rather deliberate allegorization, humor, a certain excessiveness—such are the qualities of the Gospels' treatments, the late medieval *Second Shepherds' Play*, the things that people desire to do in ordinary life in the face of this inspiration.

Look at the *Second Shepherds' Play* for a moment. Mak and Gill, man and wife, are alive strictly speaking at the time of the birth of Christ. But they are clearly too in present-day (medieval) England, suffering its conditions and swearing by Christ and Mary. Like Godard's Mary and Joseph, Mak and Gill are a modern couple who do not compare themselves to the Bible but still reflect the coming of God into life in their ordinary/extraordinary everyday lives. Mak and Gill live a life of poverty and the tensions and antics of sheep stealing, getting a sheep as if getting a child, and expecting to be saved by it.

There is constantly music in the air, as in *Hail Mary*, as in so many films. Mak comes on stage expressing a lostness and freedom, a readiness for whim, we might say; and he is taken to be singing:

Mak:	. . . thy will, Lord, of me tharns; [is lacking]
	I am all uneven, that moves oft my harns . . . [brains]
Shepherd:	Who is that pipes so poor?
Mak:	. . . Lo, a man that walks on the moor,
	And has not all his will!

Rhyme and a musical mode, and humor where we can see it, seem to express a transcendence of what things would be without these qualities. The discovery of the sheep in the cradle is a joke, despite the deadly seriousness of the crime:

Shepherd:	Give me leave him to kiss, and lift up the clout.
	What the devil is this? He has a long snout.

Soon an angel is heard singing *"Gloria in excelsis!"* and the shepherds go to see the baby Jesus, mysteriously presenting him with a bunch of cherries, a bird, and a tennis ball. They finally depart the stage calling for song, and singing.

The parallel of Mak and Gill and their sheep to Joseph and Mary and Jesus, and the parallel of Godard's characters, are suggestions in the imitation-of-Christ way of thinking about life—our life is like that of Christ and those close to him. The parallel offers a solution, a way of comprehending what happens in life, and a problem, a challenge. How *can* human life be taken to parallel Christ's? What is at issue here? What ought one to do? The characters in a story may not think about this much, but the audience may go further. The *Second Shepherds' Play* (and how much of Christian art, how much of Christian philosophy?) seeks to reassess the life of Christ, to ask again what it is and what our life is. Any such work means to "supersede" Christian art and thinking as it stands, perhaps as much as Godard's film may be thought to intend to do.

But what is Godard doing? *Hail Mary* suggests right off, and continually throughout, that the lives of its characters are in the hands of something like God, a sublime force comprehending and ordering all of life. The parallel with the life of Christ suggests even more: fatedness, even constriction, to a certain pattern of life—including salvation, of course. But the film suggests too that the whole divine dimension to these lives is a matter of the way the characters live imaginatively toward one another. The film suggests this by identifying the characters, notably Joseph and Mary, over and over with the imaginative power that generates the film, these people's lives. Call this power the director, the power of film as it comes to be this film, life itself as it comes to be film.

THE FILM BEGINS with the title *EN CE TEMPS LA* (AT THAT TIME), white letters on a black ground. It is biblical, historical, romancelike, suggesting that we shall see a fable with resonating significance. Then there is a long-held shot—with the sound of thunder—of a luminously green field on a hillside in the rain, with trees and a margin of sky in the background, dense marsh grass or some such stuff (it is blurry) in the foreground, moved by wind. It is a very vivid shot; we are brought close into the natural world. Is it the moment of Creation, as *EN CE TEMPS LA* might suggest? Or is it nature standing opposed to the literariness, the art making, the idea, of the words in the title frame? Of course, it is not nature itself but a film shot, a wonder of the cameraman's art, and rather prettily composed, when we think about it, for all its immediacy. Here the world and film art are inextricably mixed up in each other.

The title of the film and the credit titles follow (white letters on black), with shots interspersed looking down on a water surface reflecting a fixed point of light—the sun? an artificial light? And this surface is broken continually by objects—perhaps rocks?—splashing into the water and making the light ripple all over the surface. Is it the primal action, getting the world into motion? With the first title a Bach sonata for cello and harpsichord begins, which plays throughout the sequence—I will come back to this. At the same time, we constantly hear the sound of the splashing in the water and the cries of birds. The water and bird cries seem to continue the creation theme, if that is what it was, from *EN CE TEMPS LA* and the shot of the field. We are taken further into the natural world. Perhaps *Hail Mary* will make a point about the primacy of nature, albeit a *created* nature, for any consideration of the events that happen in the film.

But the sight of water reflecting light cannot fail to suggest still more: film itself as a subject for this film. The surface is like a screen. Is the light a filmmaker's lamp? Who throws the objects into the water—a director?—making the light move on the surface, bringing the surface to life? (And here the idea of water as an imaginative medium or power reflects back to the rain seen watering the earth in the film's first shot.) This business is strangely like the opening of Sternberg's *Blonde Venus* (1932), with Marlene Dietrich—just the sort of rich and conscious-of-itself Hollywood film that inspired Godard in the 1950s to begin analyzing film and eventually to make films. *Blonde Venus* gives us at its opening a shot down on a water surface rippling with light; the main title and credits come, superimposed on the water surface, and then a woman emerges as if from behind the camera, swimming and churning this surface. She will be the chief actor in the film. *Blonde Venus* suggests throughout that the woman we see living her life is a woman giving us her story, creating it, as if she were the filmmaker making the film. *Hail Mary* in the opening sequence is just before getting to the woman, but the film reveals already that the created world—of nature, or of the film—and the story that will unfold are to be seen with an unusual consciousness as tied to the *art* of a film director—to the art of a person, or to the art of God, who is like a film director.

The Bach in this sequence might be taken as on the side of art. It is art. And Godard in using it may be declaring that he is shaping the natural world and the story that is to come. He freely chooses—imposes— the music and determines the mood of the sequence. But the music of Bach has such character that it cannot merely serve Godard in this way. It takes us to God, I would suggest. Bach's music evokes the harmony of the spheres: it is unremittingly contrapuntal; it never seems to need to stop. The music makes us think of mathematics: a grasp of the things of the universe in their essentials and essential relations, and as they may, on principle, be recombined. But Bach is unpredictable, even shocking, in his moves. And his work is a great dance, animated by very material rhythms from who knows where. Bach is thus in accord not so much with law as with an unaccountable, personlike spirit at the heart of things. The quantity of Bach's music, the speed with which it must have been written, suggests God working through the hand of a man. And the work is quintessentially sacred, even when it is secular (and Godard uses plenty of both kinds in *Hail Mary*). Sacred music before Bach is *of* the church; while impressive sacred music after Bach seems music addressing its own subjects with the forms of the church taken to give guidance, for an occasion (Mozart, Verdi, Berlioz). Bach points our minds to the sacred, as happens not quite with any other music, because of his moment (which is apparent *in* his music). He represents music coming to consciousness of itself, with a destiny to be followed out, while still proceeding from a function defined by something other than music. (Consider in regard to later sacred music R. P. Blackmur's discussion of the place of Chritianity in T. S. Eliot's poetry—the Christianity is distinct from the emotional subject matter of the poems and the very pressure to speak, though the Christianity is inextricable from the poems as they finally take shape; the poetry is thus Christian but not purely "devotional" in the traditional sense—where would Godard fit in here?).

All of this is not to say that Godard will simply play a passage of Bach and thereby give his story a dimension as if coming from God. Think of the human and highly expressionistic character Bach's music takes on in Pasolini's *Accattone* and *The Gospel According to Matthew*. Godard's gesture with Bach can actually throw the film to God because of the open, intellectually free way of proceeding of this film, its light/serious touch with its range of contents. Anything might happen and might come to any significance. It is a matter of style in the fullest sense of the word.

Finally about the credits sequence, the last shot of the water surface is reddish. Probably the light source is now red; perhaps the sun is setting. In any case, something happens. We are made aware that film registers events in the passage of time. What is red and liquid? Where do we go? The story of Christ comes to blood, and the meaning of the story, its redemptive force, is subsumed in our being offered blood to drink—we are to take something within us. Does such redemption amount, now, to our being offered Godard's red water surface, the screen, the film? (The very next scene will focus on eating and drinking.) Mary tells us in the film, when she "knows" she is pregnant, that nevertheless her period "came very intense" on Friday (the day of the week Christ bled and died). We are brought to Mary and to her motherhood, and strangely at the same time to her menstrual blood. The latter, because brought up unexpectedly, seems suddenly the most important thing about her. Mary's story, epitomized in her blood, is offered us to contemplate, to taste—so we might put it—as Christ's is, and as the screen is offered us to do whatever it is we do with the screen.

Now there is a café scene, virtually a parody of 1960s Godard. A woman's voice says, "Out of my mouth is shit." We are bound to wonder if this is Mary. We know Mary is our subject, and we shall wonder about her until we locate her. Because the camera is trained on the man (Joseph, as we learn later) eating and listening and the woman's voice is from someone outside the frame, except for her hands—her executive power—we might wonder if the woman is to be identified with the film director. "Out of my mouth" means what is said, what we have, this work. The film will end with the image of a woman's open mouth—black depths within—and the final, "reconciliation" chorus of Bach's *St. Matthew Passion* pouring from the sound track, the image and the music seeming to subsume all of the film, Mary delivering God. "Shit" sounds disappointing. The woman in the present scene cannot get the man to be involved with her, to respond. But shit is also fructifying. Excrement nourishes the earth. Menstrual blood is excrement. Any blood, once it is bled, or as it is being bled, is excrement. Speech, writing, art, are all in a sense excrement.

With a cut to a view of the woman, the rattling of crockery and Godard's other café sounds give way to the opening flourish of Bach's dramatic organ Toccata in D Minor. It is the dimension of God again, but the music fits the temperament of the scorned woman angrily trying to assert herself. And this music, of all the Bach, seems to foreshadow and justify, to give birth to, in a sense, the Dvořák Cello Concerto, romantic and stormy, used so much in later scenes. The gripping solo cello entry of that piece comes with a look into Mary's face when Gabriel and the child angel discover her in the gas station, her home (where "excrement" is purveyed to keep the world running).

In sum, the woman in the café scene is identified with the director by her position outside the frame as she speaks; with God, by the music; and with Mary, by our wondering and a sort of in-advance music symbolism (organ toccata/Dvořák). Indeed, a number of women in the film are identified with Mary until a woman thanks Mary "on behalf of all women" in a scene after the birth of the child. The question of the film-author and God merges into the question of Mary and woman in general.

In the café scene, the unsatisfactory conversation brings Joseph to comment, "Men think they enter a woman," and there is a cut to the next scene,

are still with Eva, makes the airplane scene seem projected by Eva and the classroom goings-on. But it is all very soon brought home to Mary, who started everything anyway (unless it was Joseph, or the woman in the café scene or someone else). Just a moment into the airplane scene a shot of Mary looking into a mirror is inserted—as if she were seeing a movie, or running one.

With the arrival of the Gabriel figure and the child angel, the film may be said again to have belatedly really started. The story parallel to the Annunciation and the birth of Christ now begins. Also, from here on until the highly whimsical "Christmas" section at the end, the film may be regarded as a familiar Godard story, the extended emotional debate between two young people over the question of their intimacy (what is it to be, exactly?), a question that seems to subsume the questions of virginity-with-pregnancy and intervention in our lives from the outside. These latter questions can seem just wrinkles, figures, things-as-they-sometimes-appear, to be taken against the solid base of the emotional set-to between Joseph and Mary. Now we can be caught up in a story, biblical or Godardian. We can take things more crudely.

And yet from the airplane arrival scene on, the succession of images and ideas carefully develops the interests of creativity and imagination already begun in the opening sequences. Immediately now we get, with the Dvořák, a shot of a plane with lights approaching in a dark sky, seen through a mass of tangled black trees in the foreground, like the tangles of a woman's hair, perhaps—Mallarmé's *cheveux impurs*. Cut to the shot of Mary looking in a mirror, hearing, perhaps summoning, the sound of the airplane. She looks at herself in the glass, looks at an extraterrestrial, as the professor has said to do. Is she doing the bidding of a man or of God rather than her own? Perhaps she is bringing an "event" to her life. Cut to a beautiful red sun on the horizon, one of those artistic, somewhat arbitrary images that suggest a metacontext for the film—perhaps the divine realm, perhaps nature—and similar to the image of the great round moon that occurred in Mary's beginning voice-over at the basketball game. Does Mary command the divine, or nature? Cut to the plane flying into a reddish sky. Is Mary sending it into her "work," her red production? Seemingly this is the plane that lands to produce Gabriel and the child angel in the airport, what we come to next.

We see the little girl looking at us close up through a pane of glass. Is she what Mary has screened? Does the child have power to screen something? Does she, who is never named and who is not part of the original Annunciation story, represent Mary herself? Is she a projector, assistant to and instructor of Gabriel, Mary's intervention to make sure the outside coming to her does what it is supposed to do? We see Gabriel and the child awkwardly together tie Gabriel's shoelace, and the camera makes us concentrate on the silly two-toned shoe, the lace, and the hands, concentrate as if on a work, somebody's achievement, the white string against red leather like a reverse of the professor's graph, his red string upon white. Do the shoe and lace epitomize the whole scene as someone's work? Mary's? Gabriel and the child go out into a night of cars and fast-moving lights, a world like a darkened cinema hall with its flickering light, an image much repeated in the film. A car (Joseph's—but again, where does he come from?) will take them now to Mary and the moment she looks at them and at the camera, and we hear the solo cello entry of Dvořák's concerto. Mary's film brings about what happens to her.

HERE I THINK we must draw up and face an aesthetic problem. Does *Hail Mary* have to be read inch by inch, so to speak, with a very active consciousness? What about the film's larger storytelling elements, after all, its larger action?

Stanley Cavell has recently discussed *Now, Voyager*, that seemingly directorless but endlessly interesting Bette Davis melodrama where "direction" seems to emanate from Davis herself or who Davis is as Charlotte Vale. Cavell has remarked how the film—or the viewers—can seem all but overwhelmed by significance at moments, perhaps at any moment. The film, if we begin to think about it, is all but stopped by its own weight of suggestiveness about what it is saying and doing, and about what film itself is. And yet the film goes *on*. Our involvement with the film is a being torn between the potential to think in and in, with the moment, and on the other hand our interest in the succession of events, always going forward.[1]

Dramatic film would seem to ally itself with stage drama and prose fiction, where the interest, what makes drama and fiction what they are, is events that happen, what goes forward. Still—and here a connection to the Bible (or other sacred history) becomes apparent—the drama and fiction that interest us most invite, or allow, analysis, taking thought, or letting ourselves register more and more, with the moment or back and forth over the interconnections of the work. Perhaps with an interesting work we never do stop and think; we may just go forward, the work having a supercharged quality for us, like a dream. But with what interests us as action, in life or in storytelling (or story-presenting), do we not always know the *potential* to stop and reflect, maybe forever? F. R. Leavis has said that the nineteenth-century novelists are the heirs of Shakespeare. Are film directors the heirs of Shakespeare and the novelists? Are all of these the heirs of the writers, or writer, of sacred books?

Does *Hail Mary* in fact go forward? This can never be answered to the point of proof. For me, the film does move, and I am interested first and last by its large things that happen, even though, I can testify, the film on a first viewing can be confusing about characters and their relationships and what exactly is occurring. One's interest on a first viewing (as with other notable Godard of the 1980s, *Every Man for Himself* or *Passion*) may be only in how people look and how they relate to the objects in their world, and what moods in the film, taken rather abstractly, supervene upon what other moods. Further, *Hail Mary*'s action is, as films (dramas, fictions) go, highly *particular*: the direction changes often and drastically; the film seems continually to be beginning anew (compare the musical structure of Schönberg's opera *Erwartung*). And Godard's moments, more than those of most films, "tend toward" being ideas, as T. S. Eliot said of the moments and patterns of some poetry considered relatively to other poetry (in one place Eliot singles out Valéry's "narrative" *Le serpent* in this respect). Moments with Mary invite thought about imagination, when we have not developed for Mary the full emotional sense of a human being, such as we develop for characters in other films. When we stop and think with *Hail Mary*, the thinking will be relatively "intellectual." With *Blonde Venus* or *Now, Voyager*, we stop and think (about the nature of film, about the causes of this story we are watching), and our reflecting, without being any the less thinking, is more than with Godard, a flowering of our emotions, a deepening of our sympathies. To look at this Godard is more like reading Melville than, say, Jane Austen or Tolstoy.

OVERALL, THE PARALLEL of Godard's modern story with that of Mary and Joseph in the Bible is more than arbitrary because of the genuine element of whim about it, the sparks that leap to connect the two stories and that appear, all the more on consideration, to come of necessity. Consider a crucial scene and its aftermath. In the gynecologist's office, there is the question of Mary's being in pain, the question of her being pregnant (though her period came on Friday), and the question of her being a virgin (though she avers she is pregnant). These issues are not taken up and answered one by one, to say the least. The doctor appears to examine Mary vaginally and then says, "It's true." And it is not at all clear what he means to be saying. He is modest about his knowledge, perhaps with a false modesty, as he washes up and prepares to have a look at Mary: "I always wondered what we know about a woman, and found that all you can know is what a man already knew." Then he really learns his lesson about this, finding out the unclear and mysterious state of affairs Mary knows and speaks of. Yet there is a suggestion of God about the doctor: "I was there when you were born." At the end of the scene, Mary asks him to "tell Joseph," and in subsequent scenes we see Joseph being instructed by the "angels," suggesting that the doctor is in league with divine forces.

But then there is plently of evidence that the angels are projected by Mary or by Joseph, a part, or one manifestation, of either's way of communicating with the other—and the priority of either Mary's or Joseph's authorship is impossible to establish, just as in the early sequences of the film. What the film's editing presents as an exchange of glances between Joseph beside his taxi and Mary in her bathroom, just after the doctor's office scene, gives rise to an appearance of the angels to Joseph. Whose glance started this—Joseph's or Mary's? And a little later, Mary at the gas pumps at night, after reading on the spirit and the flesh, is suddenly, by a cut, made to appear as if she is the image on a screen projected by Joseph and his luminous machine, the taxi and its lighted sign, now in the foreground with Mary at a distance. Is Joseph the projector, or does Mary project Joseph projecting her? In any case, this projection carries forward in time, if we like, to the subsequent scene in the clothes shop, with the angels' crucial instruction of Joseph, and on to the scene a few moments later with Mary in Joseph's room, much of it played on or about Joseph's bed, a sort of parody of the bedroom scene in *Breathless*. (Has *Breathless* given rise to this? Or is this the essence of what gave rise to *Breathless*?) Joseph concludes here, "I'll only be your shadow [as it were, cinema image?]." Cut to a close-up of Mary, possibly in a new space—divine space?—as her voice-over begins, "God's shadow. . . . Isn't that what all men are . . . for a woman who loves her man." "Your [Mary's] shadow"/"God's shadow." Is Mary God? Is she so by virtue of loving a man?

My point about all this is that in the interview with the gynecologist and the events this seems to generate, there is an openness of terms—pregnancy, virginity, telling, and knowing—that eludes what we might expect a modern, recognizable sort of story to be. These people's story has its impossibles-to-know, its confusions, if one likes. But Godard makes us wonder, hasn't any story its impossibles-to-know, hasn't any film? This story's gestures toward God's story do not so much *explain*, or alternatively *confound*, this story as *develop* it. This film, in Eliot's phrase, "tends toward" being a recognizable modern story and also toward being the divine story, without allowing us to have it either way definitely.

What about Mary's virginity, specifically? She proclaims the truth of it first to last. It is the great issue between her and Joseph, and at the end of their long reconciliation scene in Mary's room, Joseph says, "I'll never touch you . . . I will stay." (The Roman Catholic Bible tells us in the footnotes that Mary and Joseph never had carnal relations, even after the birth of Christ.) Surely we cannot deny that Mary is a virgin *in some sense*—if she and the film tell us anything, it is that. But *in some sense* is just the point. Mary is not visibly pregnant until late in the film; and Joseph has said, in his taxi just after the doctor's office scene, "It must be mine!" Does he proceed (induced by Mary?) to make it his? Does he in fact father the child, though not in the usual— what, physical? cultural?—sense? In the reconciliation scene Mary says "no!" repeatedly as Joseph offers to touch her, but later "yes" as he places his hand close to her belly. Or is he in fact touching? One can't tell. Then he draws his hand out, as if swelling out the belly. This is a strange interchange between the two of them. Does it represent the engendering of the child, which we do not see? Does it stand for a carnal relationship in the future for these two, where this relationship is to have a different tone or nature from what we are used to think of as a carnal relationship? When Joseph says, "I'll never touch you," he is actually stroking Mary's hair. I take it that Mary's "virginity" obtains between them but that we cannot simply deny that they have carnal relations.

The Bible's Mary and Joseph minister to the spirit's becoming flesh. More and more in the film Mary ponders the spirit and the flesh, and more and more Mary's nude body is the subject of the camera (as Eva's is at one point). Is this Mary's camera, as so much in the film suggests? If so, these sequences might represent the effort of the spirit, figured by filming, and fashioning a film, to come into interaction with the body, figured as film's subject. Of course, film's subject is the body *and* the spirit, so that the spirit of film in a sense just repeats the spirit that is already there before it. If we all live by something like the act of film imagination, then we imitate Mary in bringing the spirit into a dance with spirit-and-body—a way of acting that is never of a settled sort and certainly never answers to a view of spirit and body as more than provisionally separate identities (while the body still lives, should one add?).

Mary and Joseph are not fully conscious of who they are, though they do much thinking and talking and though their situation is so suggestive. Their significance is for *us* once we get involved in the work, as is the case with other figures in imitation-of-Christ stories and art (and how much other art?). This film asks us to think of the screen as like a water surface, which might reflect us. But we may break the surface, scattering light—as it were, fashioning a film as we relish the film. We may be said even to swim in it, like Mary in her bath or the infant Christ put dangerously beneath a surface of water near the end of the film—baptized as it were by Mary, his mother acting as John the prophet.[2] The first appeal of the screen is that it reflects life (or something lifelike). But as with other poetic drama, what we become involved with on the screen may mean a shocking reforming and redirecting of our lives. We may touch divinity—it is a question in each case. The possibility is to live out in the work and to foster what we then to an extent *are*. The screen life may seem not just our reflection, or just a beyond, but our life's blood, our child.

Notes

1. Cavell discussed this point about overwhelming suggestiveness and almost being stopped by the weight of it in a lecture on *Now, Voyager* at the Boston Museum of Fine Arts in the winter of 1988, and I have heard him discuss the point on other occasions in other connections. Most of the thoughts on *Now, Voyager* were worked up into Cavell's essay "Ugly Duckling, Funny Butterfly: Bette Davis and *Now, Voyager*," *Critical Inquiry* 16, no. 2 (Winter 1990).

2. I would like to thank filmmaker Ross McElwee for calling my attention to the danger of staging and filming the scene with the infant in the water.

3

The Holy Family

Sandra Laugier

> What do we know, with all our biological and scientific knowledge, about love and its mystery? What do we know about joy? (Que savons-nous, avec nos connaissances biologiques, scientifiques, de l'amour et de son mystère? Que savons-nous de la joie?)
> —Françoise Dolto, *L'évangile au risque de la psychanalyse*

> This must then be the moment when one does not quite discover religion . . . but rather, possibly, when the sky falls in on you. (Donc ça doit être le moment où on découvre non pas la religion... mais où, peut-être, le ciel vous tombe dessus.)
> —Jean-Luc Godard, *L'autre journal*

THE APPEARANCE in early 1985 of *Hail Mary* caused, at least in France, a scandal that anticipated in a way the still more serious disturbances (in proportion, perhaps, to the film's resources or to its potential audience) that attended the release of Martin Scorsese's *The Last Temptation of Christ*. After five years, we heard the same arguments in support of what was an insupportable cause—a plea to ban, or destroy, a movie perceived as shocking. It is not my intention to compare the two films. What is remarkable, however, is the similarity of the *scandals*. What really shocks us is not the so-called blasphemy, the supposedly "pornographic" images (Mary shown naked or Jesus Christ making love). We have seen worse, even in this area. The scandal is not really in the images but in what they imply: Mary and her son seen as ordinary human beings (Scorsese has essentially been reproached for portraying Jesus Christ as a "shabby" character) who would then have *nothing extraordinary* about them. This is didactically shown in Scorsese's film and rendered immediately obvious in *Hail Mary*. Consider the gas station, the basketball game, and so on. The two movies would seem to run on parallel but inverted paths, the Scorsese showing that an extraordinary life contains (the possibility of) ordinary life—and a somewhat shabby one at that—the Godard showing that ordinary life is really extraordinary, or in any case mysterious, perhaps even miraculous. The latter idea is perhaps the more scandalous one, as we shall see.

The latter idea is the one that Godard chose to illustrate, not so much out of a yearning that was truly his own as because it represented for him the *truth* of what is in the Bible, "this big book that no one has read but everyone knows" (ce gros livre que personne n'a lu mais que tout le monde connaît).[1] It goes without saying that Godard's purpose (like Scorsese's) was not to shock or ridicule. In this sense, in fact, the polemic is absurd. On the contrary, the discussion or presentation of religious themes involves (for both of them) an entirely respectful approach. This is, among other things, what Godard had in mind when he said of church people that "it was their responsibility to make the movie" (c'était à eux de faire le film), that he had in a way made it on their behalf. And it is true that Godard in *Hail Mary* gives the impression of having made more than just *his own* movie. That may in fact be one of the film's limitations. This is not, incidentally, a criticism, since he has long been making movies "for others," in their place, possibly as late as *Every Man for Himself*: "I have long been making the movies of others rather than my own, I have made the movies that they were not making and that they would have made better than I" (Car j'ai longtemps fait les films des autres plutôt que les miens, j'ai fait des films qu'ils ne faisaient pas et qu'ils auraient fait mieux que moi).[2] Godard's modesty not being of the worn variety, what he is saying is that with *Hail Mary* he had wanted to find the truth of religion and, in a way, to make the movie that the church, the believers, the "faithful"—of whom he is not one—would make if they had the same yearning, that is, if they really wanted to show (and confront) the truth of what is in the Bible. But if such a movie were made, it would be as if "the sky fell in on us." It would be the end of cinema, rendered superfluous in the same way as, to quote from Wittgenstein, if there were a true book of ethics, it would revolutionize the world: there would be nothing left to say.

There is, then, at the start, a deficiency in the film, an incapacity acknowledged by Godard. And there is indeed a theme of deficiency in *Hail Mary* or a theme of the difficulty of meeting and possessing the other: "There is always a rending, a deficiency, an impossible encounter, and not a relationship of possession" (Toujours il y a une déchirure, un manque, une impossible rencontre, et non pas une relation de possession), wrote Françoise Dolto about "the holy family." For me, and this is my argument, it is Dolto's ideas that Godard intends to represent. They nourish the film and constitute, quite literally, its script: "The script gives birth to the plan of work, which, in its turn, will watch the script like a mother watching her child's first steps" (Le scénario enfante le plan de travail, lequel à son tour observera le scénario comme une mère les premiers pas de son enfant).[3]

Even before making the movie, Godard declared:

What I would like to do is to be able to tell the people at IBM: There, I have a book by Françoise Dolto on religion and psychoanalysis, I have two characters, Joseph and Mary, I have three cantatas by Bach, a book by Heidegger, make me a program that puts it all together. But they can't do that, and I would have to do it by myself and I have no intention of spending twenty years on it!

(Ce que je voudrais, c'est que les gens de chez IBM, je puisse leur dire: voilà, j'ai un bouquin de Françoise Dolto sur la religion et la psychanalyse, j'ai deux personnages, Joseph et Marie, j'ai trois cantates de Bach, un bouquin de Heidegger, faites-moi un programme qui m'arrange tout cela. Mais ils ne le peuvent pas, et moi il faudrait que je le fasse moi-même et je n'ai pas envie d'y passer vingt ans!)[4]

The desire to find the truth in Mary's story surely came to Godard from reading Françoise Dolto's 1977 book *L'évangile au risque de la psychanalyse* (The Gospel at the Risk of Psychoanalysis). Godard's continuous references to Dolto's book and work in *Hail Mary* have received very little critical attention despite the fact that they are obvious if not explicit. The initial chapters in Dolto's book correspond exactly to the film's *script*. And an early version or rough draft of the script, reproduced in the book *Godard par Godard* (Godard by Godard), includes passages that are exact quotations from *L'évangile au risque de la psychanalyse*.

Why have these references not been commented on, not even in *Cahiers du cinéma*, which accorded *Hail Mary* the important reception it deserved and named it best film of the year in 1985? Have the critics perhaps wanted to avoid a point of view that would make of *Hail Mary* a shallow psychoanalysis of Mary, Joseph, and Jesus—to avoid, in other words, a too obvious reading of the movie? However, Godard is thinking of *one* specific book by Dolto, one perhaps not held in high esteem by the admirers of her psychoanalytic work and one that discusses religion as much as it does psychoanalysis. And in terms of Godard's intentions, a psychoanalytical interpetation, even if obviously possible (and valuable, indeed interesting), would seem to miss the point of the film, being incapable of explaining the "shock" caused by it.

We can remind ourselves in this connection of a beautiful scene in *Contempt*, a film that also treats of gods, myth, and a couple. Fritz Lang and the scriptwriter, played by Michel Piccoli, argue about a possible interpretation of Ulysses' behavior, with Piccoli suggesting in a particularly cogent and well-argued way that Ulysses does not really want to return home and Lang pointing out that even if Piccoli is right, he is mistaken: "Ulysses is a simple, courageous man" (Ulysse est un homme simple, courageux).

"Since Jesus Christ," cinema has functioned on myth, said Godard recently in his *Histoires du cinéma* (Cinema Histories), a series produced by a French television station. Myths of Ulysses, of the Homeric gods, of Mary and Jesus: how could one "interpret" them, since they instruct? "Cinema must represent, because it is stronger than ever, something that one does not encroach upon." (Le cinéma doit représenter, puisqu'il est plus fort que jamais, un truc qu'on n'entame pas.)[5] "The sky falls in on you." (Le ciel vous tombe dessus.) For her part, Dolto answers the question "But then you psychoanalyse Jesus?" as follows: "Not at all. Reading the Gospels, as I repeat, produces at first a shock in my own subjectivity, then in contact with these texts, *I discover that Jesus teaches desire* and leads to it" (Pas du tout. La lecture des évangiles, je le répète, produit d'abord un choc en ma subjectivité, puis au contact de ces textes, *je découvre que Jésus enseigne le désir* et y entraîne).[6] From Dolto's book Godard retains first the idea that it is not so much a matter of interpreting and analyzing as learning, refinding the capacity of being educated, and that is indeed the function he assigns to cinema. Dolto says: "There is myth in these Gospel passages. When I say mythical, I mean beyond the particular imagination of each one of us; it is *a meeting of all imaginations in a single representation*" (Il y a du mythe dans ces passages d'évangiles. Quand je dis mythique, je dis au-delà de l'imaginaire particulier de chacun; c'est *une rencontre de tous les imaginaires sur une même représentation*).[7] Godard did not pick up on this passage. It would, however, serve well as a definition of cinema.

In a sense, *Hail Mary* is very much a teaching film, like all Godard's films. A professor and even classroom scenes are included in the screenplay. "In *Hail Mary* there is even the sky of science," says Godard. The figure of the teacher was already present, one should recall, in *Every Man for Himself*. And can we perhaps associate *Hail Mary* with Marguerite Duras's film *The Children*, of a year later, in which an adult child, or a child adult, refuses to go to school first because they teach "things he doesn't know," then because he learns "things he already knows"? Duras has insisted on the role of religion in her film in an interview published in *Cahiers du cinéma* of July–August 1985. If Godard is interested in the stories from the Gospels, and in Dolto's stories, it is because they have to do with education, with pedagogy. But also because both have a teaching *function*. Dolto's goal was to teach to adults and children, inseparably. It is that kind of pedagogy that Godard would like not only to show but to put in practice with *Hail Mary*.

It seems to me that Godard's movie is a perplexed interrogation on the nature of Dolto's work, work whose significance within general French culture may be difficult to assess outside France (the role played by her contributions in the specific area of psychoanalysis is another matter, which I shall not broach here). The paradox of Dolto's place lies in the double nature of her

work, at once theoretical, difficult (she was a cofounder with Lacan of the
Freudian School in Paris and the author of well-known psychoanalytical
texts) and popular. In particular, she conducted a highly popular daily radio
program, which provided material for her book *Lorsque l'enfant paraît* (When
the Child Appears), in which she would directly answer the questions that
parents ask on the upbringing of children. Dolto has popularized psychoanalysis without ever (this point is, however, at times disputed) "vulgarizing" it or
simplifying it, by handing it out under the guise of everyday advice for parents.
It is the paradox of such a position in French life that interests Godard. How
can one reach out in such a way to everyone, educate so many people? That
is exactly what preoccupies him with Mary's story. How can this story speak
to everyone? It is also what he would like to do (or at least attempt) with the
movie. "As daily bread every day comes in contact with the mouth, cinema
would have to bring the spectator into closer contact with his deep everyday
existence." (Comme le pain quotidien s'approche chaque jour de la bouche,
il faudrait que le film rapproche le spectateur de son quotidien profond.)[8]
Cinema, according to Godard, should do what, according to Dolto, the
Gospels do. She says: "It is now two thousand years that the Gospels have
been read, yet they still ring with the sound of truth in the deepest part of
any human being who reads them" (Voici deux mille ans que les évangiles
son lus, ils font toujours l'effet de vérité au plus profond de tout être qui les
lit).[9] And that is also what psychoanalysis should do: not reduce or mechanize
but show "the mystery"—what it does not know. "What do we know . . .
about joy?" (Que savons-nous... de la joie?) asks Godard, repeating one of
Dolto's phrases verbatim in his "script" without bothering to identify the
quotation with italics. The role of the psychoanalyst—especially of a child
psychoanalyst such as Dolto—is as much to learn as it is to teach. "It's true
that it's true" (C'est vrai que c'est vrai) is all the doctor has to say to Mary
after examining her. He is learning. "Maybe his name is Doctor *Freude*"
(Doctor Joy) (Il s'appelle peut-être le docteur Freude), observes Godard.[10] In
her book *La cause des enfants* (The Children's Cause) Dolto tells how, as a
child, she had wanted to become an "education doctor" (even if this profession
did not exist).

It is therefore our right to expect that cinema, like psychoanalysis and like
religious texts, teach us this truth, the truth of the everyday. "22/ Each gesture
and each word show what had been concealed since the night of time. The
only gestures, having come down from another time, and which we have to
perform day after day, whether it becomes night, whether it re-becomes day.
Each day." (22/ Chaque geste et chaque parole découvrent cela qui était
recouvert depuis la nuit des temps. Les seuls gestes, venus d'autrefois, et qu'il

faut accomplir jour après jour, qu'il devienne nuit, et qu'elle redevienne jour. Chaque jour" [Godard, script].) It is, however, a "concealed" truth, hidden by the "official" religion (the one that rejects or bans this movie as well as Scorsese's). There is a fine passage from the beginning of *L'évangile au risque de la psychanalyse* that almost describes Godard's plan. Dolto says:

> In my childhood, I would listen to the Gospel readings at church—or I would read them—as passages of a tale, the tale of Jesus and the world coeval to him and of those sunny places. Those events had taken place "in the old days," as the old people in my family used to say when they talked about their own childhood, but even earlier. They also made me dream, and then the images, the pictures, proved to me that those things caused the whole world to dream. But as for me I did not see any relationship between those stories and the life around me and in me of the Church people, the hierarchy and the "faithful" as we used to say.

> (Dans mon enfance, j'écoutais à l'église les textes des évangiles—ou je les lisais—comme les passages d'une histoire, celle de Jésus et du monde de son temps et de ces lieux de soleil. Cela se passait "dans le temps", comme disaient, dans ma famille, les vieilles personnes qui parlaient de leur enfance, mais encore plus avant. Cela me faisait rêver, et puis les images, les tableaux me prouvaient que cela faisait rêver tout le monde. Mais pour moi je ne voyais aucun lien entre ces récits et le vivre autour de moi et en moi des gens, ceux de la hiérarchie d'église ou les "fidèles," comme on disait.)[11]

One can detect in these lines a sort of film project: to show and explain what happened "in those days"—it is not by coincidence that the expression comes up at the start of Godard's film—and show that "those days" are those of everyday life. Those days are ours. We know that Godard had wanted to divide the film into twenty-four segments, as many as the hours in each and every day. "It is the same words yet they seem always to reveal a new sense *as our progress in life advances*, in the course of our experiences." (Ce sont les mêmes mots et il semble toujours révéler un sens nouveau *au fur et à mesure de notre avancée dans notre temps*, au décours de nos expériences.)[12]

In *Hail Mary* Godard wants to know about a woman, and a couple. Joseph and Mary, a couple that is at once ordinary—typically, the actors that played them are little known, and have escaped the phenomenon of "starrification" (unlike those in Scorsese's film)—and remarkable, since Mary is going to bear a child without having known any man and since Joseph is going to acknowledge the child as his. What is shown of them, by Godard as well as by Dolto, clearly involves nothing extraordinary:

A small town or even better a village. . . . Mary works in a small super-market or in a store or in a garage. She is going to have a baby, al-though she hasn't known any man really.

(Une petite ville ou même encore un village.... Marie travaille dans un petit supermarché, ou un magasin, ou un garage. Elle va avoir un en-fant, bien qu'elle ne connaisse aucun homme vraiment.) (Godard)

All of this is completely alogical, surrealistic, nevertheless they live quite obviously the life of the everyday. They leave for Egypt so that Jesus may escape the massacre by Herod's soldiers. They are not rich.

(Tout ceci est complètement alogique, surréaliste, et pourtant ils vivent tout à fait dans la vie de tous les jours. Ils partent en Egypte pour que Jésus échappe au massacre des soldats d'Hérode. Ils ne sont pas riches.) (Dolto)

The intent is twofold: to show the ordinary character of the life of the "little people" that were Joseph and Mary and to show, conversely, the extraordinary character of every encounter, of every birth. That is, according to Dolto, the truth inscribed in this story, which makes it at once a myth and a quite ordinary story. "The human density of every couple is thus found in the story of the couple composed by Joseph and Mary. But, in return, this extraordinary couple helps us discover the depth of any encounter between an ordinary man and woman." (Ainsi, la densité humaine de chaque couple se retrouve dans l'histoire du couple que forment Joseph et Marie. Mais, en retour, ce couple extraordinaire nous aide a découvrir ce qu'il en est de la profondeur d'une rencontre entre un homme et une femme ordinaires.)[13]

Godard quotes this passage from Dolto, and does so because this "ordi-nary" encounter is precisely what cinema tries to show all the time without ever succeeding. "And in a sense it is better if movies are bad, because this way they can better preserve the idea that cinema may possibly be good." (Et, dans un sens, les films, il vaut mieux qu'ils soient mauvais, car ils gardent mieux l'idée que le cinéma peut être bon.)[14] This is true also of pornographic cinema, to which this film makes passing references through its dialogue and especially its images: "It's an example of the suffering of other movies, which are incapable of showing a love scene. It is because [Catherine] Deneuve can't say 'I love you' that we make a porn film that can't say it either." (Il est un exemple de la souffrance des autres films qui sont incapables de montrer une scène d'amour. C'est parce que Deneuve ne sait pas dire 'je t'aime' qu'on fait un film porno qui ne sait pas le dire non plus.) *Hail Mary* tries to show this impossibility of film itself. Dolto talks about an "impossible encounter," but she conceives of this deficiency as positive, constitutive of the true relationship.

Therein lies the teaching of her text. "These Gospels describe how, in a couple, the other never fulfills his or her partner, how there is always a rending, a deficiency, an impossible encounter, and not a relationship of possession, of phallocracy, of dependence." (Ces évangiles décrivent que l'autre, dans un couple, ne comble jamais son conjoint, que toujours il y a une déchirure, un manque, une impossible rencontre, et non pas une relation de possession, de phallocratie, de dépendance.)[15] In this sense, Joseph and Mary form an ordinary yet "exemplary," or mythical, couple. "This is an exemplarily married couple." (C'est un couple exemplairement marié.)

An important aspect of the film is the significance (perhaps not evident at first screening) it gives to Joseph. Godard observes: "God's shadow is very simply Joseph" (L'ombre de Dieu est tout simplement Joseph).[16] Dolto likewise insists on rendering him his due. In *L'évangile au risque de la psychanalyse*, she answers the question "The angel announces to Mary: 'The power of the Most-high will cover you with his shadow.' Where is Joseph?" as follows: "But is not every man God's shadow for the woman who loves him?" (Mais l'ombre de Dieu, tout homme ne l'est-il pas pour une femme qui aime son homme?)[17] Joseph is exemplary despite—or because of—all the difficulties that come his way, for Joseph serves an apprenticeship in nonpossession and separation, thanks to Mary. "[Ultimately] nothing in Joseph is possessive about his wife. Just as, in Mary, nothing is a priori possessive about her child. While engaged, they trust in life, and the destiny of their union soars. They accept it." (En Joseph, rien n'est possessif de sa femme. De même que rien, en Marie, n'est a priori possessif de son enfant. Fiancés, ils font confiance à la vie, et voilà que le destin de leur couple en surgit. Ils l'acceptent.) They are exemplary because they learn and teach separation, the way Jesus will later teach it to them: "As every child must, Jesus castrates his parents of their possessivity. He thus shows us the exemplary development of a child in a family" (Comme chaque enfant doit le faire, Jésus castre ses parents de leur possessivité. Il nous montre là le développement exemplaire d'un enfant dans une famille).[18]

An apparently paradoxical argument. How could such an improbable family be exemplary? How do a virgin mother, a father who is not the father, and a child who leaves at twelve to go "take care of his father's business" teach us things (whether we know them or not) on the nature and difficulty of our existence? There evidently lies the "mystery": "What do we know about joy?" Psychoanalysis can explain it, describe it, without ever (much like science) making it disappear. For Dolto, it is not so much a matter of analyzing the members of the "holy family" as of showing how much like all men and all women they are. Mary is pregnant, and "like every other woman, she hopes, she yearns, to be pregnant with an exceptional being" (comme chaque femme, elle espère, elle désire être enceinte d'un être exceptionnel).[19] That is in fact part of every *yearning* for childbirth if it is a true yearning, a yearning for something new and exceptional. In *Hail Mary* there is a reflection, an investigation, on the yearning for a child, which is perhaps defined according to Godard by the woman's desire to give birth to "an exceptional being" and by the man's recognition of playing a "very small part" in the matter. "A man is never sure of being the procreator, he must rely on his wife's word." (Un homme n'est jamais sûr d'être le procréateur, il doit faire confiance à la parole de sa femme.) It is this skeptical view of paternity that is present in Joseph and translates into his doubts, his anger, his initial refusals. Since Mary's story, skepticism has been "a man's business"; however, with Dolto, we may have witnessed the emergence of a feminine form of skepticism in which knowledge *is* ignorance itself. "Mary knows that she will be pregnant. But how? She does not know." (Marie sait qu'elle deviendra enceinte. Mais comment? elle n'en sait rien.)[20] *Hail Mary* describes Mary's and then Joseph's path toward the most painful form of knowledge: I know that I do not know. And that we are separate.

What the myth of Mary says, according to Dolto, is what everyone must learn: the parent and the child do not belong to each other. Mary's "stomach ache" announces the pain of childbirth and of separation. Joseph's situation typifies every relation of paternity, and from this standpoint the question of Joseph's real paternity is entirely devoid of sense ("idiotic quibbling," says Dolto).

> It takes a man three seconds to be a begetter. To be a father is quite another venture. To be a father is to give one's name to one's child, to raise him, to educate him, to spur him toward more life, more desire. . . . It is quite another thing than being a begetter. . . . A father always has to adopt his child. Some adopt them at birth, others a few days later, others when they speak, etc. There are only adoptive fathers. [Joseph] knows one never gets the child he has dreamed about, and he adopts him.

> (Il faut trois secondes à l'homme pour être géniteur. Etre père, c'est une toute autre aventure. Etre père, c'est donner son nom à son enfant, c'est l'éduquer, l'instruire, c'est l'appeler à plus de vie, à plus de désir.... C'est bien autre chose que d'être géniteur.... Un père doit toujours adopter son enfant. Certains adoptent leurs enfants à la naissance, d'autres quelques jours après, d'autres l'adopteront quand il parlera, etc. Il n'y a de père qu'adoptif. [Et Joseph] sait qu'on n'a jamais les enfants qu'on a rêvés et il l'adopte.)[21]

Thus, for Godard, the film illustrates the everyday side of paternity. "It helps us discover" what an ordinary paternity or maternity is about. The movie should, let us repeat, "bring the spectator into closer contact with his deepest everyday existence: loving, giving life, living it, having a child" (rapprocher le spectateur de son quotidien profond: aimer, donner la vie, la vivre, faire un enfant). It is not a coincidence that *Hail Mary* closes on what, from Dolto's point of view, constitutes the essential aspect of this everyday existence, this gift of life: the separation. "To have a child" is to accept from the very start the necessity to become separated; to respect, indeed to instigate, the child's desire to leave (and all educational advice given by Dolto, whether for children or for grown-ups, through the spoken word or writing, goes in this direction, boils down to just this). "I have to take care of my father's business." The last scenes in *Hail Mary* cannot really be understood if one does not view them as a narrative of a "successful"—accepted though painful—separation. The little boy is leaving, and Mary knows she has to let him go. "But what scandalous advice for us human parents!" says Dolto. Why have a child at all if we must then separate from him or her? There is a mystery here—and an obviousness. That is what Mary understands of Jesus: "He will go and seek those life values no longer in his parents, but in Jesus." Here we finally come to the lesson, the teaching of the movie. "Who would dare say that to his child in this day and age?" (Qui de nos jours oserait le dire à son enfant?)[22] That lesson is also what the Angel salutes on his last apparition at the very end of the movie. "Il n'y a rien, je vous salue, Marie!" (There is nothing. Hail Mary.)

What is Dolto saying, and what is Godard's cinema showing, if not that ordinary life may be heroic and that what Mary accomplishes, even if not particularly extraordinary, is ultimately miraculous? The lives of the other characters in the movie, the unhappy story of the professor and Eva, could attest to that. "The life of man is the true romance, which, when it is valiantly conducted, will yield the imagination a higher *joy* than any fiction."[23]

In conclusion, what do we make of the question that should be of greatest interest to us, that of Mary's virginity? Dolto gives two answers. The first is classically psychoanalytical: "Well, it is what we encounter every day. Every child would like his mother to have been a virgin. It is a fantasy that comes from the night of time, when the child was in the uterus." (Mais c'est ce que nous rencontrons chaque jour. Tout fils voudrait que sa mère fût vierge. C'est un fantasme qui vient de la nuit des temps, lorsque le fils était dans l'uterus.) The second is the one that concerns Godard, and the one we find in the film: "Our thought may be fecundated by an idea coming from elsewhere, without knowing who gave it to us. That is what Mary represents: she is an image, a metaphor of perfect availability" (Notre pensée peut être fécondée par une idée venue d'ailleurs, sans savoir qui nous l'a donnée. C'est cela que represente

Marie: elle est une image, une métaphore de la parfaite disponibilité).[24] (This availability is also ignorance. It has not been pointed out, however, that Joseph too can represent this availability.) Godard translates: "She is a virgin image. No traces. No imprints. That's what Mary represents. *To be virgin is to be available*, to be free" (Elle est une image vierge. Pas de traces. Pas d'empreintes. C'est cela que représente Marie. *Etre vierge, c'est être disponible*, être libre). We talk of "virgin film," referring to film that has not been imprinted yet. Mary embodies the availability, or virginity, that allows the movie to be born, that allows something radically new to arise. "A story is born to us and is given to us. That is how life resuscitates through an image." (Une histoire nous est née et nous est donnée. C'est ainsi qu'à travers une image ressuscite la vie.) Cinema, born as an instrument of mourning (it started, in the era of World War I, in black and white in order to wear mourning for life, says Godard in his *Histoires du cinéma*,) may also become a place of rebirth. "The movie is the evidence that that is possible, because it happens under our very eyes." (Le film est la preuve que c'est possible, puisque ça arrive sous nos yeux.)[25] To those who in France and elsewhere speak complacently of "the death of the cinema"—and they have their reasons to do so—the message delivered here is clear: to be reborn, cinema will need to be carried forward by a new desire.

Notes

This article was originally written in French and was translated by Pasquale G. Tatò.

1. Jean-Luc Godard, "L'art à partir de la vie" (a conversation with A. Bergala), in *Jean-Luc Godard par Jean-Luc Godard* (Editions de l'Etoile-Cahiers du cinéma, 1985), 18.
2. Godard, 22.
3. Godard, 592.
4. Godard, 597 (originally in *Le Nouvel Observateur*, December 30, 1983).
5. Godard, 605.
6. Françoise Dolto, *L'évangile au risque de la psychanalyse* (Seuil, Coll. Points, 1977), 15. Françoise Dolto died in June 1988.
7. Dolto, 21.
8. Godard, 591.
9. Dolto, 15.
10. Godard, 590.
11. Dolto, 9–10.
12. Dolto, 13.
13. Dolto, 26 (repeated verbatim in Godard, 591).
14. Godard, 605.
15. Dolto, 24.

16. Godard, 591.

17. Dolto, 23.

18. Dolto, 35.

19. Dolto, 24.

20. Dolto, 26.

21. Dolto, 25.

22. Dolto, 48.

23. Ralph Waldo Emerson, quoted by Stanley Cavell at the opening of *Pursuits of Happiness* (Cambridge, Mass.: Harvard University Press, 1981).

24. Dolto, 29.

25. Godard, 591–92.

4

Marie/Eve: Continuity and Discontinuity in J-L Godard's Iconography of Women

Laura Mulvey

> Go and catch a falling star,
> Get with child a mandrake root
> —John Donne, "Song"

GODARD'S FILM OF the Annunciation, *Je vous salue, Marie*, was widely seen as the gesture of a Marxist fallen out of kilter with his politics and falling back on blasphemy to maintain a radical profile. But in fact the film manages to pay tribute to the spirit of the Christian myth and still derive from themes and motifs latent in Godard's past work, so that there are unexpected elements of continuity between this, and the older, more familiar Godard. Although politics do indeed fade from the picture, many long-standing Godardian preoccupations persist, even finding a new visibility through an altered set of conjunctures. To my mind, this film draws attention, from a new and illuminating angle, to the long zigzag path of Godard's struggle with the meaning of the feminine. I am interested particularly in the persistence of his preoccupation with the woman's body and her sexuality in the story of the Annunciation. Mary's virginity is refracted through images of desire that show continuity rather than discontinuity with his previous attitude to femininity. And while the Virgin Mary is yet one more chimeric shape in Godard's gallery of feminine iconographies, Myriem Roussel is a reincarnation of the Godardian ideal of feminine beauty.

The film dwells on Joseph's almost unbearable sexual frustration, his conviction that Mary's pregnancy proves her infidelity, his reluctance to accept chastity as a precondition of love, and his ultimate reconciliation with her soul and spirituality by accepting her virginity and her pregnancy. In the meantime, the camera, essentially destined to be voyeur rather than lover, has unlimited access to the carnal joy of her image. Godard makes no attempt to reconcile theme and image. His film shares the deep ambivalence aroused by the female body in a tradition of Christian ideology that fetishizes the virgin birth. From this perspective, the sensuality with which he depicts the Virgin may be out of keeping with her usual kitsch image, but it touches the raw nerve that female sexuality represents for patriarchal religion. At the same time, the film still manifests the deep imbrication between the cinema and desire that haunts Godard and confirms that with *Prénom: Carmen* (1983), woman and sexuality returned as a central preoccupation in his work.

Godard's career can be roughly divided into three phases. From the midsixties, somewhere around *Deux ou trois choses que je sais d'elle,* until the early eighties, draining away around *Sauve qui peut (la vie)*, Marxism was the main intellectual vehicle for his ideas. In the early sixties, his work had been almost exclusively concerned with the cinema as cinema, torn between its potential for fantasy and for reality, fascinated by its potential for illusion but morally and aesthetically committed to its ability to react to the real. During his Marxist period, this ambivalence resolved into a search for a materialist cinema, within the Brechtian tradition of radical formalism. The reality of cinema now extended to its process of production, its apparatus, its dialogue with an audience. This synthesis between cinema and politics fell apart in 1980, heralding the phase-three, post-Marxist Godard. The cinema returned explicitly, as it were "as such," with the making of the film of "Passion" within the film *Passion* (1981). And, with Isabelle Huppert's transformation from militant worker to potential entrepreneur, Godard, in Andre Gorz's words, "say[s] farewell to the working class." The (fictional) director's struggle with his images in *Passion* also foreshadows the way that Godard's own return to a cinema stripped of politics will trigger the crisis of creativity depicted in *Prénom: Carmen*. *Prénom: Carmen* (1983) and *Je vous salue, Marie* (1984–85), form a kind of diptych in which he returns to his old pre-Marxist obsession with the duality of cinema, its magic versus its reality. In *Je vous salue, Marie* Godard finds an apparently paradoxical means of restoring spirituality to realism, the unnatural nature of the virgin birth, but one that is also in keeping with the spiritual tradition of cinematic realism that links Dreyer, Rossellini, and Bresson to aspects of Godard and moments in Straub/Huillet. He subordinates the magic implied by a belief in the virgin birth to an acceptance of mystery and returns his cinema to nature through the hand of God. Only Godard's instinctive understanding of cinema's inherent contradictions could realize its paradox so precisely, and only a despairing obsession with the enigma of femininity could invoke the Virgin Mary as the paradox itself.

The problem of cinema that finds an analogue or a metaphorical representation in the problem of woman comes clearly into focus with the *Carmen/Marie* diptych. The two kinds of cinema, the cinema of magic/desire (Carmen) and the cinema of spirituality/truth (Marie), are reworked through metonymies which both link back to the place of the female body in Godard's earlier work and represent a point of crisis, a numbing realization of the inextricable involvement between desire and creativity. In his Marxist period and in his collaboration with Anne-Marie Miéville, Godard struggled to depict sexuality within the realm of the social rather than as accessible only to the discourse of desire. From the point of view of his politics, woman as prostitute and woman as consumer of commodities, indeed woman as both, could appear as a symptom of capitalist relations; these social roles also create a metaphoric merging of seduction and repression (in both its social and its sexual sense) that Godard saw as typical of capitalism. But there is still something intractable about Godard's representation of women, a "something more" that resists political rationalization. It is as though he could put a woman on the screen only if he found her fascinating and seductive. And as feminine beauty for Godard, both inside and outside its rationalization within capitalist consumerism, represents artifice, the image of feminine beauty almost inevitably becomes associated with mystery, the enigma of femininity, and ultimately with sexuality and deceit. This association between female sexuality, artifice, and deception, has, of course, a rich history in Western culture, and there are many femmes fatales who could represent the myth that he realized with the Carmen story, while only one woman, the Virgin Mary herself, could represent the other side of the antinomy.

Godard's dualistic, almost Manichean, attitudes are there at the very beginning of his work as a director, or even before the beginning when, as a critic, he first started to articulate his concept of cinema. As a critic, Godard encapsulated his ideas through names ("Criticism taught us to love both Rouch and Eisenstein"), constantly reiterating an opposition between research or documentary (Lumière) and spectacle or fiction (Méliès): on the one hand, Rossellini; on the other, Nicholas Ray. Through these oppositions, Godard tried to negotiate the problem of truth and beauty in the cinema. From the beginning, dating from Patricia's betrayal of Michel Poiccard in *A bout de souffle*, the split between feminine seductive appearance and either deceitful or mysteriously unknowable essence was a recurring theme in Godard's work. It is not only a dramatic trope but also a metaphor for the more profound philosphical problem of the split between appearance and essence. It is a problem of inscription. *Je vous salue, Marie* returns to this problem, but by a strange route, one that is mapped through/across the question of truth as the presence of the invisible and spiritual made manifest through/across the body of woman.

In the myth of the Mother of God, the engimatic and dangerous mystery of female sexuality is exorcised, but only through the further mystery of God's power. And paradoxically, this mystery can only be grasped by a blind subservience to irrational belief. Belief in God depends on belief in the woman's impossible virginity, which represents her "wholeness," an evisceration of the psychologically threatening and physically disgusting "inside." It is only as "whole" that woman can drop the mask of artifice with which she both deceives man and conceals the truth of her body. For Nietzsche, femininity cannot be separated from performance. He ends "On the Problem of the Actor" in *The Gay Science* with these words: "Finally women. Reflect on the whole history of women: do they not have to be first of all and above all else actresses? Listen to the physicians who have hypnotised women; finally, love them—let yourself be hypnotised by them! What is always the end result? That they 'put on something' even when they take off everything. Woman is so artistic."[1] It is easy to see the phrase "women are so artistic" in Godard's mind's eye. At what point does art turn into artifice and artifice into art? The aesthetic problem posed by the dissembling nature of the actor preoccupied Godard in the spirit of Nietzsche's comment: "Falseness with a good conscience; the delight in simulation exploding as a power that pushes aside one's so-called 'character' flooding it and at times extinguishing it; the inner craving for a role and a mask, for *appearance*."[2]

In *Une femme mariée*, Charlotte interrogates her actor/lover, showing the same doubts about how to read his inner being in his appearance that are more usually projected by the man onto the woman. It was this mistrust of performance that pushed Godard towards the distanciated, visible separation between actor and role that characterised his late-sixties cinema.[3] And that then engulfs the simulation and fiction of cinema itself. The woman's simulation, like the cinema's, is spectacle, and what can be seen only as a surface still conceals its secrets.

The dichotomy between surface and secret, artifice and truth, is paradoxical. The artificial surface may disguise in the woman an inside that contains a danger. Or the artificial surface in the cinema may be that of illusion, concealing the true beauty of its reality. But Godard also associated female beauty, almost ontologically, with the cinema. In an early article, written in 1952 in the *Cahiers du cinéma*, "Defence and Illustration of the Cinema's Classical Construction," he makes the following comments:

> A beautiful face, as La Bruyère wrote, is the most beautiful of sights. There is a famous legend which has it that Griffith, moved by the beauty of his leading lady, invented the close-up in order to capture it in greater detail. Paradoxically, therefore, the simplest close-up is also the most moving. Here our art reveals its transcendence most strongly, making the beauty of the object signified burst forth in the sign. With these huge eyes half closing in discretion and desire, with these blenching lips,

all we see in their anguish is the dark design they imply, and in their avowal only the illusions they conceal. . . .

The cinema does not query the beauty of a woman, it only doubts her heart, records her perfidy (it is an art, La Bruyère says, of the entire person to place a word or an action so that it puts one off the scent), sees only her movements.[4]

Reading these words, it is impossible not to think of the profoundly cinematic beauty of Godard's actresses, most of all of Anna Karina, and of her glance into the camera in *Pierrot le fou* as she lies to Ferdinand. Many critics were struck, seeing *Prénom: Carmen*, by Myriem Roussel's likeness to Anna Karina. As the Virgin Mary in *Je vous salue, Marie*, she transforms perfidy into purity. The beauty of her body can still transfix the camera, and acts as a conduit toward a new kind of cinema that can transcend materiality and fantasize liberation from an enslavement to sexuality.

While Carmen encapsulates the theme of beauty and faithlessness (and also refers back specifically to *Pierrot le fou*), the theme of the spiritual in nature, represented by Marie, resurrects the ghost of Rossellini's one-time significance for Godard. In a 1962 interview with the *Cahiers du cinéma*, he said:

Rossellini is something else again. . . . With him a shot is beautiful because it is right: with most others, a shot becomes right because it is beautiful. They try to construct something wonderful, and if in fact it becomes so, one can see that there were reasons for doing it. Rossellini does something he had a reason for doing in the first place. It is beautiful because it is. . . . The cinema is the only art which, as Cocteau says (in *Orphée*, I believe,) "films death at work." Whoever one films is growing older and will die. So one is filming a moment of death at work. Painting is static: "the cinema is interesting because it seizes life and the mortal side of life."[5]

The ideas in this quotation resurrect another, less obvious influence on Godard: André Bazin, Catholic, founder of the *Cahiers du cinéma* and its editor until his death in 1958. In his essay "The Ontology of the Photographic Image," Bazin argues that the origins of art lie in the human desire to overcome death, to mummify the body and conquer time, "the preservation of life by a representation of life." In the history of art, this "creation of an ideal world in the likeness of the real" was vitiated by the need for illusion, the "proclivity of the mind towards magic," and it was only Niépce and Lumière who redeemed art from this sin. Bazin says: "For the first time, between the originating object and its reproduction there intervenes only the instrumentality of a nonliving agent. . . . Photography affects us like a phenomenon in nature, like a flower or a snowflake whose vegetable or earthly origins are an inseparable part of their beauty."[6] And he compares the shared nature of the object and its photograph to the fingerprint.

The fingerprint, in the semiotic categories of Charles Peirce, is an index, the sign in which the object leaves its own unmediated trace, just as light in photography carries the image onto celluloid. Peter Wollen associates Bazin's aesthetic of the index with his concern for the spiritual:

> It was the existential bond between fact and image, world and film, which counted for most in Bazin's aesthetic, rather than any quality of similarity or resemblance. Hence the possibility—even the necessity—of an art which could reveal spiritual states. There was, for Bazin, a double movement of impression, of moulding and imprinting: the first, the interior spiritual suffering was stamped on the exterior physiognomy; then the exterior physiognomy was stamped and printed upon sensitive film.[7]

Here the problem of the relationship between interior and exterior, between an appearance and what it might conceal, is effaced as the presence of the deity is inscribed into the world, into nature, and into the soul of man. Thus, in turn, the cinema finds an integration between its mechanical nature and its ability to record; the split is effaced between the cinema as a surface illusion and the disillusioning mechanics that produce it. But for Godard, there is a difficult tension between the cinema's imbrication with the beauty of woman, and therefore her perfidy, and its potential realization of Bazin's aesthetic. When in *Vivre sa vie* Anna Karina as Nana weeps as she watches Falconetti's face in *Joan of Arc,* Godard is making a tribute to Dreyer's image, in which the spirituality of the soul is indistinguishable from the spirituality of the cinema. Myriem Roussel's Marie could be born out of the gap between Karina/Nana, innocent but a prostitute, irrevocably subordinated to the body and the sexual, and Falconetti's Joan, uncontaminated by the sexual and inscribed with the spiritual power of God. Peter Wollen says: "In Bresson's films Bazin saw 'the outward revelation of an interior destiny,' in those of Rossellini 'the presence of the spiritual' is expressed with 'breathtaking obviousness.' The exterior, through the transparence of images stripped of all inessentials, reveals the interior. Bazin emphasised the importance of the physiognomy, upon which—as in the films of Dreyer—the interior spiritual life was etched and printed."[8]

Raymond Bellour has pointed out that the index is both the most material and the most spiritual of signs. In his Marxist period, Godard sought truth through materialism rather than through a cinema that lay on the cusp of magic and reality. From a materialist point of view, truth lies in revealing the relations of production, whether those of capitalist society or those of cinema itself. In this sense, the beauty of the filmic image comes not from recording something mystically inherent in the pro-filmic but in the inscription of the usually obscured presence of the processes of cinema. A sense of the presence of the camera lights up the nowness of the film moment into its indexicality, and when Godard's characters speak directly to the camera, not only does documentary break into fiction, but that moment is then carried into the actual screening of the finished film, and the screen speaks to the spectator. It is as though the acknowledgment of the apparatus of the cinema, what is usually concealed and glossed over in the process of making a film, opens out the secret space of cinema's truth, just as direct address opens out the darkened space of the auditorium. The realist aesthetics of Brecht are not the same as those of Bazin. But while Godard was capable of defetishizing the cinema and illuminating the fetishistic imbrication between woman as appearance and the dissembling nature of the late capitalist commodity, his iconography of the feminine on the screen was never freed from a fetishistic gloss.

In the early eighties, with *Prénom: Carmen*, Godard's return to the cinema "as such" takes the form of a kind of despairing return to zero, ironically inverting the thrill of the return to zero in 1968 with *Le gai savoir*. If *Prénom: Carmen* marks a moment of crisis in Godard's history, it also reveals the bare constitutive elements of his late cinema—all that remains when everything else is stripped away. The return to zero is a return to the origins of the director's primal desire for cinema rather than to the point zero that investigates the social circulation and significance of images, as, for instance, in *Le gai savoir*. His struggle is now to represent what makes the making of cinema possible, its obsessive, romantic, delusory hold over the director rather than a modernist, Brechtian struggle to represent the process of production of cinema and the process of production of meaning. Although there is an obstinate courage in Godard's "self-portrait" as the director who sees the cinema slipping through his fingers, and a poetic heroism in his ability to turn even such an intimation of loss into new "sounds and images," the question persists: why, at the moment of crisis, should he return to these particular sounds and these particular images? And above all, what is the significance of the sequence in which Marie follows on from Carmen to create two polarized icons of the feminine?

In both films, the image of woman as beauty achieves a kind of metaphoric realization of the difficulties Godard faced with the destiny of his cinema. In *Prénom: Carmen*, his mood is despairing and nihilistic, as though the fascination of the cinema could only materialize through fascination with the body of a woman, which could only, essentially, arouse and betray carnal passion.

In *Je vous salue, Marie* the problem of the spiritual, as a problem of inscription, returns to Godard's cinema through the figuration of the woman's body in which the word was made flesh. But the two women, polarized though they are as femme fatale and ascetic saint, are both bitterly desired by and incomprehensible to man. Both represent the enigma of the feminine. The difficulty of seeing the soul through the body, the body as disguise of the soul, finds heightened expression in the female body. And the theme of faithlessness that Carmen incarnates is continued with Marie with Joseph's jealousy and violent accusations when faced with her pregnancy. The two films polarize femininity into a binary opposition, the carnal and the spiritual. But the simple fact of polarization will always link as well as oppose, and the attributes that separate Carmen and Marie only superficially conceal the underlying "fit" between them. Both myths revolve around mysteries of the female body and its ultimate unknowableness. Both myths symbolize a zero point for Godard at which the mystery of the feminine, profoundly destructive on one level, becomes a threshold to and signifier of other, *more profound* mysteries. With Marie, the enigmatic properties of femininity are conflated with the mystery of origins, particularly the origins of creativity, whether the creation of life or the creative processes of art.

Godard's search for purity, earlier transmuted into materialism, takes the form in these two films of splitting the component parts of the film into distinct, almost autonomous spheres. These divisions are most significant in *Prénom: Carmen*. Carmen and eroticism are a function of image, while Claire and purity materialize through the music. It is as though the elements of film that are usually wound together in a hierarchical organization have been unraveled so that sound acquires image track and image is used to generate sound track. The music is taken from Beethoven's late string quartets. A string quartet is intended for informal performance, and a "chamber" space in which the members of the quartet practice materializes alongside the space of the story to give an image to the music on the sound track. The quartet's violinist, Claire, played by Myriem Roussel, is detached from the carnal world of Carmen by the spiritual abstraction of the music. Godard had always been concerned to preserve the reality and thus the purity of his sound. Richard Roud comments:

> [Godard's] first two films were post-synchronised: *Une femme est une femme* was his first experience with direct sound and *Vivre sa vie* brought this new technique to a head. Jean Collet, who followed the shooting of the film, reported in *La revue du son* the revolutionary news that the film was shot entirely with direct sound, both dialogue and noises. And,

cause God or the power above is still felt, even by sceptics, to be the origin of all things, who holds life itself in his gift and is therefore responsible for all birth, not only Christ's.[12]

At the very end of the film, Gabriel appears for the last time to indicate that Marie is now free. He says, "Je vous salue, Marie." Marie sits alone in a car, her face in close-up. She lights and smokes a cigarette. She takes some lipstick from her bag, and as she applies it to her lips, the camera moves in to fill the frame with the shape of her mouth, which becomes dark and cavernous, surrounded by her bright, newly painted lips. The cycle is complete. The Virgin turns into a whore; the hole returns to break the abstract perfection of the zero. Mary, the Mother of God, reverts to Eve, the mother of lust.

This violent oscillation between different images of the feminine indicates that a system of belief alternates with a system of anxiety. Fetishistic belief, attributed by Freud to the child's insistent belief in the maternal phallus, amounts to a denial of sexual difference and an inability to accept the specificity of woman. Godard's cinema has always had an interest for feminists, as it came close to representing the difficulty of woman, particularly in his association between the visual construction of the feminine and the cinema, and in the metonymic links between the dissembling nature of the feminine as sexual commodity and the dissembling nature of the commodity itself. There is a common topographical structure that facilitates the construction of such analogies. It is, perhaps, as though analogy were enabled by homology.

The image of an exterior casing protecting an interior space or contents from view usually carries with it the implication that if the exterior cracks, the interior contents may disgust and possibly harm. From a psychoanalytic point of view, the protective surface is a defense constructed by the ego along the lines of a fetish. It denies the interior, but because it believes that the exterior *is* an exterior, it thus acknowledges the interior. Female beauty, in a sense, fulfills this function by fixing the eye on something that pleases it and prevents the psyche from bringing to mind those aspects of the feminine that are displeasing. So even if Carmen, for instance, brings death and destruction, the female figure who personifies her brings an image of youthful perfection to the screen. The screen itself fixes this image into an image, a shadow, eviscerated of bodily fluids associated with the maternal body. The cinema can thus enjoy the indexicality of the image while preserving the body from death and decay. Although Godard claims that the cinema films death, it is also constructing and fixing the body in its surface presence and perfection.

I have argued recently for a female spectatorship that would replace a visual pleasure, focused on fetishized feminity, with the pleasure of curiosity.[13]

Curiosity undercuts a belief system and generates a desire to see into forbidden spaces and mysteries. Curiosity has, perhaps, been associated with woman precisely because woman is, comparatively, inured from the anxiety the female body can produce. The Medusa's head may hold fears, but of a different order. While curiosity is a compulsive desire to see and know and investigate, fetishism is born out of a refusal to see, fixing instead on a substitute construction. Out of this complex of turning away, of covering over, not the eyes but understanding, the female body is bound to remain an enigma and a threat. It is interesting that Godard, no longer able to approach historical, political reality, should attempt to construct the image of the Virgin Mary as a fetishized substitute. It is, however, characteristic of Godard's rigor and his honesty that he reveals the impossibility of his own construction, just as he used to reveal the illusionistic nature of the cinema machine. But this time, there is no materiality, no knowledge to be gained, from behind the facade.

> Thou, when thou return'st, wilt tell me
> All strange wonders that befell thee,
> And swear
> No where
> Lives a woman true, and fair.[14]

Notes

1. Friedrich Nietzsche, *The Gay Science*, trans. Walter Kaufman (New York: Vintage Books, 1974), 317.

2. Nietzsche, 316.

3. See Peter Wollen, "Godard and Counter Cinema: *Vent d'est*," in *Readings and Writings* (London: Verso, 1982), 89–90.

4. Jean-Luc Godard, "Defence and Illustration of Classical Construction," in Tom Milne, ed., *Godard on Godard* (New York: Viking, 1968), 28.

5. *Godard on Godard*, 180–81.

6. André Bazin, *What Is Cinema?* trans., ed. Hugh Gray (Berkeley: University of California Press, 1967), 12.

7. Peter Wollen, *Signs and Meaning in the Cinema* (London: Secker and Warburg, 1969), 134.

8. Wollen, *Signs and Meaning*, 132.

9. Richard Roud, *Godard* (Bloomington: Indiana University Press, 1967), 74.

10. Marina Warner, *Alone of All Her Sex* (1976, repr. London: Picador, 1990), 59.

11. Nietzsche, 122.

12. Warner, 45.

13. Questionnaire on female spectatorship, *Camera Obscura* 20–21 (May–September 1989), 248–52. See also the introduction to *Visual and Other Pleasures* (Bloomington: Indiana University Press, 1989): "Like voyeurism, curiosity is active and thus, in Freud's terms, masculine, but it can confuse the binary male/female, active/passive

opposition that I associate[d with visual pleasure in 'Visual Pleasure and Narrative Cinema']. In the myths of Eve and Pandora, curiosity lay behind the first woman's desire to penetrate a forbidden secret that precipitated the fall of man. These myths associate female curiosity with an active narrative fuction." See also my paper "Pandora: the Mask and Curiosity," in Beatriz Colomina, ed., *Space and Sexuality* (Princeton University Press, 1992).

14. John Donne, "Song" (Go and catch a falling star).

5

Miéville and Godard:
From Psychology to Spirit

David Sterritt

ANALYSTS OF THE *Hail Mary* diptych tend to concentrate their energies on the second and longer portion, directed by Jean-Luc Godard, passing more quickly over Anne-Marie Miéville's briefer introductory work, *The Book of Mary*. One reason may be that Miéville's contribution is more conventional than Godard's in narrative flow and visual complexity and therefore provides a less imposing stimulus for the decoding and interpretation in which Godard watchers habitually engage. Miéville's film may also seem more "obvious" than Godard's since she uses fewer distancing devices and since her Mary figure is somewhat easier than Godard's to identify with on a psychological level.

Yet closer observation reveals that Miéville's film has enough depth and density to make it a fitting match for Godard's, and conversely that Godard's film operates more intensely on a psychological and emotional level than many of his earlier, more ideologically and theoretically determined works.

It is not difficult, for example, to approach the Mary figure and the Joseph figure of Godard's film in terms of psychology and emotional response. This is noteworthy since Godard's films are often very resistant in these respects. From the beginning of his career he has been concerned, to a greater or lesser degree in any given film, with distancing his audience from the hearts and minds of his characters so that neither psychological identification nor narrative momentum will obscure the ideological or theoretical issues that are his primary concern. Unlike the characters in, say, *Weekend* or *Numéro deux*—to name representative films made (respectively) before and after Godard's problematic Dziga Vertov group period—the Mary and Joseph figures of *Hail Mary* are immediately accessible as real, vulnerable, multidimensional human personalities with problems that adult viewers can speculate on from the vantage points of their own experiences. The complexities and eccentricities of Godard's narrative style and editing strategies provide a healthy measure of characteristically Brechtian distancing and alienation, but the fundamental humanity of the central characters stands side by side with their symbolic, metaphorical, and paradigmatic functions.

Since he has avowedly chosen in *Hail Mary* to deal with matters of "chastity and virginity" in a quasi-religious context of "Catholic images and Protestant music,"[1] it seems safe to speculate that Godard is here attempting to confront a level of experience that could be called spiritual in a general sense, an area with which his previous works have rarely been concerned. In earlier films as different as *Masculin-féminin* and *Sauve qui peut (la vie)*, Godard has insisted on distancing his audience from his characters so that ideological constructs and conceptual juxtapositions can be readily perceived through a deliberately thin veil of narrative and characterization. *Hail Mary*, by contrast, marks an attempt to deal with spiritual issues that are closely interwoven with the humanity of his characters, and particularly with the confusions and sufferings brought to them by inchoate spiritual yearnings, anxieties, and epiphanies. Here distancing devices serve not so much to throw ideas and concepts into relief as to point up a nonmaterial dimension of experience that cannot be approached through narrative and characterization.

To state the matter from a slightly different perspective, in earlier works, Godard eschewed psychology in favor of what he perceived as a higher and more abstract level of ideological construction. In *Hail Mary,* his partial erasure of psychology and conventional narrative serves the different purpose of exposing a nonrational and largely affective layer of experience. This nonrationality is something different from, and more mysterious and profound than, the irrationality of social and cultural arrangements in contemporary European and American life, which Godard posited and criticized in many earlier films. It is a spiritual rather than a psychological or sociological phenomenon, and although he makes little attempt to define or depict it in concrete terms, it lies at the heart of *Hail Mary*, explaining and justifying its unconventional cinematic tactics.

One precedent for this in Godard's work may be found in a key sequence of a key film, *Vivre sa vie*. In a brief speech, visually heralded by a camera movement that purposefully isolates the speaker, a character quotes from a child's essay on the subject of barnyard animals, saying (in more colloquial language) that removal of the outside reveals the inside, while removal of the inside reveals the soul. This is an apt metaphor for Godard's method, or at least his aspiration, in many of his most complex and interesting films, including those that have no overt religious or theological content. Getting beyond the "outside" of his characters—beyond appearance, manner, gesture, behavior—is one of his chief aims and purposes in cinema. Hence he rarely tells straightforward stories about people; but neither does he stop at revealing their "insides," or psychological states. Indeed, the activity of psychological exposure, which constitutes an ultimate goal for many thoughtful filmmakers, is only a first step for Godard. Having established special conditions—the absence of traditional narrative and the presence of exposed psychological mechanisms—he then seeks to use these conditions to reveal new insights regarding the social, political, and behavioral interaction of diverse people in specific social and cultural situations. Hence the strong, even obsessive sociological and political dimension of most Godard films, from the early *A bout de souffle* and *Le petit soldat* through such later efforts as *Sauve qui peut (la vie)* and *Prénom: Carmen.*

Hail Mary takes this exploration into new territory, going beyond socio-political and psychological analysis to a quest for awareness on a still deeper experiential plane—removing the "outside," like other Godard films, and then proceeding to remove the "inside" to expose something that might be called the soul. Since he evidently considers the soul discoverable through close examination of characters in states of confusion and suffering, Godard allows more emotional resonance to his characters (especially to Mary and Joseph, but to others as well) than one finds at any point in such signature films as *Weekend* and *Numéro deux.*

More important yet, in a step that might seem regressive were it not tied to some of Godard's most innovative maneuvers in other respects, he ties this emotionality directly to the psychologies and personalities of his characters. The receptive spectator can find an emotionally expressive dimension in all of Godard's works; even a compulsively alienating film like *Weekend*, with its radical and continual use of long shots, shock cuts, printed words, and narrative fragmentation, is designed not to replace emotionality with cerebration but to evoke on *both* levels a sense of Godard's sociopolitical concern. He continues to operate on an emotional as well as an intellectual level in *Hail Mary*, but here the primary vehicle for emotive content is less the film's cinematic style (which *is* the primary vehicle in *Weekend* and many other works) than the experiences of the main characters and the acting of the performers who play them. For all its density and complexity on a cinematic level, *Hail Mary* thus emerges as a less "abstract" and more immediately human work than many others in the Godard canon, even excluding the films of the Dziga Vertov period. This is a logical consequence of the film's attempt to confront spiritual and theological issues, which Godard sees as intimately connected with characteristically human vulnerability, uncertainty, and suffering.

Miéville's film, *The Book of Mary*, prepares the spectator for the mingled

intellectual and emotive operations of *Hail Mary* with its relatively straightforward telling of an extended anecdote about a girl whose parents are having
an emotional conflict. It also serves as an elegant and purposeful introduction
to formal concerns that will continue to make themselves felt in Godard's
film.

To a greater degree than most filmmakers, Godard considers image,
speech, and music individually manipulable (although closely related) elements of the cinematic experience. Hence his longtime willingness to combine
(or uncombine) the three in ways that may seem arbitrary and eccentric by the
standards of conventional narrative-based film. His remark on the "Catholic
images and Protestant music" of *Hail Mary* shows him to be, once again,
at least as concerned with pictorial and musical content as with narrative
development. *The Book of Mary* serves as a formal prelude to *Hail Mary* by
isolating and calling attention to three essential cinematic elements: image,
word, and music. It does so through artful use of its main character, who—
three times in the course of the film—ceases being a character in a convention-
ally arranged scene and becomes the sole focus of the film's attention.

The first occasion is a scene that shows young Mary sitting at a table with
her parents. Shortly before this moment, Mary's mother has expressed a desire
to "see clearly." She repeats this wish, then wonders aloud why people are
afraid of clarity. Also present is Mary's father, ironically wearing dark glasses,
as if he embodied an attitude exactly opposite from that of his wife. Evidently
hoping to fend off unpleasant dinner-table conversation, Mary suddenly
launches into a lecture on the eye, taking the metaphorical idea of "seeing
clearly" and literalizing it into a momentary obsession with the optical mecha-
nism itself. This moment serves two functions. First, it calls direct attention
to one of cinema's key elements, the image, which is perceived through
the eye. Second, it leads immediately to thematic material that plays a part
throughout the *Hail Mary* diptych. As a model of the eye, Mary uses a bisected
apple, which has strong Old Testament connotations. (Apple-eating figures
prominently in both parts of *Hail Mary*.) She then places a nut into the center
of the apple half—an image recalling a conjoined sperm and ovum—and
specifically refers to it as resembling a baby in a mother's womb. She further
comments that the eye is made largely of water, thereby introducing the water
references and water imagery that recur in both films.

In the very next scene, Mary again takes the film into her hands. She is
reading Baudelaire from a printed text, introducing the importance of words
as references, referents, and solid presences in both *Hail Mary* films. The
poem concerns the loss of volition, the loss of control over one's destiny, and

fear at this prospect, concepts that will become increasingly important in both films. Here verbal activity, a second pillar of cinema, becomes momentarily the entire focus of the film.

The third key Mary scene is the sequence when she plays music and dances. Here music replaces the word as the primary focus, and Miéville takes great care to announce that this is happening. An excerpt from a concerto was played on a phonograph in a scene just a bit earlier, and the generic structure of concerto form was specifically compared (in dialogue) with conversation. The concerto is now replaced by a symphony, erasing the conversational (and implicitly dialoguelike) implications of the concerto. Once the word has been wholly displaced in this manner and symphonically structured music has filled the available aural space, Mary proceeds to fill the screen with the visual equivalent of music—choreography.

In these three scenes, the film moves through a series of three distinct emphases: (1) imagery and the eye, (2) the spoken and printed word, (3) music and choreographic gesture. As if completing this cycle, the most striking characteristic of Mary's choreography is the resemblance of her gestures to swimming. This recalls the water reference in the earlier apple/eye scene and consolidates the importance of water as a theme of both *Hail Mary* films, with forceful connotations of birth and death.

Mary has *The Book of Mary* to herself once more before it ends—in the coda, when she seats herself before an egg and breaks it. The roundness of the egg prefigures many other round images (from moon to basketball) that form a major leitmotif of both *Hail Mary* films. It especially prefigures the image of Mary's mouth at the end of Godard's film, sharing not only its temporal placement at the conclusion of the narrative but also its silence, its openness, and its generally enigmatic quality. The opening of the egg can be construed as an opening into the next film: From this ruptured ovum will erupt everything to come in Godard's movie. This raises the fascinating question of what is to erupt from Mary's open mouth at the end of *that* film. The answer must be something indefinable (hence her silence) and, in keeping with Godard's spiritual quest on this occasion, perhaps unnameable and ineffable.

The mysterious and seemingly arbitrary quality of the final imagery in *The Book of Mary* and *Hail Mary* is perhaps the clearest indication of both filmmakers' wish to capture some hint or echo of a nonphysical, nonpsychological reality. Since the vocabulary of cinema is rooted in materiality and physical appearance, this endeavor necessarily entails some negation or erasure of normal cinematic mechanisms and methodologies. Godard and his colleagues have not been hesitant to attempt this negation in the past; it has been noted how thoroughly many Godard films eschew commonplace approaches to editing, mise-en-scène, and narrativity.

Godard's coda to *Hail Mary* represents one of his most audacious steps in this direction, however. The close-up shot of Mary's mouth resonates with many potential meanings, including the suggestion of sexual penetration (in the mouth's relationship with Mary's lipstick). It also echoes imagery in other Godardian work, from his own first feature, *A bout de souffle*—wherein both Jean-Paul Belmondo and Jean Seberg trace the outline of their lips with their fingers[2]—to Miéville's *Book of Mary* coda. The latter scene, with young Mary facing her ruptured egg, is uncommonly bold in its almost dreamlike unconventionality, but the concluding shot of *Hail Mary* is stronger yet. I have already noted that its most important qualities—the mouth's roundness, openness, mysteriousness, and silence—are shared with Miéville's egg image. Yet the last of these qualities, silence, takes on a new importance since an egg is naturally silent, while the adult Mary's mouth has *not* been conspicuously silent over the course of her film; indeed, she has done a good deal of verbalizing about the conditions visited on her and the events in which she has participated. Her silence at the end of her story stands in contrast to her earlier verbosity, just as her chastity has stood in contrast with the sexual behavior that would be considered "normal" for a young person of her time, place, and relationship with a potential lover.

This suggests that her silence and her chastity may have common roots in both her personality and the supranormal events that have marked her life. Looking first at her silence, one recalls the semiotic distinction between language as *parole* and language as *langue*—the first connoting the individual act of speaking, the second connoting the overall construct of a language as a whole, which is never reducible to actuality (as *parole* is) because it embraces all possibilities available to all speakers of the language. By refusing to speak a concrete word, Mary leaves open all possibilities of verbal expression and interpretation. This echoes her earlier decision to remain celibate and her suggestion that, by avoiding an individual sex act with an individual man, she has remained open for (and open to) all possibilities of love. Mary's silence and chastity are therefore not negative acts but supremely positive ones, courageous (like the filmmaking of Godard and Miéville themselves) for their openness to ambiguity and their willingness to avoid the verbal, visual, and behavioral reductionisms that reside in most narrative cinema.

It can be noted as well that Mary's silence is also Godard's silence, since he is the *auteur* of her story. We can therefore look to her statements about her experiences within the film for clues to Godard's spiritual aspirations and feelings. We find Mary celebrating, at key moments, a transcendence that goes beyond intellectual or psychological fulfillment—just as the filmmaking of Godard and Miéville seeks to go beyond those levels, too. Mary says she is not "resigned" to what has happened, since one cannot be "resigned" to being loved. She also says, "I am joy," not only accepting but embracing the things that have happened to her and the inner transformations they have brought. Transcendence and transformation—real in Mary's case, vicarious (perhaps wistfully so) in Godard's—can also be felt in her strong words about God's power, which she finds so great that it must be felt rather than named or measured. That is to say, identification and quantification are too limited to be useful in assessing the supranormal realities that have touched Mary's life.

Accordingly, Godard and Miéville have used radically unconventional cinematic methods in an attempt to bypass the usual forms of motion-picture portrayal and construction. Their two-part film is not a depiction but an exploration. Neither filmmaker may have had a precise idea of what he or she was after in attempting it, and there is room for debate as to whether the Godard-Miéville team (or we ourselves) have a deeper or stronger awareness of nonmaterial realms—realms of spiritual possibility rather than physical or psychological actuality—after encountering *Hail Mary*. But the boldness and commitment of both *Hail Mary* films are unquestionable, and the two Marys themselves are important icons of what critic Paul Schrader calls "transcendental style" in film, even if the Godard-Miéville methodologies have little in common with the formulas that Schrader identifies as producing transcendental experiences in more straightforwardly narrative movies.[3] From the opened egg of the child and the open mouth of the adult spring more expressive and interpretive possibilities than most reality- and convention-bound films begin to offer.

Notes

1. Godard interview with Giuseppina Marin in *Corriere della Sera*, April 25, 1985.
2. Gerald O'Grady has pointed this out.
3. Paul Schrader, *Tanscendental Style in Film* (Berkeley: University of California Press, 1972).

6

Jean-Luc Godard's *Hail Mary*: Cinema's "Virgin Birth"

Inez Hedges

THE FRENCH New Wave will always be remembered as a movement that opened up new possibilities for cinema as an art form. The potential of the film medium was enriched by the French *auteur* theory, the play on Hollywood genres, and the exploration of film as language and hence of filmmaking as a kind of writing.

The *auteur* theory has been the New Wave's most lasting legacy; the legitimacy of other national cinemas has ever since been staked on auteuristic claims. Whether they be those of New German cinema's Herzog and Fassbinder, Australia's Peter Weir, or Britain's Derek Jarman or Peter Greenaway, films are marketed in the authorial mode.

It is all the more significant that Jean-Luc Godard, a film author by anyone's measure, should have voiced dissatisfaction with the concept of directorial authorship in statements and interviews published in the 1980s. For him, the emphasis on authorship is a sign that the essentially collaborative medium of cinema has gone off the track. Even people involved in making films are so impressed by the director-author that they fail to contribute to the full extent of their capacities. As a result, he says in an interview published in *Artpress*, films today exploit only 10 percent of the capabilities of the medium and the talents of those who make them.[1]

Godard's preoccupation with film language (the metacinematic dimension of his oeuvre) has meant that he has always been concerned with the medium as such; all of his films, from *A bout de souffle* (*Breathless*) onward, have addressed themselves to this issue. If Godard now turns to the biblical story of Mary and Joseph, we can be sure that one of the reasons is that this story enables him to say something about the film medium that no other subject could offer him. I will therefore be discussing Godard's treatment of his subject as a metaphor about filmmaking, an approach that substantially ignores what has caused the greatest controversy about *Je vous salue, Marie*— the apparent religious subject matter of the film.

In the interview previously mentioned, Godard has underscored the fact that the French language makes it possible to speak of the "virgin" celluloid (*la pellicule vierge*) imprinted by the body of the camera. We may thus take Godard's thematization of virginity in this film to stand for the entire complex of theories that he has attached to cinematic representation. In his total oeuvre, the image of virginity is strongly counterbalanced as well by the thematization of prostitution in such films as *Vivre sa vie (My Life to Live,* 1962), *Alphaville* (1965), *Deux ou trois choses que je sais d'elle (Two or Three Things I Know about Her,* 1966), and *Sauve qui peut (la vie) (Every Man for Himself,* 1980).

Godard's view of cinema has consistently been a transcendent one: he advocates a cinema that does not "prostitute" itself as entertainment. As a member of André Bazin's *Cahiers du cinéma* coterie in the 1950s, the young filmmaker came into contact with Bazin's theory that the cinematic medium allowed people to come one step closer toward the age-old dream of reproducing reality in art.[2] Ideally, Bazin wrote, the screen should function as a window, letting reality transpire through it; at the same time, filmed reality will be *visioned* reality, a heightened and intensified experience of the real. For the sake of consistency, Bazin was obliged to advocate a cinema in which montage (the editing together of shots taken from different angles to make up a scene) was reduced to a minimum and the technical supports of the medium were effaced. He advocated the use of deep focus, the long take, and conveying meaning as much as possible through mise-en-scène.[3] But in doing so, he came up squarely against the paradox that the film image is a frame, even when it is a "window"—any image operates within the constraints of selection from the elements of the real world that it reproduces. And the meaning intended by a filmmaker will come from his or her manner of framing. As Dudley Andrew explains, "The screen as 'window' is a place of perception; as 'frame' or border it delimits and organizes perception for signification."[4]

Godard was thus obliged to adapt Bazin's philosophy to his own filmmaking practice. In the important essay "Montage mon bon souci" (Montage My Fine Care), published in the *Cahiers du cinéma* in 1956, Godard uses the Bazinian criterion of naturalness to defend montage: "When montage effects surpass those of mise-en-scène in efficacity, the beauty of the latter is doubled, the unforeseen unveiling secrets by its charm in an operation analogous to using unknown quantities in mathematics."[5] For this reason he suggests that directors must be intimately involved in the editing of their own films and that editors and cinematographers need to participate in and contribute to the particular vision of the director. Godard's first movies were more than attempts to put life on the screen; they were snatches of life itself. "The originality of the New Wave," he says, "comes from the fact that we made films before we had lived."[6] Living and filming were one and the same thing.

The stake that Godard has in defining his life through films brings with it many dangers. Over the years, the filmmaker has used the theme of prostitution as a way of critiquing film language. In *Alphaville*, the visiting journalist Lemmy Caution finds that a "seductress" has been routinely assigned to him at the hotel. In his room, the first thing she looks for is his "Bible," a dictionary placed in the nightstand of every hotel room. Later, Natasha von Braun explains to him that words are made to disappear every day in the city. The inhabitants are not allowed to use any word that does not appear in the "Bible," which is issued by the central government. Words like *conscience, tenderness,* and *autumn light* have already disappeared. At a ceremony, the journalist watches several executions of people accused of showing emotion. The loss of love and the loss of language are seen to go hand in hand with degraded sex. The hero's confrontation with the central computer, Alpha 60, ensures the metacinematic dimension of Godard's meaning, as Lemmy answers the question "What brings light out of darkness?" Lemmy's answer, "poetry," suggests that cinema, the language of light, will triumph over the bleak world of *Alphaville*. In *Vivre sa vie*, cinematic representation is once again presented as a mode of redemption; Nana is shot at the end of the film, but not before she has found true love in a young man who reads to her from Poe's story "The Oval Portrait." The story of the model who expires just as the painter exclaims that he has managed to paint life itself on the canvas prefigures Nana's own apotheosis as the most lifelike heroine Godard has ever shown on the screen.

In more recent films, the tone of Godard has turned dark. *Sauve qui peut (la vie)* includes a memorable scene in which a customer directs two prostitutes in chain-reaction sex that is supposed to mime the negative mechanics of the television industry ("We've got the image now, let's add the sound," he says). Increasingly, Godard has found it difficult to find the kind of collaborators who will make it possible to inscribe the real onto the screen. The era of risktaking, of improvisation and free invention, is over. Cinema is commercialized—prostituted.

In *Je vous salue, Marie*, Godard confronts this problem head-on. This film should be considered in tandem with *Scénario du film Passion*, the 1983 film whose very title announces its metacinematic dimension. This time the discussion of the mode of composition is included in the opening moments of the film itself, where Godard's voice is heard offscreen: "For the story there were certain givens, but one had to see whether they could exist . . . that's the work of the script, afterwards you make the movie. But you must create, not a world, but the *possibility* of a world. The camera is there to do the work, to make this possibility probable or rather this probability possible, to see; to see the invisible and to see what happens if the invisible becomes visible."[7] Ironically, it is Godard, whose works have been the most engaged in the concept of film as *text* (witness the collage of quotations in such films as *A bout de souffle* or *Weekend*), who now gropes for a cinema beyond words.

The figure of Mary is one to which Godard would naturally gravitate in pursuit of this project since she stands in Western culture as the feminine counterbalance to organized religious mythology that gives primacy to the word. Julia Kristeva has explicated the dual nature of Christian faith: "On the one hand, the difficult adventure of the Word: a passion; on the other, the reassuring cloak, the preverbal image of the mother: a love."[8] Godard chooses the figure of Mary to embody his concept of a virginal cinema, a film in which the celluloid, even though it passes in front of the aperture of the lens, though it receives an inscription (an impregnation) by the opening of the camera (which is a body), still communicates an unmediated image. This is what Stanley Cavell has called the "automatism" of film—the sense that cinema reproduces the world while confirming the filmmaker's absence from it.[9]

If Godard now finds it necessary to confront this issue directly by telling the story of the virgin birth, it is important to note that this is not a new preoccupation. Certain moments of his previous films seem graced by the transparency that becomes the central issue in *Je vous salue, Marie*. In *Weekend*, the errant couple come upon a pianist who has set up his grand piano in a barnyard; the camera makes two counterclockwise pans around the barnyard, then one clockwise turn, while the pianist plays a Mozart sonata. In the end, the Mozart piece appears to motivate the images rather than the other way around. The laborer who walks by with his shovel seems an accompaniment of the music. There is the sense of stopped time, of a moment eternalized. This scene, which retrospectively reads as one of the finest in Godard's film-making, as one of the most consistent with his blending of thematic and formal concerns, was understood very differently at the time. Robin Wood, not incorrectly, stressed the political content, seeing the scene as a joke about Minister of Culture André Malraux's policy of bringing culture to the people: "The thrice-repeated circuit of the farmyard conveys a sense of enclosure, insisting on the total irrelevance of the Mozart performance . . . to the world of pileups and general disintegration outside."[10]

Today that political reading seems overshadowed by the scene's obvious connection to Godard's formal experimentation, what David Bordwell has called his "parametric" style of narration.[11] Bordwell notes that it is important to distinguish between the subject matter of Godard's films (which may appear political) and the films' approach to it (in which the concern for form predominates). The publicity attending upon *Je vous salue, Marie* and the attention paid to it by the Catholic church ("Banned in Boston") seem particularly misplaced in view of the fact that Godard's real subject matter is the search for cinematic form.

Je vous salue, Marie should be taken seriously as a dramatization of the crisis that pervades today's cinema. In the *Artpress* interview, Godard says that he considers the film a failure because the collaboration necessary for the production of a great film proved elusive. He describes his mode of filmmaking as essentially passive; you have a basic idea, then wait for the film to happen (as you wait for a miracle, a manifestation of God—what else can explain our fascination with the virgin birth?). Even though the filmmaker says the actors failed to show any curiosity about this project, and even though the film in a sense never "happened," "there were moments in which I ended up believing in the Holy Ghost. . . . When we needed a snowfall, we got it, and if we missed her, she made us believe that she wouldn't come a second time."[12] The astonishing shot of a jet airplane crossing the sun—made possible by chance—which becomes a metaphor for Mary's fertilization by the Holy Ghost, is perhaps the most obvious instance where the filmmaker's readiness to use accidental material offered by the real world has paid off.

The way Godard lies in wait for events to "happen" in front of his camera resembles the surrealist theory of objective chance, the idea (as Bréton wrote in 1920) that mind and the world are consonant in privileged moments. Artistry consists in being aware of such moments. When captured on film, when integrated in a meaningful montage, they truly can become instances in which the world seems to speak through film, when the seen vision succeeds in magnifying everyday perception. Godard states that those moments come for him only rarely now.

There is in Kristeva's discussion of Mary a startling passage in which she reveals her feelings about her motherhood, in which the body of woman is described as a cross, a receptacle-womb anchored by thighs and traversed by limbs. Kristeva sees woman as a cross but also as a crossing, a meeting of paths (*carrefour*).[13] Godard's plaintiveness makes one think of these cruciform and crucified mothers: he—and his film with him—is a fertile crossroad on which technicians and actors walk endlessly back and forth without feeling. If in *Je vous salue, Marie* he has not succeeded in the mise-en-scène of a miracle, at least he has conveyed the powerlessness of words to convey our real experience. And we should not forget that Anne-Marie Miéville's short film *Le livre de Marie* forms a diptych with Godard's. Here all along was that moment of suspended time that Godard had so laboriously sought. As Miéville's Marie dances by herself, we suddenly experience one of those privileged moments in cinema when we seem to be looking through the window into another world that exists apart from us and is more perfect, more innocent, more real, than our own.

Notes

1. Dominique Paini and Guy Scarpetta, "Jean-Luc Godard et la curiosité du sujet," *Art Press*, special series no. 4 (1984–1985): 9–10.

2. André Bazin, "The Myth of Total Cinema," in *What Is Cinema?* vol. 1, ed., trans. Hugh Gray (Berkeley: University of California Press, 1967), 21. Bazin writes that the myth that guides all the techniques of mechanical reproduction of reality in the nineteenth century was "an integral realism, a recreation of the world in its own image, an image unburdened by the freedom of interpretation of the artist or the irreversibility of time."

3. Bazin, "The Evolution of the Language of Cinema," in *What Is Cinema?* 23–40.

4. Dudley Andrew, *Concepts in Film Theory* (Oxford: Oxford University Press, 1984), 43.

5. Jean Norboni and Tom Milne, eds., *Godard on Godard* (New York: Viking Press, 1972), 39.

6. Paini and Scarpetta, 14.

7. Jean-Luc Godard, "Scénario du film Passion," *Avant-Scène Cinéma* 323–324 (1984): 81.

8. Julia Kristeva, *Histoires d'amour* (Paris: Denoël, 1983), 239.

9. Stanley Cavell, *The World Viewed*, enlarged ed. (Cambridge: Harvard University Press, 1979), 23. I would like to thank Professor Cavell for the many pleasant conversations that helped me in writing this article. The relevance of Julia Kristeva's work to this whole question is, in particular, one of the insights for which I am indebted to him.

10. Robin Wood, "Godard and *Weekend*," in Jean-Luc Godard, *Weekend and Wind from the East* (New York: Simon and Schuster, 1972), 11.

11. David Bordwell, "Godard and Narration," in *Narration and the Fiction Film* (Madison: University of Wisconsin, 1985), 311–57.

12. Paini and Scarpetta, *Art Press*, 7. My awkward translation tries to convey the sense that "*chute de neige*" is feminine and hence seems personalized in Godard's discourse.

13. Kristeva, 240–41.

7

An Alternative to Godard's Metaphysics: Cinematic Presence in Miéville's *Le livre de Marie*

Ellen Draper

IN *Je vous salue, Marie* the dogged intelligence of Godard's filmmaking is as clear as ever. Some of the film's images, both verbal and visual, are haunting. Yet as much as I respect Godard's meditation on the virgin birth, I do not *like* the film. As a whole, it seems to lack depth: its contradictions and discrepancies are all on the surface, and its philosophical dilemma is predictable if not tiresome.

Taking the virgin birth as its story and Godard's inevitable alienation from the virgin birth as its real subject, *Je vous salue, Marie* casts woman as a transcendental cipher. She turns out to be a disappointment in the role; the role itself turns out to be a disappointment; and the film ends by recognizing Mary as a merely human other. This is not the first Godard film that concludes with the image of a woman standing for the limits of (masculine) knowledge. Since the last shot of *A bout de souffle*, Godard has used the otherness and venality of women as conclusive representations of the limits of cinematic signification. In *Je vous salue, Marie*, however, the stakes are particularly high, for Mary's mystery is divine, and Godard's film knows that it is not.

A barrier of sacred sexual difference looms between Godard and Mary and inevitably becomes the central theme of the film. No resolution is possible, so the film forces its viewer into the subject positioning epitomized by Joseph, who is bullied by Gabriel until he agrees to look at Mary without touching her. In a similar fashion, the viewer is pummeled by Godard's camera work and editing into an acceptance of Mary that precludes the possibility of empathetic interaction. Something like Joseph's resignation to his role ("Je resterais," he tells Mary) consigns the viewer to the uncomfortable position of watching Mary exposed physically and emotionally by Godard while the viewer is held at a distance via cuts and camera angles. The shots of Joseph's taxi waiting patiently that are intercut with scenes of Mary struggling to accept God's (and Godard's) role for her are particularly annoying. What if the viewer is not patiently waiting but impatiently wishing to feel closer to Mary or to be done with the whole business?

Mary is not the only mystery held at a distance by Godard's film. The glorious shots of sunsets, fields of grass, and lakes stand for the mystery of the universe without making it present. No person appears in these shots; they are devoid of psychological inflection, devoid of human scale. The embodiment of Godard's philosophical meditation apart from Mary, the shots of the natural world are cool, abstract. The film accounts for this abstraction and distance in the figure of the exiled professor who wonders at the complexity of the cosmos, until he is seduced by Eve. That story, running in counterpoint to Mary's pregnancy, serves to remind us of the mortal need for salvation and returns us to the problem of Mary's mystery.

What are we to make of the last scene of the film, when Gabriel greets Mary as the mother of Christ and finally speaks the film's title "Je vous salue, Marie"? All the transcendental gestures of the film are gathered in the angel's recognition of this woman's potential power of redemption. Yet the film then follows Mary as she buys and applies lipstick, and the last shot of the film is a close-up of Mary's gaping painted mouth, open as if to swallow the camera in a gesture of fellatio.[1] Is it possible to take seriously Gabriel's dictum, "A hole is not a hole," in the face of such a crudely human abyss?

It is specifically unclear what sort of a claim to know, or not know, Mary this last shot of the film might be. Is the camera poised to penetrate Mary as the Holy Ghost did, as a man might, or as a camera must? Godard's inability to penetrate the meaning of Mary's divinity and femininity may stand as a measure of the limits of masculine knowledge, but need it stand as a woman's cinematic cogito? All that is really conclusive is that Mary, a woman after all, cannot stand as an adequate signifier for Godard's faith and his doubt.

The problem is not that in making the film Godard somehow went astray; it is rather that he felt called upon to make this film in the first place. Once the cinematic project was under way, who could fault Godard's pervasive skepticism, questioning every basis for knowing Mary? Everything must be doubted. Yet the simple—or, depending on how one looks at it, enormously complex—bond of gender similitude is unavailable to Godard's meditation on what he can know and doubt of Mary as the mother of God. In some sense, then, *Je vous salue, Marie* is from the outset not only an impossible quest for understanding but an insignificant claim to knowledge of uncertainty. Godard's arpeggio of doubt cannot question the essential issue of Mary's femininity.

When in the last shot of the film Godard reveals the limits of what he can know and question, it is too late for the viewer to decline to share his struggle.

Perhaps a man watching the film could accept this failure of conclusion as a matter of course. For a woman, it is especially difficult, for the epistemological issues at stake have been cast in terms of gender by Godard at the expense of the female viewer who assumed that she had a role in the film's questioning.

HOWEVER DISENFRANCHISED, irritated, or bored the female viewer may feel watching *Je vous salue, Marie*, there is comfort to be taken in the fact that Godard and his collaborator Anne-Marie Miéville have decided to program Miéville's own short film, *Le livre de Marie*, along with the Godard film. The Miéville film is as deeply and successfully feminine as Godard's film is ineffectively masculine.

Because *Le livre de Marie* is shown before *Je vous salue, Marie* and Miéville's film is about a young girl named Mary and Godard's is about a young woman named Mary, we are tempted to read the two films as a single linear narrative. Postulating that the Mary in *Le livre de Marie* grows up to be the Mary of *Je vous salue, Marie* brings another layer of complexity to Godard's already complicated meditation on the virgin birth. It is not just possible but in some way undeniable that Miéville's Mary provides a psychological history for Godard's Mary. The girl who watches her parents' marriage break apart and concludes *Le livre de Marie* by breaking an egg is metaphorically, if not literally, the young woman who struggles with the idea of a virgin pregnancy in Godard's film. As the first section of a diptych, Miéville's film offers us the story of a child in a reassuringly straightforward narrative before Godard's film unleashes its dazzling play of dualities and adult doubt.

To read the two films as a single work, however, is to risk relegating the Miéville film to the role of prologue. Unlike *Je vous salue, Marie*, *Le livre de Marie* does not stridently insist upon its own ambiguity, and the film's accessibility may seem to be a weakness rather than a grace. Because Miéville's film does not make recognizing the limits of interpretation a condition of understanding its narrative, we may be tempted to undervalue the film in our estimation of Godard's work and as a result either dismiss the Miéville film as inferior cinema or misrepresent its complexities by describing them in Godard's terms. It does not explain the complexities of Miéville's film to assert, as Peter Harcourt does, that "the film [*Le livre de Marie*] is full of binary oppositions! In a most classical structuralist way, *Le livre de Marie* opposes the beauty of images of nature to the ugliness of disputatious speech; Nature to Culture; woman to man; yin to yang—literally "v" to "∧" in this film; when Marie visits her father and they study triangles together, she is forming a trough with her hands, he a roof."[2] As a description of Godard's film, such emphasis on binary oppositions would be appropriate, but as a description of Miéville's film, it is misleading. The dramatic force of *Le livre de Marie* is not built from such a dialectical struggle. It gathers in more subtle ways, and achieves a remarkable resonance that is commemorated in Mary's dance to Mahler's Ninth Symphony near the end of the film. No oppositions underwrite this moment; it is a demonstration of the power of sheer cinematic presence.

Without denying the way *Le livre de Marie* functions as part of the larger cinematic work that comprises both films, I want to consider Miéville's film as the equal of Godard's film rather than the introduction to it. *Le livre de Marie* and *Je vous salue, Marie* are complementary but quite different accounts of the transformation of Mary into the mother of Christ, and considered on an equal footing, the films demonstrate the fundamental differences between a woman's act of creation and homage and a man's.

At the heart of each film lie questions about sexuality, creation, human limitation, and transcendence. For Miéville, these questions become the basis of a parable of instruction; for Godard, they serve as the basis of a metaphysical meditation. Surely it is not a coincidence that Miéville has created an integral text—a book of Mary—where Godard has created a fragmented one, a salutation that cannot escape the first person.

Le livre de Marie does not ignore the possibility of fragmentation or the isolation of a subjective point of view. In fact, the film addresses these concerns in its opening shots. The first shot is of a lake seen through the balusters of a porch rail. From offscreen, a man's voice says, "So what do you think? That if you're alone you'll escape routine?" Another shot of the lake through the balusters replaces the first. The framing is identical, but the focal depth and light are slightly different. It is just possible to tell that this is another view of the scene. A woman's voice replies, "No, it's not that. . . ."

As the woman goes on to voice her complaint, the film cuts to other shots, and over the developing quarrel on the sound track the film shows us a montage of ravishingly beautiful images—the sun half hidden by clouds, lawns, a rose, fruit in a bowl. We begin to see shots of the principals in the quarrel. The schism between image and sound track grows. In some shots the woman is seated in a white chair; in others she is unaccountably absent. While we hear her voice on the sound track we see her sitting silently. It is tempting to try to interpret the fragmentation of this sequence—for example, the woman's first absence from the white chair occurs as the man says, "You can't face up to things"—but my sense is that such an attempt would ultimately be more frustrating than fruitful. What seems most significant about the disparate shots is the fact of their disparity, the way they disrupt the narrative of the film and call into question the cinematic process of signification.

Because the fragmentation of this montage is anticipated in the first two shots of the film when the camera takes up the different views of the lake as a way of reminding us that Mary's father and mother see the same thing differently, the disruption of the film's signification remains anchored in the narrative of the film. As the film goes on to elucidate the difference between Mary's father and mother, it begins to cover over, repair, the initial fragmentation by fully voicing the difference that precipitated the quarrel. For Miéville, the articulation of difference is not divisive or limiting. It is the necessary development of meaning in a world that might otherwise remain picturesquely mute.

The measure of the difference between the man and the woman, and hence the measure of the film's recuperation of its initial fragmentation, is Mary. Throughout *Le livre de Marie* Mary appears as an integral character, a resoundingly whole person in a world of adolescent chaos. Much of the confusion is sexual. She is a young girl on the brink of womanhood, and her identity is being forged in the collapse of the archetypes of Mother and Father. The collapse threatens on every level, including the film's process of signification. Mary holds the film together as she holds herself together, and she becomes mysterious as she does so. Like characters in Hitchcock's late films (I am thinking of Norman Bates in *Psycho*, Melanie in *The Birds*, and Marnie), she speaks with an authority we can neither fully interrogate nor dismiss.

Mary is a cipher, a prophet, a teacher, a pupil. From her first appearance at the lunch table, where she unfolds the parable of the eye to her parents, she speaks a language that begs for interpretation but holds its origins within itself. Asking her father, who is wearing sunglasses, if his eyes are hurting him, and responding to her mother's stated wish to see more clearly, Mary presses a nut into half of an apple and launches into her story. The nut is compared to the pupil of an eye, floating like a child in his mother's belly. It has had a shock, and Mary is going to operate. The operation can be performed once only; if it is not successful, the eye withers.

This parable represents at once the project of the film and Mary's role in it. She is a pupil as well as an educator. She has had a shock, has been terrorized, by her parents' violence. Now she is undertaking a therapeutic operation, and what is at stake is vision—hers, her parents', ours. Like the fragmented opening sequence, however, what is most important about this scene may not be the interpretations one can draw from it but the manner of its presentation. The breach between Mary's father and mother is recognized by Mary's parable but contained by the act of storytelling. Thus the disrupted signification of the film's first sequence gives way to an inclusive symbolism that embraces all the disparities of the film.

Because the film allows us to measure the differences in Mary's parents only through Mary's presence, she becomes an embodiment of both the tension in the film and its containment. Once she appears at the lunch table and offers her parable of eye surgery, Mary appears in every scene. She enacts the narrative's need for resolution and at the same time emblematizes the film's process of signification, its continual appropriation of difference into the integral wholeness of parable. Mary's next parable casts her as a teacher dictating Baudelaire to students whom she repeatedly admonishes to silence. Silence is of course our lot as we watch the film, and it is perhaps the most appropriate response to the knowingness with which Mary speaks.

If *Le livre de Marie* confers grace upon our silence by characterizing it as the respectful silence of pupils undergoing instruction, it suggests that Mary shares this scene of instruction, and this silence, with us. She is never cast as an other to the viewer. Indeed, as the film progresses, it becomes more and more difficult to isolate Mary as the object of the camera's view, and it becomes hard to tell what we are to make of Mary as the subject of the film.

The camera takes up Mary's point of view most explicitly in the scene where she and her father discuss triangles. Being themselves two-thirds of the love triangle in the film, they are invoking meaning beyond their literal discussion of geometry, but it is not clear what authority Mary and the camera wield. Like the resonance of other scenes, the symbolism of this scene is so widely applicable that it remains essentially obscure, and the relation of Mary to the unfolding meaning of the film narrative is hard to determine.

In *Soft Talk on a Hard Subject between Two Friends*, a video Miéville and Godard made in association with Channel 4 in France the year after *Le livre de Marie* and *Je vous salue, Marie*, Miéville describes filmmaking as a place without landmarks: "It was an immense, infinite space stretching in infinite directions. A space where sentences didn't follow each other but interwove in infinite interaction. They were no longer sentences but gifts of the inexpressible—gifts of life, gifts of creation embracing the world conceived by a previous consciousness." This is a useful description of *Le livre de Marie*. What appeared to be fragmentation in the opening scene of the film was instead the basis of differences that are recuperated as the film begins its interweaving. What Miéville calls "sentences," the basic units of cinematic signification, are not exposed in their limitations but celebrated as "gifts of the inexpressible—gifts of life, gifts of creation." Mary is the emblem of this creation.

The insistence on Mary's presentness as the measure of Miéville's film comes to a climax when Mary dances to the haunting music of Mahler's symphony of death. This scene follows Mary's visit to her father, with whom she can listen to music but no longer live. For all we can tell, Mary has purposely withheld the record of Mahler's Ninth from her father's collection. The interpretive dance she performs is certainly the most authoritative expression she proffers in the film, but it is also clandestine, all but private. As Mahler's music swells, Mary transforms the living room that was the scene of the initial quarrel into a performance space. The shot of the lake that first registered the different views of her mother and father becomes the backdrop for part of the dance, with the doorway serving as an ad hoc proscenium. All by herself, Mary recuperates the differences of the film in her performance.

It is exactly the point of Mary's dance, I take it, that we have no ordinary words to describe the feelings she makes manifest. If we had words, we would not need this moment of cinematic catharsis. *Le livre de Marie* insists that this is a moment of catharsis. At a climactic point in Mahler's music, Mary collapses on the floor, into a silence and a stillness that is broken when her mother enters the room. "Are you dead? or just tired?" her mother asks, to which Mary replies, "Dead." A moment of crisis has been reached, and the crisis is one of cinematic signification as well as psychological motivation.

As with the end of Godard's *Je vous salue, Marie, Le livre de Marie* posits as its climactic moment the collapse of Mary as a signifier. Yet whereas in the Godard film what collapses is the filmmaker's ability to find meaning in Mary's femininity, in the Miéville film what collapses is Mary's performance. Godard offers us the futile violation of women as an expression of masculine skepticism. Miéville offers us a young woman's gesture of finitude, made in accordance with the camera's presence, and made in recognition of our presence as witnesses.

Miéville has made this crisis of signification an all-or-nothing proposition. The possibility of cinematic failure broached at the climactic moment in *Le livre de Marie* is finally attributable not just to Miéville or Mary but to us. Mary's dance ends in her "death" either because we have failed to see its meaning or because we have seen in it a possibility of transcendence that no mortal can maintain for long. If Mary's dance has not moved us and does not stand for us as the condensed presence of the film itself, Miéville's cinema has failed. Failing to see the meaning of Mary's dance is tantamount to failing to see the point of the whole film. If Mary's dance has meaning for us, the crisis of death and rebirth that Mary enacts holds out to us the possibility of our redemption as viewers in a way the crisis at the end of the Godard film cannot. Instead of Godard's metaphysical speculation on the limits of knowledge, in *Le livre de Marie* we are given—and we help create by being witness to—an enactment of faith in cinematic presence and process as we watch the film.

In *Soft and Hard*, Miéville goes on to say, "I think some things are inaccessible and can't be shown. For instance, when it comes to love relationships, love scenes, once you go beyond the Hollywood kiss you don't know how or what to show. You can only show other images of a process at work. If we go back to the image of the chicken and the egg . . . if you really want to show an image of the egg . . . perhaps you can indicate that while the egg is apparently motionless . . . all sorts of invisible things are happening inside it." The stunningly beautiful close-up of the egg that brings *Le livre de Marie* to its conclusion simultaneously demonstrates the motionless, mute wholeness of the world of the film and summarizes the "process at work" in the narrative. The egg cannot be subdivided; it can only be broken. To make an omelet, or end a film, one must break the egg, and yet as Mary rattles off a string of platitudes about eggs, Miéville reminds us that saying this is a truism. The difference between saying and doing is everything here.

It is fitting that Miéville's film avoids representing the miracle of Mary's conception of Christ. Godard tackles this problem of representation head-on. Where Godard's film continually discovers the limitations of its mortal genesis in comparison with the virgin birth, Miéville's act of creation takes upon itself Mary's role of procreation. *Le livre de Marie* is no more or less mortal, no more or less divine, than Mary is as she dances. The film does not presume to represent Mary's divinity but to make it present to us.

Mary's dance to Mahler and her collapse into a deathlike swoon are not the end of the film, it turns out, but the beginning of another moral tale, this one told by Mary's mother, who points out to her daughter that her name, Marie, is an acrostic for *aimer*. Before the triviality of representation sweeps back into the world of the film along with Mary's platitudes about eggs, a woman reminds a girl that her identity is an arrangement of love. If we accept this blessing, as Mary does, the film stands as a glowing tribute to the filmmaking as an act of love and an affirmation of relationship. This is Miéville's "process at work." The egg is only *apparently* motionless at the end of *Le livre de Marie* as the knife swings down to break it.

Notes

1. Peter Harcourt proposes that this shot of Mary putting on lipstick—"always for Godard, an indication of prostitution"—is the only indecent shot in the film. See Harcourt, "Metaphysical Cinema," *CineACTION* 11 (December 1987): 6.

2. Harcourt, 3.

8

One Catholic's View

Robert Kiely

IN HAWTHORNE'S *The Marble Faun*, the New England heroine rushes around Rome in a moment of anguish looking for consolation at one of the hundreds of shrines to Mary. An aesthete and a Puritan, she has no luck. None of the Marys satisfies her "fine sense of the fit and the decorous. . . . She never found just the virgin mother whom she needed. Here, it was an earthly mother, worshipping the earthly baby in her lap, as any and every mother does."

It is difficult to imagine a Catholic (of whatever kind) reading this passage without amusement. More than any other element in our tradition, certainly more than the pope, Mary is peculiarly ours. Though there is a theology of Mary, most Catholics have only the vaguest notion of it. In a fairly typical conversation among adult well-educated Catholics the other day, I heard someone ask why the feast of the Immaculate Conception was not nine months before Christmas. The person asking the question had forgotten, as many Catholics do, that the feast refers to the conception of Mary, not of Jesus. There are also dozens of books about Mary, including pious prefeminist ones and irreverent postfeminist ones, which most Catholics never read.

The Catholic experience of Mary is not abstract or analytical but concrete, ordinary, and intimate. Most Catholics, even today, have mothers or grand-mothers who say the rosary. Each bead calls for a recitation of the "Hail Mary" or a reflection on one of the "joyful, sorrowful or glorious mysteries" (moments) of Mary's life. Most Catholics have been exposed over a lifetime to countless images, cheap and plastic or rich marble and paint, of Mary enthroned, Mary in agony beneath the cross, Mary with the angel Gabriel, or simply Mary in a blue veil with outstretched arms. Catholic monasteries and convents close each day, as they have for centuries, with the "Salve Regina" (Hail, Holy Queen) or "Regina Coeli" (Queen of Heaven). And, of course, all Catholics know the "Hail Mary"; indeed, for many, it is the first prayer they have learned and remains, therefore, the simplest, most basic, and most innocent expression of faith: "Hail Mary, full of grace, the Lord is with thee, blessed art thou among women and blessed is the fruit of thy womb, Jesus.

Holy Mary, Mother of God, pray for us sinners, now and at the hour of our death. Amen."

The way the prayer ends, asking Mary to pray for us "now and at the hour of our death," reminds us of an ancient Catholic tradition which holds that Mary is with us, as she was with her son, in our dying moments, that she is one who helps us to die. This is one of the things Catholics know, not as a formal article of belief, but as a fundamental understanding of the way things are. Hawthorne's heroine's search for the "virgin mother whom she needed" seems unnecessarily anxious and egocentric. Implicit in the Catholic understanding of Mary—an assumption coincidental with her name—is that she is the one who is present in time of need. We may call on her, but we do not conjure her up. She is "full of grace," and grace, by definition, does not withhold itself. Even the Puritans liked to say that "grace abounds," though Catholics tend to be less restrictive in their sense of the breadth and length of the field on which it plays.

Looking for the "right" image of Mary—especially one that is not "an earthly mother . . . like every other mother"—seems, according to my sense of the Catholic tradition, an appalling act of idolatry. Perhaps it is a form of idolatry that only a cultivated New Englander of the nineteenth century could practice. For the Catholic, all images of Mary are the "right" ones and the "wrong" ones. No representation can fully capture Mary. Yet from the religious point of view, the plastic image on a dashboard has exactly the same value—no more, no less—than a Bellini or Donatello icon. As non-Catholics often feel puzzled by the mixture of high and low art forms in Catholic churches, so Catholics almost invariably feel uncomfortable in churches that are so exquisitely decorated as to have nothing out of keeping. More is at issue, of course, than taste or cultural norms. Fundamental to the Catholic understanding of Mary is that she is, of all the expressions of divine love, the most accessible to every class and age. That there are literally thousands of common garden-variety statues of Mary is a reminder that she is not a decorator's dream or a museum piece. Insofar as there is a theology of Mary, it must accomodate itself to the fact that she is infinitely hospitable to aesthetic vulgarity.

In one sense, Jean-Luc Godard's film is in perfect keeping with the long line of vulgar artifacts that have been associated with Mary. Yet, unlike plaster statues, it is not particularly accessible. It achieves a certain postmodern aura by reassembling fragments of popular culture in such a way as to make them unavailable to anyone unaccustomed to seeing French art films, which means most people. Mary is depicted as a contemporary urban working girl who pumps gas in her father's station and belongs to a women's basketball team.

But Mary's working-class origins and athletic ability are even harder to believe in than the virgin birth. The role is played by a fragile, pale, delicate actress who never looks dirty or sweats and whose abundance of leisure time suggests that the gas station and basketball game are a form of symbolic tokenism not meant to be taken literally. To an American viewer, the basketball scenes are particularly artificial and choreographed. The ball does go through the net, however, and one cannot fail to pick up connections with other visual and verbal references to things passing through holes—as in sexual intercourse, giving birth, eating an apple.

The film ends with a close-up of Mary's open mouth as she applies bright red lipstick to her lips. The notion of Mary as a cipher, an orifice, an enclosed space through which divinity passes, touches on questions of sexual and religious importance. Mary is "favored" by God in having been chosen to give birth to the Messiah, yet she is shown in the film to be alienated from the world because she has not known man. Pregnancy itself, dwelled on in some detail by the camera, is shown to be a time of isolation in which the woman is cut off from "husband" and child. Conception and birth, the embodiment of the other, exist in the past and the future. In sexual as well as metaphysical terms, husband and child hover between immanence and absence in the space provided by the woman. Meanwhile, it is the woman who frames memory and expectation and provides the shape—at first slight, then swollen—of the immediate reality.

The film is peculiarly French in its tendency to present and explore theological and biological questions in abstract form. The technical common-places of contemporary film—rapid cuts, abrupt shifts in mood and place, the foregrounding of background sounds, the repetitions of phrases and gestures, the parallelism of character types—create an impression of impersonality. More important than individual psychology and motivation, or class as a historically determined condition, or gender as a category rooted in biological and cultural ground, is the quest for a satisfying recombination of forms. There is a Rubik's cube quality to the film. With each repetition of the words *EN CE TEMPS LA* (AT THAT TIME), the viewer is not simply reminded of the biblical convention for beginning a story but taken back to approaching the same puzzle once again with a fresh start. The phrase, thus repeated, is not so much a sign of rhythmic inevitability as an admission of a previous false start and a determination to try once again to solve the still unsolved problem.

What the film fails to bring into dramatic focus is the perspective from which the problem is perceived and attacked. Whose problem is this? And why? One seemingly obvious answer is that it is Mary's. She is the one who has been singled out and who is undergoing the physiological consequences. Since scripture has relatively little to say about Mary's reactions, the film's most contemporary and radical opportunity for speculation would seem to be dwelling on the young woman as she lives through her pregnancy and tries to explain it to herself and to others. There is little question that the film is serious to the point of grim determination in placing Mary at the center, as though it is making up for what the Bible failed to do.

But in its privileging of the character of Mary, the film is at its weakest. Godard chose to concentrate his camera on Mary's body. Mary in the bathtub, Mary removing her panties on the doctor's examining table, Mary writhing in bed, Mary wandering around her flat in her undershirt, undoubtledly upset many viewers. Such a reaction is both easy and difficult to understand. For some people, nudity is shameful and Mary too sacred a figure to be associated with it. However, if one believes that no shame is attached to a naked body and that Mary was human and therefore in possession of a body like everyone else, no offense need be taken. But beyond this rather simple and obvious way of thinking about the problem is the more interesting and subtle question of the semiotics of nudity. One need not have seen hundreds of French films in order to recognize that female nudity is to many French directors what special effects were to Cecil B. De Mille. When you run out of original ideas in Hollywood, you call in the makers of thunder and lightning and, if the film is biblical, the parters of the Red Sea and the choirs of heavenly angels humming to the strings of Mantovani. In Paris, you haul out the naked woman, with or without cigarette.

Godard's reliance on this most worn-out of French film clichés is not outrageous or offensive, but predictable and flat, and, at times, it borders on self-parody. In one sense, it might be thought of as an honest admission of defeat. Once having chosen to sketch in the narrative where the Bible is relatively silent, the director was stumped. In order to fill the time, he found himself pushing a familiar button. It is true, of course, that an admission of defeat is a perfectly respectable subject for artistic examination, especially in the twentieth century. Many might reasonably argue that this is a film about the impossibility of making a modern film about the virgin birth. Further-more, in keeping with the abstract pattern of circles and holes through which things pass, it could be said that Mary cannot be depicted as a believable person because she was the "handmaid of the Lord," an instrument of a male God's will, a cipher.

Such a conclusion may satisfy the need for mathematical neatness, but it is a too conveniently schematic resolution. It is also an unimaginative conces-sion to the feminist critique of Mary as passive and characterless. That the evangelists were males in a patriarchal culture writing about a male Messiah is incontrovertible, but that their reticence about Mary must necessarily leave us with an impression of weakness does not follow. Given the unconventionality of her marriage, pregnancy, lying-in, exile in Egypt, and her son's behavior, it is highly unlikely that Mary was a person without a clearly defined will and character. Scripture does not say much about her, but there are important clues that might well provide material for an original modern film. For example, early in her pregnancy Mary goes without Joseph to visit her cousin Elizabeth in another city. The greeting of the two women is the occasion for one of the great poems in the New Testament (an echo of the song of Hannah in 1 Samuel 2) and the source of innumerable and powerful paintings of female bonding. The two women remain together for three months—an important, perhaps crucial period in Mary's pregnancy.

Godard's film makes no reference to this episode, perhaps because he could not imagine what it was like. St. Luke may not have been able to imagine how the women spent their time either. But he points to the episode and to the potency and joy in the female embracing the female. Godard instead shows the pregnant woman alienated and alone, stroking her own body. This is his way of placing Mary at the center of the stage and showing her wrestling with the problem, but the perspective is not convincingly Mary's (since she is a cipher) or woman's because the camera eye is that of a male. The female body and mind are as impenetrable to Godard's camera as an immaculate virgin's would be to a curious but somewhat obtuse suitor.

The most credible and human perspective in the film is Joseph's. Godard takes the biggest liberty with Joseph's characterization not because he makes him a cabdriver instead of a carpenter but because, in contrast with tradition, he makes him young. Joseph has been Mary's boyfriend for some time and he is passionately in love with her. Though he has not slept with her, it is quite clear that their relationship has been intimate and affectionate until suddenly she will not allow him to kiss her or even touch her. Joseph wears shades, slicks back his hair, dresses cool, and is in every way an average, healthy dude. His frustration and bewilderment with Mary's altered state and her terse and unconvincing insistence that she has not slept with a man are among the few recognizably human responses in the film.

One can feel sorry for Joseph or laugh at him. Two of the most arresting and perhaps the only comic moments occur when the angel Gabriel and his teenage sidekick literally accost Joseph. In one scene Gabriel slaps Joseph and calls him an "asshole," and in another he jumps him and wrestles him to the ground. Joseph is cowed and ultimately tamed. Mary teaches him to touch her belly and declare his love as an act of reverence rather than desire. In some combination of awe, disappointment, tenderness, and resignation, he learns his lesson and promises his unpossessive love. In short, Joseph steals Mary's line—"Let it be done to me according to your word."

Since scripture pays even less attention to Joseph's reaction than to Mary's, this depiction of Joseph is one of the film's most original touches. After all, though he did not carry the child in his own body, he also had to live through the mystery, humiliation, and scandal Mary's pregnancy must have caused. Portraying Joseph as a comic-pathetic figure is not biblical, but it is not a postmodern innovation either. In medieval iconography (as for example in the carvings of capitols in the cathedral of Auxerre, in the portico of St. Benoit-sur-Loire, and in the cloister of St. Trophime in Arles) Joseph is depicted on one side of the column shrugging his shoulders and looking quizzical, while on the other side, the angel Gabriel is announcing to Mary that she will give birth to a son.

If Godard does not give Mary the comfort of Elizabeth, he does not really give her the comfort of Joseph either. In presenting Joseph's "let it be done," Godard reveals an insight into an aspect of male psychology and simultaneously (and perhaps accidentally) into an important element in the Christian tradition of the virgin birth. Joseph, like Mary, was chosen to play a mysterious and honored role and, at the same time, his sexual identity has been strangely mocked. Mary attends the Lord, and Joseph attends Mary. His lack of genital responsibility for the Messiah breaks the Hebraic patriarchal line forever. The Gospel of Matthew traces Jesus's royal lineage through Joseph, but the mystery of the virgin birth places such genealogies into a precarious relationship with the Savior. The parenthood of Mary and Joseph is bound together in the same mystery, yet for Godard, the two remain oddly separated. Their behavior is more like that of a couple alienated from one another than like one united in the anticipation of a new life.

In contrast with the troubled, scrupulous, unconsummated relationship of Mary and Joseph is the affair between the Czech professor who believes that human beings came from outer space and one of his students, Eva, whom he insists on calling Eve. The professor expounds his theory: Eve/Eva bites an apple; they make love (offscreen); she walks around smoking a cigarette in the nude (on-screen); he takes a train back to Czechoslovakia and his wife; she tells him he is a real "nothing." Once again, the image of an empty circle, a zero, pops up. His theory is full of holes. So apparently are his declarations of love. If the film took itself a little less seriously, this "subplot" might have been a hilarious spoof of the pretensions of postmodern filmmakers. But because the focus and perspective of the entire film are so unclear and unsteady, neither parody nor satire can really come into being. In the theology of St.

Paul, there is an implication of sisterhood as well as difference in the references to Mary as the new Eve. In its muddled abstractness, the film dehumanizes the sisterhood and blurs the difference.

The later part of the film, which shows sky and fields and the child Jesus running away from his parents, is particularly anticlimactic. The film's hallmarks, if not exactly its strengths, have been a certain claustrophobic monotony and concentration. One almost sees the traces of the wrinkled brow of the director confronting an impossible task. But the last scenes are particularly slack, a visual floundering without tension.

One of the great religious films of all time is Pasolini's *The Gospel According to Matthew*. Godard must have seen it. In any case, he uses the same chorus from Bach's *St. Matthew Passion* as background music. Whether the quotation is intentional or unintentional, the comparison it brings to mind is unfortunate. In seeking so diligently to update the image, Godard sacrifices the spirit and the earthiness of Mary to an abstract problematic. Yet Catholics are accustomed to finding grace in even the shabbiest icons of Our Lady. When near the end of the film a voice calls out to Mary as she is getting in the car, she asks what he wants. His answer is a greeting: "Je vous salue, Marie" (Hail Mary). The celebration of the feminine and the recognition of mystery for one moment ring true.

9

A Failure to Make Contact

Gayatri Chatterjee

IN FRENCH, Mary is spelled *m-a-r-i-e,* for it contains the verb *a-i-m-e-r,* explains Marie's mother in Anne-Marie Miéville's *Le livre de Marie.* But after the woman director opens with this short film, introducing Marie lovingly in her girlhood, the male director cannot or does not do his part, calling it *Je vous aime, Marie.* The attempt of the woman filmmaker is to portray Marie as a person, not as a sacred virgin performing miracles, aloof and demanding veneration, so that poor mortals cry out from afar, *nous vous saluons.* Miéville's Marie wants to say and hear the three words *I love you (je t'aime).* Then why can this T-shirt-clad Marie, dancing out her agonies to Mahler's music, not make Godard tell her that, even though Joseph cannot?

As I was getting ready to see the film, I was thinking of Godard's cinema and cinema in general. The last two letters of the word *cinema* are *m-a.* We Bengalis call our mothers by this name, as do many others. In most languages, mothers are called by words that approximate to that sound, "ma." It has been remarked that cinema replaces the biological mother early in life, fulfilling her role and performing certain "duties" while the natural mother often fails. Television goes a step further by becoming both a surrogate mother and a surrogate babysitter. Man's relationship with cinema (most filmmakers have been male; even now there are comparatively few women filmmakers) has been quite tempestuous and full of passion. It is also remarkable that the Oedipus complex and allied problems and questions have never found a better medium. It was love at first sight for most audiences, and there was fear too (going by reports of the first screening of Lumière's *The Arrival of a Train* or when Griffith showed the close-up of a face without trunk and limbs). Never was any art medium so hurriedly absorbed and adapted for mass consumption. Never, it seems at times, will any art medium be left so misunderstood or little understood. The attempts to understand this "mother," the analytical or critical theories around cinema, have not had a slow evolutionary process of development, as with criticism of literature, painting, and other arts. The portrayal of women, and male-dominated visual and pleasure principles working behind the film image, always called for a feminist criticism. This, though, has been slow in coming, and is it adequate now? But for cinema, the need is imperative.

Among contemporary filmmakers who seem to be developing over an entire career span trying to understand cinema and make it understood and "better its image" (in both senses), Godard's name shines bright. If God has made man after his own image, what kind of image should be created to depict, discuss, and criticize that image? What does one do with the image when one is dealing with the image of an image? And if cinema contains the image, carries and gives birth to it, then surely all manipulation, all misuse or abuse, is a rape; to appropriate "her," to sell "her," is prostitution. Godard's concern has been the rampant practice of the prostitution of the image, and the ways of bettering the situation. Godard has wanted us to forget what we think of and love as cinema in order to purge this medium of all such practices. I can say for India that though a very small percentage of the film audience see or get the chance to see Godard's films, among film students, film-study people, and film-society personnel, Godard is always considered as the "guru;" not followed, perhaps, but seen with love and regard.

Another French speaker, Derrida, writes, "West is Image, East is Stage" (*Dissemination*). I am from the East, and the West's fascination with the image fascinates me. Of course, India, and the East in general, also have a rich heritage of images and imageries; the East has various modes of representation. But all these images and modes of representation are closely connected with a sense of performance. All arts are in that sense performing arts. Icons and deities are not merely representations or symbolic abstract meaning systems but are played with, fed and clothed, sung to and danced with, apart from being worshipped. The world is the manifestation of God's play. He realizes himself and enjoys himself through his creation. Man's life is a play too, illusory and yet repetitive (repeating in various lives). Man tries to find transcendence from his play, from this enactment of everyday chores and artistic practices, with or without gods.

This view gives rise in India to a surfeit of performance, an overdoing of things, that can be called overacting. In this supposed effort at transcendence there is, as it were, a spilling over of all that does not get transformed or transported "above," causing an excess, a hysteria or melodrama. In the intoxication of performance, East sometimes forgets to contemplate the subject and its object. The image and the performance suffer.

Still, performance is potentially something that takes place between two, whereas an image is created by one and can remain for just one. I stand before the mirror; I see my image in it (and perhaps it sees me). The question of the nature of this "I" and the question of the nature of this image of the "I" revolve around each other and become a trap. That it is a trap, the fact that there are such traps, West admits again and again. But the point is, this question revolving around itself has produced fatigue and ennui. The circuiting causes short-circuiting too. (Isn't this one reason for the success of melodrama and violence in the arts in the West?)

I find that for the first time in his career Godard, willingly or unwillingly, is entering this trap. The quest for the *other* is reinforcing the sense of loss more than the excitement or the sheer joy of the quest. Or is it a sign of fatigue in a person who has harped on one thing for too long? Godard must know that his audience has been absolutely convinced that the image need not be raped, sold, consumed, manipulated—at least not theoretically. If practically this cannot be avoided, is *Hail Mary* his way of admitting it? When his Marie bares herself again and again, what is he saying?

Maybe ancient Joseph's anger and suspicions were ignored or stifled by the evangelists; maybe this twentieth-century Joseph must try to establish his male and paternal rights. Perhaps AT THAT TIME (which time, *EN CE TEMPS LA*?) matriarchy and patriarchy were in perfect balance. Wish for a balance is indicative of a time when hopes reign. Is the balance now tilting hopelessly toward patriarchy? Is the balance lost forever?

Why must the probing fingers of a mortal and male doctor verify a virginal conception? If a penis is not required to bring the Son of God to this earth, why should a woman's womb be required to contain the holy fetus? It is not a denial of the need for a paternal identity in order to retain a pagan matriarchal supremacy. Isn't the requirement of a virgin a male demand? Why cannot the man and the woman join in a holy communion? If not, then let the Son of God walk down from the clouds or burst forth from a pea pod.

Both the body and the soul of man (I hope the status quo of the patriarchal language has now lost its power through our awareness) are today tired of conflicting with each other. Set them free from the still image of themselves in battle, as we see it in *Hail Mary*, and let them do something *together*. Can't we harness all these *together*—our body, mind, and soul?

All these questions are being directed not only through Godard and his film *Hail Mary* but at Godard. For, perhaps for the first time, Godard is not asking the medium to acquire a definitive attitude toward itself; nor is he giving a positive directive about what this medium is, should be, and ought to do. Instead, he is talking about someone called Jean-Luc Godard.

Godard's agonies at man's separation from woman have found expression in other films (from the first film, *Breathless*, onward). But all his angst before has been of a general contemporary kind, and he has used the exploitation of sexuality in cinema to laugh at the audience or make them laugh, asking them to break out of their conditioned unprotesting stupor. The first sequence of *Weekend* after all these years is as valid as ever. But *Hail Mary* does not make us laugh, nor do we see a laughing Godard.

It is very interesting to see Godard in person, so to speak, in *Hail Mary*, very heartening in a way. But he seems, to me at least, to be admitting that he is in a blind lane and to be showing a certain acceptance of it. It reminds me of another phenomenon of the sixties, from Liverpool, singing of finding himself in times of trouble. Mother Mary comes to him and speaks words of wisdom, "Let it be," "Let it be." But I cannot rest at the "Let it be."

10

Mariology, or the Feminine Side of God

Harvey Cox

IT IS IMPOSSIBLE for me to watch *Hail Mary* without seeing it within a much larger, even global, cultural context. That context is one in which we have witnessed the unforeseen renaissance of traditional religion not too many decades after we had been assured that it was disappearing. This renewal is taking place at all levels of society, elite and popular, and in most places on the globe, not only within the Christian ambience.

Why is it happening? I believe it is because the world of "modernity," which was understood to be a rejection of, indeed a going beyond, religion, turns out to be a kind of pseudoreligion itself. Modernity is a "religion" in that it proffers a comprehensive meaning system, with its own set of answers to the existential questions which are of interest to Godard in this film, questions such as the nature of consciousness, the beginning of life, physical and spiritual love and their relationship to each other, and the inevitable impact on all of us of uncontrolled and unforeseen circumstances. Each of these perennial questions can be viewed either as a *problem,* which is the characteristic "modern" perspective, or as a *mystery,* which is the traditional "religious" one. I think that what Godard does in this film is to remind us that these questions are, at least in some measure, *not* just problems, but mysteries. He thus tries to reintroduce a religious dimension into an ailing modernity.

My theological teacher, Paul Tillich, used to say that theology has to do with relating the answers of faith to the questions posed, not necessarily explicitly, by human existence. The answers of faith in any religious tradition do not usually appear in discursive formulations. They are expressed, rather, in the form of a symbol, a story, a metaphor, a tale, a liturgy, a song. I would add that religious symbols also sometimes raise questions about conventional answers. This is the case in *Hail Mary* where we are seeing the utilization of traditional religious symbolism and stories to raise questions about what has become an increasingly implausible "religious" system—modernity. The fact is that in many people's minds modernity is becoming increasingly implausible as we discover its lethal consequences if we continue to move in the direction it is carrying us. But, one might ask, Why Mary?

When Pope John Paul II decreed a "Marian Year" beginning in April 1987, he invited a new interest in that branch of theology called "Mariology." I think of Mariology not just as the study of devotion to Mary but also as the study of this devotion as one example of the much larger, comprehensive, and global religious renaissance that one can discover in Shinto Japan, the Muslim Middle East, Catholic Latin America, or all over the world. By Mariology I mean the attempt to understand both the symbolization of Mary throughout the centuries of Christian history and the "feminine side of God," a reality that in our Western history was to some extent repressed during the Reformation but, like all repressed elements, keeps coming back at the popular and the intellectual level. This film is about "Mary versus modernity." And not just Mary. It is about the "goddess" as well, and the juxtaposing of Mary to the moon reminds us that, historically, the moon is the symbol of other female deities.

There are two phases in this brilliant juxtaposition of Mary and the goddesses with the deteriorating fabric of modernity. The first shows that for many people—Godard included—modernity's answers are no longer final, authoritative, or satisfying. There is a growing awareness of this in all of us. As Mary says in the film, "I had only the shadow of love. Only the shadow of love." Many of the most eloquent critics of modernity have focused on the loss of love under its regime. I think of Walter Percy's *Love among the Ruins* and François Mauriac's *The Desert of Love*. The list is endless. Godard's second phase is to try to show how the symbols of traditional religion, reformulated or reinterpreted, provide not just questions but more satisfactory responses to these mysteries than those offered by modernity.

I think Godard has done very well—brilliantly, in fact—at the first phase, but not so well with the second. He has demonstrated the bankruptcy of modernity, but he fails to show how traditional Christian responses might be more satisfying. Would that have been too much to do in one film? Perhaps. This film is therefore what we might call in theology prolegomenon. It raises the question. It sets out the issue to be attacked. Now someone else must attempt to do the second phase.

I want to remind you that Godard is a part of a much larger trend—the unexpected revival of certain aspects of Mariological devotion in the Catholic world. Ironically, at both the left edge and the right edge of world Catholicism, we see a reemergence of Mariological devotion. Mariology has reappeared among the liberation theological movements in the revolutionary wing of

Catholicism in South America, where Our Lady of Guadaloupe, as a kind of fighting Madonna, has been popular. This image is drawn from the Magnificat, where Mary says that the "mighty will be thrown from their thrones, and the hungry fed, and the rich sent away empty." And we have Mariology on the extreme right of popular Catholicism, for example in the apparition of Our Lady of Bayside, Long Island, where a small cult listened to her pronouncements that we should not have altar girls, that the nuns should return to their habits, and that we should get the guitars out of the churches. Our Lady of Bayside is apparently uncomfortable with many of the reforms introduced by Vatican II.

Why do we have these two opposite wings both turning to Mary? I think it is because both represent parts of Catholicism that are critical of that church's compromise with bourgeois capitalistic modernity, but from different perspectives. Consequently they both draw on this distinctively *pre*modern Mariological material to make that statement in their own symbolic ways. Now Godard enters into this same process, drawing on Catholic symbolism. He uses Protestant music, but he uses Catholic imagery, not just because he is Swiss-French but I think in some measure because Catholicism was never quite as compromised with the emergence of modernity as Protestantism. Remember, Protestantism appeared historically just at the beginning of the modern period. Therefore, it has an element of involvement with modernity that in most instances does not characterize Catholic imagery. Godard succeeds in part, so why does John Paul II feel he must point out the flaw? I do not know, and I also believe the flaw he points out is not the real one. What is the real flaw?

In early 1987, the pope issued an encyclical, *Redemptoras Mater,* about Mary and the place of Mary in Christian ecumenism, criticizing that form of Mariological devotion that makes Mary into a goddess on her own and breaks her relationship to Jesus. This is just what Godard seems to do in this film. He is interested in Mary the goddess, and he minimizes her relationship with Jesus. I think this may be the reason the myth of Mary in this film succeeds in the first phase (the critique of modernity), but fails in the second (the reinterpretation of the traditional myth). It puts too much weight on Mary. It tries to combine in one person both sacred and profane love. This is one of the basic underlying themes of this film. But it fails.

Little wonder. It does not succeed because it cannot succeed within the idiom Godard works with, an idiom in which it is always the *woman's* body and the *man's* eye that focus the action. Within this patriarchal pattern we always end up either with virginity and celibacy on the one side or with some kind of rape and domination on the other. This is the focus Godard uses, so the problem perpetuates itself. I am afraid it will do so as long as these are the terms in which it is presented. If Jesus' critique of patriarchy could have been included, the result might have been quite different.

I congratulate Godard for having succeeded so well in one part of the task, and for having juxtaposed these elements—sacred and profane love—so brilliantly. When I say he succeeds only partly, I must immediately add that he should not be expected to do the work that theologians do. Still, I appreciate his preparing the ground.

11

Virgin Soiled, or a Woman like the Others?

John Gianvito

A. Promo

> There's only one knowledge and that's the knowledge
> of what makes people come—what makes them go:
> "Oh, God!"; like when you first hear a new Rolling
> Stones song that's perfect; like when *Paperback Writer*
> first hit, or a Phil Spector song, or a Rimbaud poem
> or . . .
>
> —Patti Smith, *High on Rebellion*

FEW PLEASURES I have experienced match the pure visceral excitement of a new Godard film. It is both the most manifest and the most ineffable characteristic of Godard's work, overshadowing all analysis and argument. Bearing in mind Rilke's caution to young Kappus that "with nothing can one approach a work of art so little as with critical words,"[1] I am increasingly wary of the value of any criticism that does not partake of pleasure. Pleasure, either in pure response to the subject or in the critiquing of the subject, even if condemnatory, must propel analysis from its launching pad.

Can one truly have encountered the films of Godard if in the face of such recent aesthetic provocations as *Everyman for Himself*, *Passion*, *Grandeur and Decadence of a Small-Time Filmmaker*, and *Hail Mary*, one has not felt strong emotion, not had the *pleasure* of seeing these films? Godard stirs things up. With the heart of a classicist and the eyes of a modernist, with inexhaustible *jeux d'esprit* combined with a pessimism often veiled beneath a comic veneer, with the most conspicuous cinematic zealousness since Mack Sennett and an unswervingly quixotic regard for the marketplace, Godard with each new film sends me reeling as if shot into a futuristic pinball machine where sounds, images, and ideas ricochet off each other and off the viewer in dizzying poetic frenzy.

With the exception of two or three of the sketch films and whatever the latest film is, I have seen all of Godard's films (even those that put to the test nearly everyone's enthusiasm for Godard). It's a personal thing. I am well aware that for some, he is the most infuriatingly difficult, some say sexist, some say obscurantist, some say blasphemous, of all contemporary filmmakers. Still, no matter how one finally brushes up against Godard, there is no denying his absolute and prodigious presence in the art of the twentieth century. He is a figure who with each passing year appears more noticeably irreplaceable, ever more solitary, a man increasingly free to speak.

B. Recess of the Spirits

> Reason's last step is the recognition that there are a number of things which are beyond it. It is merely feeble if it does not go as far as to realize that. If natural things are beyond it, what are we to say about supernatural things?
>
> —Pascal, *Pensées*

That Jean-Luc Godard at fifty-five should turn toward the contemplation of his navel must be seen as a sign of hope.

That *Hail Mary* should prove so controversial gloriously ensured its financial success and the potential for Godard to continue down his path with, at least for the moment, a little less difficulty.

Stemming initially from a common preoccupation of children, today the expression "to contemplate one's navel" is used to express a waste of time and energy. Art, however, is the domain of unruly children. Kindled by the rubbing of one's soul against all the stuffs of life, the making of art, at any age, requires a serious form of playfulness in order to catch and flare. In the work of many this initial stage of conceptual play is eventually covered over, its tinder and stoking sealed up within the final version. With Godard, it is always transparent. Each elliptical edit, each disruptive sound cut, each kinetic intermingling of actors, feels as if one could see, in a sense, the still-wet paint flying off each stroke. We simultaneously participate in the making of the film and the watching of it. Because of their unique cubistic construction, the experience of watching Godard's films is that of grappling with each distinct moment, reconsidering and rearranging the moments as they climb rapidly on top of one another in dialectical formation, all combining to make a single (motion) picture.

While this quality remains part and parcel of Godard's style, with the advent of *Hail Mary* a new shift has emerged that should not go unacknowledged. Having turned his gaze directly toward the spiritual, toward mystery, Godard in *Hail Mary* appears to have pushed deeper into himself, executing more struggle and care upon a film than ever before. Given the subject matter, this is natural enough, the result being a film a bit less spontaneous in appearance but more memorably visual, a film whose conceptual wrestling to life, fraught with typical behind-the-scenes turmoil and complications, is perhaps discernible only in the suffering faces of the performers. *Hail Mary* is set down in an altogether more serene and controlled universe than that witnessed before in any Godard film, its anguish posited in a structure that feels tighter, more considered, than usual, and consequently more contained. It is as though having come face-to-face with a transcendental pulse beat, Godard, with his frenetic barrage of stylistics, found himself subdued by the calming influence of imperturbable reality.

Godard has reported how in the midst of shooting he found himself uncustomarily overbudget and had to stop and take on the directing of *Detective* in order to plow his salary back into *Hail Mary*. "The directing [of *Hail Mary*] lasted seven months, for an hour of film! We had to redo everything four or five times, everything!"[2] In the nature sequences alone Godard summoned from himself and his cameramen the patience and alertness of Bel or Van Lawick.[3] "We set up a camera and were waiting, waiting, waiting until a certain time when you get the exceptional in everyday natural things. I mean, we shot the sun, but we needed to have a plane cross the sun, and it doesn't happen every second! It's a one-time thing."[4]

Here there is no second-unit work, no purchasing of stock footage. And the fruit of Godard's laborious looking: a thin sliver of late-afternoon sunlight caresses a meadow as a single strand of silken cobweb stirs in a breeze; before an immense sinking sun, two swallows suddenly soar and weave in intersecting patterns directly toward the camera; a full moon gently rolls out from behind a mottled bank of high clouds. This is nature in its most primordial and pristine glow, unadulterated by man and the debris of man, except for the repetitive passing and roar of jet planes. Symbols, in part, of male power and enterprise, the planes also seem to offer the suggestion, as did the descending planes in Herzog's *Fata Morgana* (seven of them as in the week of creation), of primeval earth having been impregnated by vehicles from outer space.

If Godard's recording of nature at its most simple and elemental strikes us as too clichéd and worn-out to evoke profound sensation, perhaps the problem lies in our own incapacity to push our stares as Godard has his to the other side of these images. We hold back and resist letting our dulled senses reawaken to the consciousness of our surroundings, to acknowledge, truly and with humility, the palpable breathing of some kind of mystery behind all things. Listen to Godard the intellectual talking: "I had the feeling in *Hail Mary* that there was an immaculate screen, and it was saying to me,

'Don't stray too far, or don't come too close. Or come closer. Or don't come.'
I had the feeling of a voice there."[5] Muse? The subconscious? God? The Force?
No matter how one defines it or takes exception to his method, the evidence
stands that Godard's search in *Hail Mary* is for spiritual enlightenment. Who
has the right to take anything away from that? The world has had its Jobs and
its Thomases, its Caravaggios and its Pasolinis, and each had his part to play,
each putting his imperfect shoulder to the heavenly wheel.

I maintain that not only does *Hail Mary* not rape nature, as some cynics
would have it, lost within confused notions about the appropriation of reality
and the possessive power of images, but that far from being a defilement of
either Mother Nature, the Blessed Virgin, Myriem Roussel, or the Sacred
Mysteries, the film stands as a sincere and self-admittedly perverse paean of
love to them all.

C. Seeing or Believing

> There is no film without love, love of some kind.
> There can be novels without love, other works of art
> without love, but there can be no cinema without love.
> —Jean-Luc Godard, "The Carrots Are Cooked"

Godard is unabashedly an aesthete. He likes to look at the beautiful,
whether it be women or horses or sunsets. Those who criticize *Hail Mary* as
merely a succession of beautiful images make their first mistake with the word
merely. To render beautiful that which is already beautiful is not easy. To
create beauty where it had not previously existed through a cut, a composition,
or an idea is an achievement. Moreover, beauty is a value in and of itself and
needs no further justification. Why do so many people still bother looking at
ancient sports footage from the 1936 Olympic Games if not for its sublime
transfiguration in *Olympia*?

For those who fail to perceive the beauty and love behind *Hail Mary*, the
first evidence ought to be inclusion of Anne-Marie Miéville's film *The Book of
Mary*, which precedes *Hail Mary*. Shot independently without foresight of
their accompanying each other, the two films are now bonded, the distributor
being required to market both films as if they were one. And with *The Book
of Mary*'s frequent cutting to black, there is nearly a momentary disguising of
when one film ends and the other begins as *The Book of Mary*'s last image of
the severed egg cuts to black, followed by a shot of rain-swept meadow, which
is only then followed by the first credit shot for *Hail Mary*. This unusual
attachment of short film to feature film, unheard of these days in the world

of film distribution, bespeaks a gift of love to Godard's friend and longtime collaborator Anne-Marie Miéville. (Reciprocally, so is Miéville's having young Marie sit in front of the TV watching *Contempt*, although there are other textual significances to this choice as well. Similarly, as has always been Godard's fashion, *Hail Mary* contains a variety of reverent filmic references, including ones to Dreyer's *Vampyr* and Bresson's *Au hasard, Balthazar*).

Yet another reflection of love of beauty is the casting of Myriem Roussel (the ringer in the chamber quartet in *First Name: Carmen*). There have been remarkable-looking women in Godard's films, and more often than not he has chosen women with whom he was personally involved (Anna Karina, Anne Wiazemsky). It is only natural—one films what one loves.

Myriem Roussel, whose gentle features, earnest wide-eyed gaze, and graceful womanly figure are frequently cradled in the most delicate composition and drapings of natural light in *Hail Mary*, by the film's end is herself as much the subject as the character Mary. Commenting upon the experience of working with Godard, she has said, "I do not feel myself an actress with him: It is a lot more personal than professional." It is through *Hail Mary*'s intense, personal, and nearly obsessive fixation upon Roussel, and particularly upon her nude body, that Godard has sought "to make the audience see not a naked woman, but flesh if that's at all possible."[6] And just as he attempts to suggest that which lies behind nature, Godard strives here to see not only flesh but beyond the flesh to the mystery that stirs beneath.

Some years ago, a related cinematic attempt was undertaken by French director Marcel Hanoun in his 1976 film, *Le regard*. Hanoun sought to show a man and a woman making love in such a way that would be perceived as neither erotic nor pornographic. Freed from narrative and traditional contextualization, *Le regard* was a rare attempt to make a film where one might be able simply to *look* at this most crucial human interaction while having consciously to come to terms with one's feelings regarding voyeurism. Unfortunately, Hanoun's attempt seems to have been met with general bewilderment and like most of his work, remains largely unsung. People could not venture beyond pedestrian responses to explicit sexuality on screen; they could see no broader or deeper signification. They got stuck at skin level.

A parallel can be seen in the controversy that arose around *Hail Mary*. As with Hanoun's film, much of the heat of *Hail Mary*'s controversy stems from audiences stuck at skin level, able to perceive only a prurient display of exhibitionism. Further complicating matters, *Hail Mary* asks one not only to see the miraculous in the ordinary but to look beyond images of divine significance (the virgin birth, the Holy Family, the presence of angels) to their more commonplace associations.

"People think of their bodies as territories," Godard says. "They think of their skin as the border, and that it's no longer them once it's outside the border. But language is obviously made to cross borders. I'm someone whose real country is language, and whose territory is movies."[7] The major mistake many critics of *Hail Mary* make is a failure to grasp the film's study of the virgin birth as a metaphor encompassing a far more wide-ranging and everyday involvement with the miraculous surrounding all human activity. We know biologically how children are conceived, but does that truly explain where life springs from? Darwin and his successors have uncovered much, but does it fully explain man's appearance on the earth or the why of his appearance? What is this "silent power . . . vast as a mountain or the sky, that you can't measure or name, but only *feel?*" "Does the soul have a body?" Such are the questions of *Hail Mary*. And at the heart of all this yearning, at the center of this "labor of love," is a young woman, naked.

A friend of mine once said to me, "You hate beauty because you love it so much." I have passed women on the street so stunningly attractive, I wished I had not seen them, but of course I still look. This reaction, I should make clear, comes not from any sense of sinfulness in lust. Perhaps it is because the beauty of strangers is so fleetingly cupped, vanishing into the crowd before it can be savored. Or perhaps, closer to the mark, it stems from an unrealizable desire to know intimately (some might say possess) each unique and alluring beauty. There is, I think, something of this in Godard. Like an active child fascinated by hurling the biggest rocks he can find into the serene surface of a pond, Godard in *Hail Mary*, as in the preceeding *First Name: Carmen,* both praises the feminine form and rails against it. But unlike *Carmen*, the struggle in *Hail Mary* extends beyond the theme of the femme fatale and the seduction of appearance to an inquiry into that which "man *cannot imagine* a woman to be." As Mary's doctor says as he washes his hands, "I've always wondered what we know about a woman, and I found that all you can know is what a man already knew: There's a mystery there."

The old notion of the feminine mystique, tempting though it may be for men, is not a concept I endorse. While many things remain to perplex human beings, I'm not convinced that feminine psychology is one, at least no more so than the workings of any mind, male or female. Addressing this myth, Simone de Beauvoir wrote, "Mystery is never more than a mirage that vanishes as we draw near to look at it."[8] Perhaps in his pursuit to understand the ways of women, Godard has yet to move in close enough in his films, and when he has, it has more often been with the confused and aggressive angst of a Joseph. I was intrigued by a remark Godard made in a British rock magazine at the time of *Hail Mary*'s release. When asked if he considered himself a feminist, Godard replied, in part, "I would have called myself a feminist, but really I'm not much of one: I probably fear women too much and that's why I pretend I respect them."[9]

Where *Hail Mary* makes some progress in this regard—and it is for me the climactic moment in the film—is in the sequence where Mary teaches Joseph the proper way to say "I love you." Continually denied direct physical contact with Mary, Joseph beleagueredly repeats the words "I love you" and reaches out to Mary only to encounter her sharp cry "No!" At last, with great gentleness, Joseph presses his palm lightly upon Mary's belly button and softly and with ease says, "I love you." For Mary, it is the right way, perhaps because the reverence bestowed on the navel indicates an acknowledgment of a mystery greater than oneself, than one's own flesh. It is the beginning of respect. If elsewhere in the film Godard betrays this respect, at least he is honest enough to display his attitudes, warts and all.

"The cinema is an x-ray machine in which you photograph your own disease,"[10] Godard once keenly observed. And as the first step to a cure is self-examination, by having the courage to look squarely at his own symptoms, Godard must inevitably reflect, in some way, our own.

Vast regions of inquiry and debate are opened up by a film such as *Hail Mary*, and I am happy that Pope John Paul II has helped to put them in a wider spotlight. Still, as original an entry as it may be in Godard's career, *Hail Mary* but continues to confirm and affirm something Godard wrote as far back as 1952, seven years prior to *Breathless*, in a small article, entitled "What Is Cinema?" "Art," he wrote, "attracts us only by what it reveals of our most secret self. . . . So, to the question 'What is Cinema?,' I would first reply: the expression of lofty sentiments."[11] And to the question, What is *Hail Mary*?, I would first reply: Cinema!

Notes

1. Rainer Maria Rilke, *Letters to a Young Poet*, trans. M. D. Herter Norton (New York: Norton, 1962), 17.

2. Louis Skorecki, "Godard: Fragments d'un entretien impossible," *Libération* (Paris), January 23, 1985, 24.

3. François Bel is a French documentarian whose renowned animal films, *Le territoire des autres* (1970, codirectors Gérard Vienne and Michel Fano), *La griffe et la dent* (1977, codirector Gérard Vienne), and *L'animal et son territoire* (1987, codirector Alain-Marie Thomas) are the result of several years of filming followed by a long period of editing and scoring. Hugo Van Lawick is one of the greatest wildlife photographers, dividing his time equally between still photography and filmmaking. His film documentaries include *People of the Forest* (1988, a twenty-year portrait of

the chimpanzees of Gombe) and *Cheetahs, The Blood Brothers* (1990). He frequently collaborates with zoologist Jane Goodall.

4. Katherine Dieckmann, "Godard in His 'Fifth Period,'" *Film Quarterly* no. 2 (1985–1986): 3. The interview is reprinted in this volume.

5. Dieckmann, 6.

6. Dieckmann, 3.

7. Jonathan Rosenbaum, "Bringing Godard Back Home," *The Soho News*, September 24, 1980 (from an unpaginated reprint by Godard's distributor).

8. Simone de Beauvoir, *The Second Sex*, trans. H. M. Parshley (New York: Bantam, 1961), 240. De Beauvoir further elaborates: "Of all these myths [regarding women's nature], none is more firmly anchored in masculine hearts than that of the feminine 'mystery.' It has numerous advantages. And first of all it permits an easy explanation of all that appears inexplicable; the man who 'does not understand' a woman is happy to substitute an objective resistance for a subjective deficiency of mind; instead of admitting his ignorance, he perceives the presence of a 'mystery' outside himself: an alibi, indeed, that flatters laziness and vanity at once."

9. Nigel Matheson, "The Creator" (interview), *The New Musical Express*, October 12, 1985, 7.

10. Jean-Luc Godard, "What Is Cinema?" in *Godard on Godard*, trans. Tom Milne (New York: Viking, 1972), 31.

11. Vincent Canby, "Second Thoughts about the New York Film Festival," *New York Times*, October 12, 1980 (from an unpaginated reprint by Godard's distributor).

12

Godard's Vision of the New Eve

Vlada Petric with Geraldine Bard

AMONG ALL *nouvelle vague* filmmakers, Jean-Luc Godard has exhibited the greatest concern for female characters. He presents them on the screen as protagonists of his stories; he focuses on their psychological uniqueness; and he analyzes the roles they play as women in society, family, and male-female relationships. From his first feature, *Breathless* (1960), Godard has assigned to his female protagonists a significance uncommon in traditional cinema. These protagonists are seen as equal to, or more powerful than, their male counterparts.

By the end of *Breathless*, Patricia has evolved into a complex person with great integrity and enough strength to ignore the sardonic accusation by her lover-crook of being "disgusted" (*degueulasse*). In *A Woman Is a Woman* (1961), Angela (played by Anna Karina, then Godard's wife) succeeds in persuading her lover to accept the child she has conceived with another man. In *Vivre sa vie* (1962), Nana (again Anna Karina) emerges as a heroine who "like Lola Montes, is able to safeguard her soul while selling her body" (Godard's characterization of his heroine). *A Married Woman* (1964) deals with a woman's infidelity in a way that ideologically, and radically, defies the conventions of both the Hollywood romance genre and bourgeois morality. In *Masculine-Feminine* (1966), Madeleine comes through as a self-aware, mature person in contrast to the depressed psyche of her lover (Paul), who in many ways reflects Godard's own grim state of mind at that time. Most of all, Juliette Jeanson (Marina Vlady)—the "her" in *Two or Three Things I Know about Her* (1967)—is metaphorically depicted on the screen as a physical/ethical/ideological center around whom all the other characters, as well as the camera, rotate.

Such a dramatic and graphic foregrounding of the female characters in Godard's films is particularly noteworthy when one sees that the women are always placed next to or against strong male personalities, often interpreted by famous French actors like Jean-Paul Belmondo and Jean-Pierre Léaud. But even in the films that do not feature well-known players, the emphasis on womanhood imbues the narrative with a feminine worldview, as with the more recent Godard films such as *First Name: Carmen* (1983) and *Hail Mary* (1985), in which the leading parts are portrayed by rather obscure actresses, which intensifies the authenticity of the worlds presented in the films.

At first glance, *Hail Mary* appears to be a film about religion, a narrative recapitulation of essential elements from the canonical text. It is a modern recounting of the events associated with the life of Mary, Joseph, and their son Jesus (with direct references to the Annunciation, the Nativity, the Incarnation). Godard, however, transcends narrow religious connotations by developing other themes, such as comprehension of the fact that unpredictable and uncontrollable outside forces can disrupt human relationships; the contrast between female and male attitudes toward love, sex, and marriage; the painful nature of consciousness in relation to procreation and the difficulties of existence; religious and secular assumptions concerning the origin of the human species; the politics of conventional sexuality and its alternatives; the inevitable liberation of members of the traditional family unit; the emotional ties between parents and their children; the reconciliation of physical and spiritual love; and, above all, woman's ability to maintain her integrity in adverse psychological and social circumstances. All these themes reflect Godard's unorthodox attitude toward women and their position in a contemporary society governed by traditional ethical principles. The film's biblical references appear as a background against which a philosophical discussion concerning essential problems of humanity can take place.

By focusing on the biblical story concerning the Holy Family, Godard's film emphasizes a dramatic paradox: situating the sacred legend within a modern milieu (a small city in contemporary Switzerland), he highlights the absurdity of a miraculous event occurring in the contemporary world, while acknowledging the mythical significance and powerful psychological impact of such a phenomenon as a virgin becoming pregnant. There is a complicated point being made. But the integration of contemporary characters within the biblical narrative has naturally evoked disquietude in those viewers who, as the pope claims, have absolute trust in and reverence for the Bible. The Vatican states that Godard's film "insults and deforms the fundamental tenets of the Christian faith . . . deeply injuring the respect for the sacred and the Virgin Mary."[1] Surprisingly, Godard's response to the pope's accusation seems to be quite conciliatory:

> There is something true in what the Pope says. Mystery cannot be shown. It can be approached, but not shown. But in my opinion, there has been a misunderstanding and it's given some Catholics the chance to create a fuss. . . . I believe in something, though I wouldn't necessarily call it God. I don't know anybody who doesn't believe in something.

And even Marie is blasphemous, and why is that so bad? Blasphemy has a part to play in religion. Even saints can be blasphemous. Look at Peter, founder of the Catholic Church, who denied Christ three times. I believe that *Mary* has a religious strength to it. Maybe my faith is that I believe in looking to the stars and receiving light. Movies are just receiving light.[2]

Hail Mary (1985), eighty-six minutes long, has been distributed along with a thirty-minute feature, *The Book of Mary* (1985), by Anne-Marie Miéville, which is about the separation of a husband and wife as experienced by Marie, their eleven-year-old daughter. Godard opted for what can be considered a cinematic symbiosis, obviously not because his film was too short for adequate distribution (some of his other works of the same or even shorter length have been shown alone) but because he saw Miéville's short feature as an appropriate introduction to his film. Even with this indirect focus on Marie's childhood (totally ignored in the sacred Gospels), Godard confirms his feminist orientation toward his protagonist, acknowledging not only her present life but her past. She is a real woman with a history.

The Book of Mary depicts a child's response to parental conflict and the separation of the parents. Marie's contemplative nature, especially her spontaneous understanding of poetry, music, and life in general, reveals her as an extraordinary human being from the beginning of the film. Some of Marie's ideas are extremely sophisticated for a child, as when she links the musical structure of a concerto to that of a conversation: "[The concerto] sounds like talk, don't you think, Father? People in a discussion . . . a bit of both . . . agreement and disagreement. Changes of mood produce exasperation. I demand fire, error, horror, suffering." Such an extraordinary statement parallels the way Godard's protagonist examines the dichotomy of the soul and body. Preoccupied with the internal aspects of her being, Mary steadfastly maintains that she is a "soul inhabited by a body."

At the end of *The Book of Mary*, the viewer is tempted to ask, what kind of human being will Marie be as an adult? Acquainted with the experience she has undergone in her childhood, the viewer finds it likely that Marie will become an integral character capable of making autonomous decisions in life, courageous enough to face even the most painful of circumstances, and likely to continue to react to things with extraordinary emotions and intelligence.

The girl Marie cracks an egg at the breakfast table, and as a shot of the cracked egg fades to black, a white intertitle appears (occupying the center of the black screen): AT THAT TIME (*EN CE TEMPS LA*), introducing Godard's film. The intertitle is followed by a shot of a green meadow foregrounded by weeds visibly pummeled by rain and wind. Then the film's main title, *Hail Mary*, appears, and the credits follow, alternating with shots depicting water, periodically disturbed by ripples (caused by rocks thrown into the water from offscreen).

The viewer, though startled by the unexpected appearance of Godard's film credits, is instantly conditioned to accept the previous portion of the screening as a prologue to the main film. This perception is reinforced if one thinks back to the series of opening (stationary) shots of *The Book of Mary*—flowers, sky, fruit, water—that anticipate the repetitive use of images of nature throughout *Hail Mary*. The narrative correspondence between the two films is most directly underscored by the actual opening sequence of *Hail Mary*, which presents a young woman seated at a restaurant table talking with a man positioned across from her. The viewer spontaneously perceives this dark-haired young woman (Juliette, one of Joseph's two female companions) as the grown-up dark-haired Marie from *The Book of Mary*. In the next sequence another dark-haired young woman (this time it is Godard's protagonist) sits on a bench watching a basketball game as Juliette's voice-over continues (carried over from the restaurant setting). The confusion is reduced in the subsequent shot when Mary begins her warm-up exercise behind the players seated on the bench as Juliette and Joseph's (offscreen) conversation continues (Juliette: "How are you doing with Mary?" Joseph: "That's my business."). Two succeeding shots—a long view of the basketball game followed by a close-up of Mary—finally identify the actual protagonist as the coach says, "Listen, Mary, when there is a break out, move fast." By now, the audience is certain that the film's title refers to the dark-haired young basketball player, Mary, particularly when her own voice-over begins to accompany her close-up ("I wondered if some event would happen in my life").

As Mary's voice-over continues, accompanying the shots of the full moon and the basketball game, the image of Mary becomes more complex. Intensely contemplative, she is preoccupied with concerns uncommon to the two other women in this film, Juliette and Eva. Mary struggles with her unusual experience of love. Finding herself in a most peculiar situation she would "never have wished for herself," she is aware that there is no simple way to escape it. Her frustration is emphasized by a complex audiovisual symbolism, which is meant to elevate the filmic structure to the sphere of cinematic abstraction.

Accompanying the shot of the full moon, Mary's meditative voice states: "I had only the shadow of love, in fact, the shadow of a shadow, like the reflection of a water lily in a pond. . . . Not quite, but shaken by ripples in the water. So that even the reflection is deformed and not yours." Recurrently appearing on the screen, representing steadiness and the power of the universe, the shot of the full moon floating in space becomes emblematic of the entire film's point of view. Together with other images of nature, it appears at crucial points of the narrative development. Graphically, the circular shape of the moon in the sky is associated with the shape of the basketball in Mary's hands, thus establishing a link between Mary and the moon, setting up metaphoric correspondences. As events develop, the moon—and the sun—is directly associated with Mary's destiny, symbolically exemplifying her obsessive search for an answer to her extraordinary physical condition (her mysterious pregnancy). Such metaphoric association invites the viewer to see the film as a modern parable loosely based on biblical myth, with a broad philosophical significance relating to humanity's place and function in the universe.

This issue of humanity's place is directly addressed by the professor during his lecture to the students about the origin of life, especially when he quotes a contemporary British scientist: "Life appeared entirely by chance. . . . What if it wasn't by chance? . . . If it came from elsewhere, from space. . . . It can only be explained . . . by something in this cloud [distant in the universe] intercepting light . . . at a specific wavelength . . . which establishes a very strong presumption that life exists in space. We're from there." In *Two or Three Things I Know about Her* (1966), Godard makes a similar comment in his own whispering voice over a cup of coffee on whose surface a galaxylike structure is formed. He contemplates mankind's future "when the lightning advance of science [will] give to future centuries a haunting presence, when the future will become more present than the present, when distant galaxies will be at my door, my likeness, my brother." As the coffee foam assumes an even more "astral" configuration, Godard's voice asks, with an evident hesitation, the primal question—about the origin of the universe: "Where does it begin? But, where does *what* begin? God created the heavens and the earth, which is, of course, a bit cowardly, and easy to say." The ironic rhetorical counterquestion, "But, where does *what* begin?" is resolved in *Hail Mary* by a supposition that the "what" may be the distant cloud that intercepts light at a specific wavelength, indicating the presence of bacteria life—a proposition that can be taken as both a pantheistic and a materialistic concept of evolution/creation.

In none of his other films has Godard associated a woman so excitingly with nature, especially with its energy and beauty, as he does in *Hail Mary*. Already as a young critic he exhibited great admiration for Bergman's metaphorical use of nature: "In Bergman's aesthetics, those shots of lakes, forests, grass and clouds.reflect the psyche of his characters at a particular moment."[3] Different attitudes in the two directors, however, are pronounced. While in Bergman's films nature functions as an environment *within* which his characters' anguish takes place, in *Hail Mary* Godard associates various symbolic details of nature with his disturbed heroine, revealing his philosophical attitude toward life. A frequent appearance of the images of nature (mostly depicting environment) in Bergman's films is closely related to his characters' acute emotional condition; the shots of nature in *Hail Mary* stand as the filmmaker's comment on the character's worldview and the direct revelation of Godard's own understanding of the universe. This understanding is a mix of dialectical materialism with an instinctive deism.

THE BASIC NARRATIVE flow of *Hail Mary* evolves realistically regarding the action within the shot, while the order of the shots continually transcends common linear sequentiality. In addition, the sound track is stylized in the way the dialogue and especially the music and sound effects are mixed together. The inconsistency of the compiled sounds, their discontinuity with the images, subverts the diegetic wholeness of the presented events while giving them a certain mythical "air." The viewer is encouraged to search for metaphoric links between the modern and biblical implications of the narrative. Yet these two parallel significations of the narrative (modern and biblical) defy each other at critical dramatic points. One must look for a deep meaning in things, but it must be a meaning other than the biblical one.

From the beginning of the film, the visual progression is accentuated by frequent intercutting of seemingly alien images. Representing natural elements—water, rock, earth, flora, sky, sun, and moon—these stationary shots signify a universal permanence against which the uncertainty of the protagonists' personal lives is contrasted. The inserted images of nature persistently disrupt the narrative flow by triggering contradicting associations, mostly in relation to the dialogue and commentary accompanying the image. Accentuated by equally disturbing sound effects, the inserted images are typical of Godard's "cinematic essayism," whose ultimate goal is to achieve integration on the level of ideas out of the "incoherent" image/sound relationship and the events that lack common linear narrative progression.

For example, during Mary's traumatic soliloquy, heard over her spasmodic thrashing as she lies in bed, the inserted stationary images of the sunset, reeds, water, full moon, evoke stability, independence, and unresponsiveness. Mary's inner monologue indicates that the source of her distress is an incapacity to reconcile the soul/body dichotomy (earlier she has confided this problem to her physician, explaining that it is her soul that contains a body; "the spirit acts on the body, breathes through it"). At the peak of her internal struggle now, she cries; "I am a soul imprisoned by a body," then looks upward as if pleading for God's mercy.

In the closing sequence of the film, when she finally accepts a mundane way of life, which is nature in another guise (symbolized by her application of lipstick), Mary's voice-over reiterates her psychological frustration: "My body left only an imprint on the soul that helped me." The dialectical contradiction between the auditory and the visual is obvious. The spoken text underscores the importance of the spiritual over the physical, while the image suggests the unmatched power of the nature to which Godard's heroine must adjust if she is to survive. Otherwise, she is doomed either to complete her self-destruction or to rise to sainthood—either option incompatible with Godard's view of women.

In contrast to Godard's earlier experimentation with "cinematic essayism" (*Le gai savoir*, 1969, and *Vladimir and Rosa*, 1971), *Hail Mary*'s visual symbolism is embedded in the mental, emotional, and corporal conditions of the film's characters. For example, the two-shot of Eva and the professor discussing the balance of nature is followed by a long shot of two eagles circling each other in the sky. Accompanied by the music of Dvořák, the inserted image has two functions: it represents the professor's actual point of view as he looks upward and talks about the permanent balance between the universe and nature, and it metaphorically relates to Mary and Joseph, especially when in the subsequent shot their gestures parallel the circling birds as Mary unsuccessfully attempts to elude Joseph's touch. During this confrontation, the professor's offscreen remark, "Won't our decedents try to preserve life," attaches a universal significance to Mary and Joseph's intimate relationship.

After two shots depicting Joseph's assault on Mary as he pins her down on the hood of his cab, an insert of the sun partially obscured by dark clouds is again accompanied by the professor's voice: "A prior intelligence programmed life, which struggled to exist in a pitiless universe." This is meant to raise a question about the protagonists' personal conflicts. The point is reinforced by part of the professor's lecture concerning the origin of life on earth, delivered earlier in the film: "Life appeared entirely by chance. . . . It came from elsewhere, from space. . . . There is a very strong presumption that life exists in space. We're from there." Sensitive viewers are expected to establish a connection between Mary's personal trauma and the idea that she is, as a human being, manipulated by a "superior power." The professor's tirade provides an option to consider Mary's painful condition as imposed on her by an irresponsible force against which she tries uselessly to fight. But by accepting the biological function of having the child, she is set free to reintegrate into secular life not restricted by canonical dogma. Through personal mental growth, at the end Mary turns in a completely opposite direction, one that is fully identified with life *here and now.*

In the sequence in which Joseph assaults Mary in front of his cab, another shot appears that cannot be justified from a diegetic perspective—a repetition of the shot immediately preceding it in which Joseph pins Mary against the hood of his car as she eludes his kiss by turning her head aside. This repetition has a certain "mysterious" implication, as does the reappearance now of the intertitle AT THAT TIME, which evokes fatalistic overtones—namely, that the resolution of male-female antagonism is dependent on forces outside human power. What are we to make of this? the film blatantly asks.

The intertitle underscores Mary's need to understand what she instinct-ively feels is located outside herself as her feeling of alienation increases throughout the film. She is often shown, mostly in close-up, looking toward the sky as if asking for help. After a close-up of her in the bathroom, there is a shot of a huge plane disappearing "slowly" (with the use of the telephoto lens) into the blue horizon over trees and airport signaling equipment, and this long shot of the airplane is reinserted several times in the film, following shots in which Mary (and sometimes Joseph) looks upward. The plane is associated with Gabriel (he is first seen at the airport arriving with the young girl whose cherubic features suggest an angel). But although it seems problem-atic to associate the airplane with the notion that Gabriel is God's messenger, it is natural to connect images and sounds of the plane with the ideas of flying, transition, freedom, and ascension—all central to this film's general philosophical interests. Once Mary reconciles the dichotomy between the micro and macro dimensions of her existence, once she realizes the "mythical chain" that binds her inner being with nature, she appears like a new Eve, capable of accepting—and experiencing—secular life.

There are only two instances in the film of blatantly supernatural occur-rences, both connected not with Mary but with Joseph, when he still proves unable—and unwilling—to accept Mary's virginal pregnancy. The first "mira-cle" takes place when Joseph is about to enter his cab. Unexpectedly he "sees" Gabriel standing in front of the car holding a child by the hand. Surprised, but not fascinated, Joseph walks to where Gabriel was standing, only to discover (in the subsequent shot) that nobody is there! This shot can be read as a visualization of Joseph's altered state of consciousness (i.e., mirage) caused by his frustration, as opposed to Mary who, struggling to live with her condition, experiences no perceptual distortion of the outside world. As Gabriel predicts, all Mary's problems, including the actual delivery (not shown on screen), are gradually ameliorated. After the initial torment caused by her intense feeling that she is going to deliver a baby without having had intercourse with a man, she finally becomes reconciled with her destiny ("The hand of God is upon men and nobody can interfere. . . . All this doesn't happen every day. . . . The spirit affects the body. . . . We cannot escape each other as we cannot escape Him").

Another "miracle" occurs during the climactic confrontation between Mary and Joseph in her apartment. After Joseph grudgingly acknowledges Mary's claim that a superior "Rule" exists, Gabriel suddenly reappears (again as deus ex machina) in the subsequent shot. But unlike the former materialization, which can be interpreted diegetically as the product of Joseph's fantasy, this appearance and disappearance of a character represents structural intervention by the filmmaker, made possible by the editing procedure. Godard "meddles" with the diegetic world to make clear his point. Joseph tries to touch Mary's bare stomach (as he utters, "I love you"), but she resolutely prevents him from doing so. In a medium close-up of Mary's abdomen, an arm suddenly enters from the left, shoving Joseph's hand away. Cut to a close-up of Mary, her mouth open in astonishment, accompanied by a strong musical accent. Then, a long shot taken from a high angle, showing Gabriel throwing Joseph to the floor while chiding him for his unwillingness to keep his hands off Mary.

The representational inconsistency and shock of introducing Gabriel is typical of Godardian editing technique aimed at conveying an idea of the filmmaker's coming from outside the diegetic world. The auditory-visual execution here enhances the mysterious "air" of the film, associating the story with the supernatural in the biblical myth. But the directorial gesture contributes to Joseph's final acceptance of Mary's condition in a way that expands and intensifies Godard's feminist message: Mary accepts her condition through inner struggle, while Joseph relinquishes his resistance only after the direct "intervention" of a higher force.

IN SUBVERTING the narrative, Godard utilizes a procedure characteristic of silent cinema; the visual continuity is repeatedly broken by the insertion of written information. The central intertitle AT THAT TIME (whose literal translation from the French would be "in that time, there"), first appears as part of the film's credits, then recurs three times in conjunction with the three women (Mary, Juliette, and Eva) and the men with whom they are associated (Joseph and the professor). In the fifth and sixth appearances, it is used to link the professor's lecture about the origin of life on earth with the conflict between Mary and Joseph. The seventh and eighth times, it is inserted (with only one shot—water—between them) in the boat-harbor sequence when

Mary and Joseph are temporarily reconciled. The ninth and tenth appearances of the intertitle function as a framing device: the title opens and closes the montage sequence signifying Mary's delivery. In addition to shifting the story from a visual to a literary level, the recurrent use of the same intertitle intensifies the segmented, yet circular, structure of the narrative, with its spatiotemporal inconsistencies. The viewer is forced to reflect upon the philosophical dimension of the action and the spoken words rather than identify with the characters.

The intertitle AT THAT TIME provides ironic overtones. The written text often intrudes into the intimate relationship between the two protagonists, suggesting (with its biblical sound) correspondences between the biblical and the modern male-female relationship, particularly regarding a woman's maternal status. It is probably the film's ironic tone attending the recounting of the sacred myth that led the pope to accuse *Hail Mary* (apparently without seeing the film) of "mockery of the religious feelings of believers and desecration of the spiritual significance of the Virgin Mary." The choice of words— *EN CE TEMPS LA* (in French, the emphasis is on the final word, *là*, "there")— is meant to link the contemporary story consisting of ordinary facts with the extraordinary circumstances of mythical antecedents.

But the rhetorical repetition of the same phrase, reminiscent of the standard beginning of fairy tales ("once upon a time") encourages the viewer to observe the events at a distance, so much so that the most literal biblical references in the film provoke laughter in the audience (as when Jesus renames his playmates or tells his parents that he must "attend to his father's affairs"). It would be unwise to believe that such humorous responses are unintended by Godard. It is more conceivable that they reflect the filmmaker's intention to demonstrate the absurdity of traditional beliefs, however entrenched in collective consciousness. Consequently, it is also not accidental that at the junctures where the film's diegesis most closely parallels the Bible's text (e.g., Gabriel's announcement of Mary's pregnancy, Jesus' embarking on his messianic journey), the diegetic world on the screen becomes most incoherent. This again provides grounds for the audience to become suspicious.

THE DIALOGUE and soliloquies in *Hail Mary* are less manifestations of dramatic conflicts than rhetorical statement, while references to the biblical story ebb and flow. All of this forms a broad metaphorical network for a philosophical interpretation of the diegetic world. During the most dramatic moments, the spoken text usually begins as a realistic verbal exchange between the characters and subsequently turns into refined, often convoluted, philosophical eloquence. Thus, for example, once the conflict between Mary and Joseph reaches its dramatic climax (when he finally touches her swollen abdomen), the nature of the conversation changes from ordinary ("I love you." "No!") to sophisticated ("We are speaking and we are speaking of the word. . . . Then you won't leave me"). (See the shot breakdown for *Hail Mary*, shots 175–96.)

This sequence exemplifies the method by which Godard transcends the diegetic meaning of the verbal exchange and integrates it with intimations of his protagonists' extraordinary destiny. Their disjunctive dialogue is further disrupted by sounds mixed in with their independent tonal and rhythmic patterns. The dense noises that arbitrarily appear and disappear in the course of the sequence, without diegetic justification, play against musical fragments from classical pieces, thus contributing to the self-substantiality of the auditory track, which parallels and comments on the structure created by the film's diegetic world and biblical references. The fragmentation of music is clearly intended to frustrate the viewer's natural desire to enjoy the melodic development and rhythmic buildup of the score. Whenever the music achieves a certain harmonic identity, it is precipitously cut off, causing an auditory shock that matches the already subverted narrative flow. In many ways, Godard's practice of relating image and sound is reminiscent of Eisenstein's concept of sight and sound counterpoint, which considers the auditory track neither an illustrative nor even a complementary counterpart of the image but a vehicle for challenging the visual continuity on both narrative and sensorial levels, thus underscoring the author's attitude toward the presented event(s). In Godard's film, the sound (especially the music) is persistently barred from continuing its development, paralleling Mary's abortive attempts to evade her painful situation, instead producing even more pain. Just as Mary is prevented from having full enjoyment of everyday life, so the viewers are left short of having full melodic satisfaction of what they hear. Only at the very end, after Mary has made her final decision to embrace reality as it is with her entire being, is Bach's melodic phrase allowed to flourish. Thus, the veiwer's "pleasure" is fulfilled *outside* the biblical context.

THE ORDER of the sequences can be apprehended only on an associative level. For example, the conversation in which Mary and Joseph agree to stay together is followed by a sequence depicting Eva and the professor separating. Before boarding a train, the professor walks away from the car in which Eva sits watching him. This sequence provides a contrast to the spiritual love sought by Mary (characterized by her insistance that Joseph accept her unexpected pregnancy). We now see the physically possessive love of Eva, who is angry at the professor's decision to return to his family. The final shot in this sequence presents a distant full moon occupying the upper right corner of the frame above a yellow diagonal strip formed by a moving train, cutting off the lower right corner of the dark screen. This graphic composition of the sacred (the moon, associated with Mary) and the profane (the train, associated with Eva) links the personal lives of the characters to the universality of the inserted image of nature or the profanity of the image of a mechanical vehicle. As if in response, Mary's close-up, following immediately after this sequence, opens her long soliloquy expressing her anguish and her doubt about the supreme "Rule" she is expected to obey.

According to the structural principle of narrative discordance and acquiring meaning by association, Mary's soliloquy is intercut with images of nature: the convulsion of her body on a bed (reminiscent of the girl Marie's prostration on the floor after dancing to a Mahler symphony in Miéville's film) is constantly "severed" by close-ups of the outside world. Mary's inner monologue reflects the disturbed consciousness of a young woman thrust into a situation that produces suffering while (as she states) God "profits" by providing orders ("Rules") for her and no real aid. Helpless, yet not wanting to give in to the pain that is imposed upon her by an outside force, Mary utters sentences as if she were a spiritual medium unaware of the meaning of the words:

> "What makes a soul is its pain. . . . God's a creep, a coward who won't fight, who counts . . . on ass alone, that is, on a quiet heart, for existence. . . . I want no carnal joy; I don't want to wear out my heart in one go, or my soul, in one go. . . . It will always be horrible . . . for me to be the Master, but, there'll be no more sexuality in me. I'll know the true smile of the soul, not from outside . . . but from inside. . . . Wanting isn't expanding by force. It's recoiling into oneself . . . from level . . . to level, for eternity. . . . God is a vampire who suffered me in him . . . because I suffered and He didn't, and He profited from my pain. Mary is a body fallen from a soul. I am a soul imprisoned by a body. My soul makes me sick at heart and it's my cunt. . . . I'm a woman . . . though I don't beget my man through my cunt. I am joy. I am she who is joy, and need no longer fight it, or be tempted . . . I am not resigned. Resignation is sad. How can one be resigned to God's will? Are we resigned to being loved? This seemed clear to me. Too clear."

The images that accompany Mary's stream of consciousness (quoted above are selected phrases from a longer text) appear in the following order:

> moon/train, Mary's face, Mary's body, sunset with clouds, city street, moon, Mary's face, reeds, Mary's face, Mary's body, reeds, Mary's writh-

ing body, reeds blown by wind, Mary's hand on lower abdomen, Mary's body turning, reeds blown by wind, Mary's hand on abdomen, Mary's head, reeds blown by wind, setting sun, lake, sky, sun, sun with clouds, water, sun with clouds, weeds, porcupines, sky with clouds, Mary's body, pedestrians on street, Mary's body, Mary's hand on abdomen, Mary's face, full moon.

Juxtaposed, the shots of Mary's contorting body and the images of nature imply the dialectical linkage between the two realities: the consciousness' inability to cope with its problems, typical of human beings; nature's steadiness and its uncontrollable power—rain, wind, storm (the majority of the exterior shots in the film are stationary, thereby underscoring the perpetuity of natural phenomena). The montage interaction between the spasmodic motion of Mary's body, her frustrated soliloquy, and the stationary exterior images testifies to Godard's philosophical thinking, emphasizing not Mary's conscious renunciations but the instinctive reconciliation with nature she is painfully accepting as an integral part of her existence.

THE DELIVERY SEQUENCE exemplifies Godard's elliptical editing procedure, used to transpose concrete (representational) denotation of the shots into their abstract connotation. After the closing sentence of Mary's speech of anguish ("Too clear"), there is a cut to her and Joseph watching a basketball game, followed by the intertitle AT THAT TIME, which marks a transition to the sequence foreshadowing and then evoking Mary's delivery (after which the intertitle appears for the last time). The length of the shots in this typical fast-paced montage segment is brief, creating an intense visual pulsation on the screen. (See the shot breakdown for *Hail Mary*, shots 242–63.)

Note that the shot at the end of the basketball game (the immense moon) is succeeded by a shot containing the curve of a white globe (a lighted lamp) while Mary and Joseph expectantly look upward. The (invisible) object of their attention is apparently the tiny full moon depicted in the next shot, which is followed by two shots of water, the waves of which move toward the camera. This series of suggestive shots is cut off by a long shot of the gas station in winter (with the clearly visible word *Self* from the *Self Service* sign), which is followed by the recurrent metaphoric shot—the plane taking off above a silhouetted forest. Then appears the final, tracking shot, photographed from a car moving behind a snowplow shoveling back the snow as we hear a baby's cries.

These twenty-two shots are framed by the last two appearances of the intertitle, after the second of which comes a medium shot depicting a cow licking itself. Finally, a series of diegetically unrelated shots—cherry blossoms, horses, fruit trees in bloom, a donkey—functions as a montage transition to a shot of Mary sitting in her car and handing the baby to her father, whose farm they are visiting. Elliptically depicting Mary' delivery, this whole sequence provides a reference to a miraculous birth, but only so as to confirm Godard's acknowledgment of the mystical—and unreachable—significance of life and its origin as it is, in nature. Men and women are to be integrated with the universe and have no capacity to exceed nature. They may challenge it, as they always do, but only to realize that they are an aspect of the physical world. This is so even when men and women discover a new, previously unknown fact about life.

After Mary's delivery, her father suggests that she tell her son that Joseph is not his *real* father. Holding the baby in her hands, Mary responds, "That's life," with the same calmness she exhibited when she accepted the "Rule" (i.e., stopped questioning the incomprehensible situation imposed on her). Joseph, preoccupied with the more mundane aspects of existence, comments: "I've come to talk about the [gas] station. . . . I've figured it out. We can pay it back in two years." On the auditory level, choral music announces the appearance of another pregnant woman, who, encountering Mary, joyously greets her: "Thanks, Mary, for every woman!" This explicit biblical reference is followed by another series of symbolic shots depicting trees in bloom, sun, sky, and water, intercut with a long shot of Mary in a body of water, the baby in her arms bursting forth from beneath the water's surface—all of this accompanied by fragmented passages of Bach and children's yells. After this metaphoric baptism, the son (young Jesus) assumes the central role until the film's epilogue, which refocuses on Mary, presenting her in a completely different context, expounding her new attitude toward life.

In comparison with the introductory *The Book of Mary*, which functions as an organic prologue to *Hail Mary*, Godard's finale, showing Mary's son selecting and renaming his playmates, is an appendix insufficiently integrated within the main film's diegetic world. Unlike the Miéville narrative, which metaphorically overrides the biblical text, the finale of Godard's film mechanically recounts Jesus' encounter with the apostles and their embarkation on a messianic journey. Such a *literal* biblical allusion lacks a deeper symbolic meaning. But after the boy runs away from his parents, the film abruptly returns to its central theme by reestablishing the question regarding the heroine's transformed attitude toward life, now focused on her reintegration within a particular social reality.

THE CONCLUSION of *Hail Mary* begins with three high-angle medium shots depicting the lower torso of a young rapidly walking woman, followed by a man (only his lower torso and tricolored shoes, associated with Gabriel, who wears them earlier in the film, are visible). The subsequent long shot reveals Gabriel as he greets Mary with the salutation heard earlier in the film: "Hail Mary!" Standing by her car, Mary (who now has wavy chestnut hair) glances upward—a gesture she makes so often throughout the film—and gets into her car. The next few close-ups show Mary smoking a cigarette, holding a tube of lipstick close to her lips, followed by a detail including only her face from eyes to chin as her hand hesitates in a repeated attempt to apply the lipstick. Mary's final statement, coming offscreen, overlaps the penultimate shot, a tight close-up of Mary resolutely applying the lipstick. "I am of the virgin, and didn't want this being. . . . I only left my imprint on the soul that helped me," heard against a motif from Bach.

By the power of screen augmentation (enlargement), the final shot of Mary's wide-open mouth appropriates a cinematic dimension disassociated from the film's actual story and is thus highly intensified in its metaphoric connotation. The shot's graphic composition (Mary's mouth) carries a strong sensual implication: the position of the lipstick in relation to the open mouth suggests penetration (especially because of the compositional emphasis on the tube of lipstick, which earlier in the film Mary considers buying). Apparently Mary has reached psychoemotional maturity. After experiencing motherhood, she is ready to embrace her womanhood. Overcoming her initial hesitation, she decides to use the lipstick, one of the most characteristic ordinary gadgets in an adult woman's life—here, a symbol of sensuality.

While consuming the lipstick, her open mouth, covering the entire screen, is a black hole, creating the film's ultimate visual metaphor, graphic and convoluted: the universe. Bounded by the horizon line of her upper lip, Mary's wide-open mouth, evoking speechlessness, further symbolizes the fathomlessness of the psyche, the intricacy of sensuality, and above all, the mystery of human existence. Mary is at one with the universe, in harmony with nature; and there is an unreachable mystery about life, though not a supernatural mystery. This final visual accent of the film produces an emotional overtone that retroactively permeates the entire narrative, stimulating the viewer to rethink and reinterpret the story.

The film's three diegetic lines of development (Juliette and Joseph; Mary and Joseph; Eva and the professor) represent three types of relationships shared by men and women. The story of Juliette and Joseph focuses on a woman attempting to consolidate the liaison with her lover by asking him to marry her and offering to conceive a child with him. When Joseph responds indifferently, Juliette feels victimized and spiteful. Eva and the professor represent another cultural pattern, that of a married man who after a brief

Godard's Vision of the New Eve 113

involvement with an unmarried woman, reassumes his marital obligations; he uses and then abandons his mistress. As the professor's student, Eva initiates an affair with him but fails to develop a deeper relationship, and when she is informed of her lover's decision to rejoin his wife and child, her behavior is that of a person who feels exploited and punished.

Antithetical to both, the third couple, Mary and Joseph, represent a relationship in which the female partner struggles to redefine the role she is forced to assume counter to her own desire. Unlike Juliette or Eva, Mary struggles with the established conventions of male-dominated courtship. She says no to Joseph, who wants to sleep with her, and she justifies her behavior by being committed to a more powerful force (the "Rule") which Joseph fails to grasp. The film shows the "Rule" not to make sense as a divine or biblical one; instead, it is the mystery of nature itself. Even though Mary does not understand the exact significance of such a power, her instinct tells her to obey it, and after a long battle she succeeds in persuading Joseph to do the same. Thanks to her sensitivity and instinct, the relationship between Mary and Joseph is gradually transformed from conventional male-female antagonism to mutual acceptance and understanding. As a reward, they are granted an exceptional child, and they find the strength to let him leave their home to fulfill his mission. After her inner struggle to defend her identity, Mary embraces ordinary life, which turns out to demand a new, right, and natural sacrifice—separation from her son.

The ending of the film indicates that a resolution to the body/soul dichotomy as experienced by Mary can be achieved. After their initial conflict and misunderstanding, a deeply spiritual affinity unites the couple. Once she persuades Joseph to trust her feelings, Mary preserves the family while maintaining her integrity. In light of the view held by biblical scholars who regard Mary as the new Eve, Godard's Mary emerges as a still newer Eve, one who has evolved into an earthly human being who against all odds overrides the contradictions of existence that threaten to break apart her soul and body. In these terms, Mary's final cry—"I am of the virgin, and I didn't want this being. . . . I only left my imprint on the soul that helped me"—can be interpreted as evidence of the ultimate reconciliation of the spiritual and physical. The body seems to speak here, taking the active, "spiritual" role and showing that the old disruption of body and soul no longer applies.

Godard's feminist preoccupation in *Hail Mary* can be summarized as "the search for woman's freedom." As she sees her son leave home, Mary feels liberated. Reintegrated into ordinary life, attractively dressed, she walks through the city while Gabriel acknowledges her with his salute, making the final reference to the relationship between Godard's protagonist and the biblical Mary. The "Hail Mary" salute can be read as Godard's (or God's, for that matter) pronouncement that the next stage of Mary's life is just another beginning. This is underscored visually when Mary, departing from Gabriel, gets into her car, lights a cigarette, and points the lipstick directly at her mouth as if committing a cardinal sin. The point is that she is decisive in experiencing this with all her being, as Godard's filming of the scene indicates. She is free and not afraid to cope with any obstacle.

The closing shot—the close-up of Mary's wide-open mouth—is a metaphor for the interminable universe with which Mary has tried *in vain* to establish a rational, verbalizable rapport. The graphically implied speechlessness reiterates the film's central message: there are circumstances in human existence that by their nature are incomprehensible and therefore must remain inexplicable. However abstract, the film's last image, a cinematic sign par excellence, belongs to Godard's heroine, ready to embrace life without traditional or ecclesiastic moralization. At the same time, this image is the director's final gesture, meant to discredit the biblical connotation of the film's narrative while creating a cinematic metaphor representative of modern woman and modern feminist aspiration.

Notes

1. *L'Osservatore Romano*, April 23, 1985 (from a reprint by New Yorker Films, Godard's distributor).

2. Godard interview, *Corriere della Sera* (Milan), April 26, 1985 (from a reprint by New Yorker Films).

3. Jean-Luc Godard, "Bergmanorama," *Cahiers du cinéma* 85 (July 1958), reprinted in Tom Milne, trans., ed., *Godard on Godard* (New York: Viking, 1972), item 37.

Contributors

Stanley Cavell, named a MacArthur Fellow in 1992, is a professor of philosophy at Harvard University. His books include *Must We Mean What We Say?*, *The Claim of Reason*, and two books on film, *The World Viewed: Reflections on the Ontology of Film* and *Pursuits of Happiness: The Hollywood Comedy of Remarriage*. He is at work on a book on film melodrama.

Gayatri Chatterjee is an independent film scholar in Pune, India, where she has taught at the National Film Institute and the University of Pune. She is the author of monographs on Raj Kapoor's *Awaara* and other early Indian films, and she is at work on a book on the great Bengali director Ritwik Ghatak.

Harvey Cox is Victor S. Thomas Professor of Divinity at the Divinity School of Harvard University. His books include *Many Mansions: A Christian's Encounters with Other Faiths*, *Religion in the Secular City*, *The Feast of Fools*, and *Just As I Am*.

Ellen Draper teaches film at Simmons College. She has published essays in *Wide Angle*, *Film Quarterly*, *Velvet Light Trap*, and *Inventing Vietnam: Film and TV Images of the U.S. Vietnam War*.

John Gianvito is a filmmaker, curator, and teacher, currently an assistant professor of film and video at the University of Massachusetts at Boston. His films include the feature *The Flower of Pain* (1983) and *Letter to a Romantic Ideal* (episode in the film *Address Unknown* [1985]).

Inez Hedges is a professor of French, German, and cinema studies at Northeastern University in Boston. She is the author of *Breaking the Frame: Film Language and the Experience of Limits* and *Languages of Revolt: Dada and Surrealist Literature and Film*.

Robert Kiely is Loker Professor of English at Harvard University, master of Adams House, and former chairman of the Department of English. A Roman Catholic and Benedictine Oblate, he is the author of *Reverse Tradition: Postmodern Fictions and the Nineteenth Century Novel*, *The Romantic Novel in England*, and *Beyond Egotism: The Fiction of James Joyce, Virginia Woolf, and D. H. Lawrence*.

Sandra Laugier teaches philosophy at the University of Rennes. She has published articles on Stanley Cavell's work, is editing a book of essays on Cavell, and is translating several of Cavell's books into French, including *Pursuit of*

Happiness for *Cahiers du cinéma*'s book series. She is the author of *L'anthropologie logique de Quine* (Quine's Logical Anthropology).

Maryel Locke is an editor and a lawyer. She is secretary of the Steering Committee of Friends of Film at the Boston Museum of Fine Arts and a former officer of Boston Film and Video Foundation and of Center Screen, Inc. Her memoir, "Anne Sexton Remembered," recently appeared in *Rossetti to Sexton: Six Women Poets at Texas*. She is a former editor of *The Radcliffe Quarterly*.

Laura Mulvey is a filmmaker and a film and cultural theorist. She is the author of *Visual and Other Pleasures* and has written repeatedly on Godard. Her films, codirected with Peter Wollen, include *Riddles of the Sphinx* and *Crystal Gazing*. She is a senior lecturer in film practice at the London College of Printing.

Vlada Petric is the curator of the Harvard Film Archive and a senior lecturer in the Department of Visual and Environmental Studies at Harvard University. He is the author of *Constructivism in Film: The Man with the Movie Camera* and editor of *Film and Dreams: An Approach to Bergman*. He has directed several experimental films and TV plays. **Geraldine Bard** is an associate professor of English at Buffalo State College, New York. She has written articles on film and semiotics and directed medical films.

David Sterritt is film critic for *The Christian Science Monitor* and Monitor Radio. He teaches film at Columbia University and has served for several years on the New York Film Festival selection committee. He is the author of *The Films of Alfred Hitchcock*.

Charles Warren teaches English and film at Tufts University. He has taught previously at Harvard University and at The New School for Social Research, New York. He taught film for a year in Europe, India, and East Asia for the International Honors Program. He is the author of *T. S. Eliot on Shakespeare*.

Interviews with Godard

Godard in His "Fifth Period": An Interview

by Katherine Dieckmann

GODARD SITS ALONE in a plush room at New York's Park-Lane Hotel, puffing on what has become his trademark cigar. A French edition of Rilke's *Letters to a Young Poet*, a stack of newspapers and an unopened bottle of Jack Daniels are on the desk before him. His English is excellent. He speaks softly, sucking in a little breath of air at the end of his sentences which threatens to make the final word disappear. One hears in Godard's answers the desire for pared-down explanations, ones like Gabriel's response to Joseph during a scuffle in *Hail Mary*. Joseph asks over and over why he may not touch Mary, and Gabriel, catching his opponent in a stranglehold, shouts abruptly: *"Parce que!"* (Because!).

Katherine Dieckmann: Are you a Catholic?

Jean-Luc Godard: No, I was raised a Protestant, but I don't practice. But I'm very interested in Catholicism. I think there's something so strong in the way the Bible was written, how it speaks of events that are happening today, how it contains statements about things which have happened in the past. I think, well—it's a great book! And somehow I think we need faith, or I need faith, or I'm lacking in faith. Therefore maybe I needed a story which is bigger than myself. I like it that *Hail Mary* is being really discussed. Instead of people saying, "Oh, it's directed by Godard," people are talking about the subject of the film first. Later they say, "It's by Godard."

K. D.: It's a sincerely spiritual film. What about it do you think is offending the Catholics most? The obsessive nudity?

J-L. G.: Probably. But you know, our purpose was to try and shoot a woman naked and not make it aggressive, not in an X-rated-picture way. There are several shots which have more the purpose of an anatomical drawing. Maybe the nudity's a bit much. It encounters the risk of becoming sinister. Or sin, even. Perhaps it's too big a word. But it was difficult to know how to show it. Very often in painting, the Virgin is depicted half-naked, or at least with the breast naked or revealed, because of the Christ child. This has always caused problems: in the time of Martin Luther, there was a great deal of opposition to Raphael, for instance. The German soldiers came to Rome and

This interview was published in *Film Quarterly* 39.2 (Winter 1985–1986): 224–32 and is here reprinted by permission of the author. The original interview included five introductory paragraphs of explanation and comment on the film that are generally covered elsewhere in this book.

scratched up many Raphael paintings. They thought it was offensive, too much of a *Playboy* style of painting. In *Hail Mary* I was trying to make the audience see not a naked woman, but flesh, if that's at all possible. And the difference between—a feeling of something fleshy. And we had thought of having Joseph be naked also, as we had a nude male in *First Name: Carmen*, but decided the audience wouldn't understand, they would immediately think Mary and Joseph were going to have intercourse. So it was absolutely impossible. And I'm a man, still, I like to look at women naked!

K. D.: You're dealing with this opposition between science and nature, or logic and illogic, in this movie. The men are associated with the logical, the women with the intuitive. And you're using a very different set of symbols. Usually your films are full of quotations from popular culture, with bits of traffic signs, neon, advertisements, cartoons. The signs in *Hail Mary* are very pure: a moon, a sun, water. Apples. Some of the images are even a little corny, like *National Geographic* photography.

J-L. G.: Well, women are more casual. They accept more things. Whereas men always feel they have to master, to understand. As for these symbols, we shot exactly like old-time Walt Disney documentaries were shot. We set up a camera and were waiting, waiting, waiting, until a certain time when you got the exceptional in everyday, natural things. I mean, we shot the sun, but we needed to have a plane cross the sun, and it doesn't happen every second! It's a one-time thing. That's why we went over budget with *Hail Mary* and had to stop and shoot *Detective* to make some money, and then go back and finish *Hail Mary*, which was very disruptive. I didn't want to make *Detective* at all, though I don't mind it now that I've done it. But it was an unwanted child, and then what do you do? You have to take care of it. What we wanted to show in *Hail Mary* was signs in the beginning. Signs in the sense of signals, the beginning of signs, when signs are beginning to grow. Before they have signification of meaning. Immaculate signs in a way. And not just to give a feeling of nature, in order to be poetic, but to show the physical process of making nature possible. A philosophy of nature, just as we tried to show the spirit and flesh of Mary. Also to bring science close to the natural, not to show them as oppositions. Because there's a scene where the professor is talking about creation—the text comes from the work of a British physicist—and it sounds very biblical or religious. We are an extraterrestrial people, as it says in the film. We come from the sky. And it's not by chance, but by design.

K. D.: And you have so many images of the circle, in nature and elsewhere, which gives the movie a strong feeling of unity.

J-L. G.: Yes, the circle. We used it metaphorically: the woman as circle, and the plane flying toward it. That's one signal: coming to a woman's center. But at a certain point there's no difference between metaphor and actuality. I had no idea we'd shot the moon so many times, but suddenly we had all these shots of the moon, and I discovered then that the moon was like the basketball in Mary's games. So it was the same: Mary was playing basketball with the moon.

K. D.: Tell me about the use of sound, because it's very complex.

J-L. G.: I try to work not with an idea of vertical sound, where there are many tracks distinct from one another, but horizontally, where there are many, many sounds but still it's as though every sound is becoming one general speech, whether it's music, dialogue or nature sound. *Hail Mary* had more of a documentary use of sound than other films I've done. It's simple in a way: there's dialogue, direct sound, and music. The story was known, more or less. And I knew that the only music that would work would be Bach. I tried to put in all sorts of Bach: violins, church music, piano, choral. The picture could be described also as a documentary on Bach's music. And it couldn't have been Beethoven, or Mozart, because historically Bach was the music of Martin Luther. And as I was saying before, Martin Luther was attacking the Catholic church, specifically the way the Catholic church makes images. Probably in his time Bach was immensely popular, because his music was played in churches that had no heat, and it was probably very cold in church, and you needed a strong and passionate music. It's a strange thing, but if you have good speakers and play Bach very, very loud—even if it's just a smooth piano piece—it sounds like rock music. Bach's music can be matched to any situation. It's perfect. When you play it in reverse, it sounds almost the same. It's very mathematical. You could play it in the elevator, like Muzak. It blends itself. Bach is the perfect musician for the elevator.

K. D.: Before you shot *Hail Mary*, you said "it will be about what Mary and Joseph said to each other before having a child." Does this still apply now that the movie's done?

J-L. G.: Yes, exactly. What could they say to each other? It's a major problem, because from the Bible we know of only two or three words that Mary spoke, and from Joseph absolutely nothing. And they must have talked together! So it was difficult to invent the dialogue, because nobody knows.

K. D.: You've also said that one film always leads directly into the next with you. So how does the story of Carmen become the story of Mary?

J-L. G.: Well, Carmen leads to Mary, though of course they're very different. Carmen is more what men imagine women to be. And with Mary, it's more a matter that a man can't imagine what a woman is. And, of course, one story ends well and the other ends quite badly. . . .

K. D.: Do you go to the movies a lot? I know when you were young and writing for *Cahiers du cinéma* in the fifties you were notorious for spending all day in the cinema.

J-L. G.: No, no, I don't go very much at all. I have a feeling these days that just by knowing the names of the directors and actors involved, and by looking at the ads in the paper or on the street, I've already seen the pictures.

K. D.: Are you still living outside Geneva? And why did you choose to shoot *Hail Mary* in Switzerland?

J-L. G.: Yes, I live in Switzerland, though I have a company located in Paris. I've shot there before—*Every Man for Himself* was shot in Switzerland, and parts of *Passion*. I've been there since my childhood. I was raised there, had family there, though I also have family in Paris. I've always been crossing borders. I belong to two countries, even if I have only one passport, Swiss. I choose Switzerland to shoot in because—I don't know, already I've used Paris and Parisian streets so much, in my earlier films.

K. D.: Let's talk about your work in general, or the way it's been periodized. In 1970 a lot of books came out dealing with your work in the sixties: there was this impulse to talk about Godard. And then in the seventies the image is that you drifted off, got involved in video and political projects. Then when *Every Man for Himself* came out in 1980 you described it as "your second first film."

J-L. G.: It works in periods of ten years, yes, because we live in a decimal system. We have ten fingers. So we always invent in periods of ten. Ten years after ten years. I'm past 50 now, so I speak of myself as being in my "fifth period." I began shooting in 1960, I mean really shooting, and then in 1970 I changed more or less, and then in 1980 I started up again. . . . I'm very regular! Now it's 1985. I have to wait until 1990.

K. D.: You're at the midpoint of the third chapter, because now you've amassed an entire second set of feature films: *Every Man for Himself*, *First Name: Carmen*, *Detective* and *Hail Mary*.

J-L. G.: I'll use the same words as Picasso, not to compare myself to him, but because they fit. He said, "I will go on painting until painting refuses me and doesn't want me anymore." I'm trying to do this with motion pictures. To go until motion pictures refuse me. Not an audience, and certainly not the industry—the industry already did! But to go until the screen says: No. I had the feeling in making *Hail Mary* that there was an immaculate screen, and it was saying to me, "Don't stray too far, or don't come too close. Or come closer. Or don't come." I had the feeling of a voice there.

K. D.: Have your working methods changed after twenty-five years of making films?

J-L. G.: I am closer to images now. Part of this comes from working in video, which I'm doing more and more. I use video to help me see and work better, because I can shoot something and see it immediately, all the while imagining a real screen behind. Video lets me look first, and then I can begin to write from what I see. Before—just like most movie-makers and industry executives—I always wrote first, and then let the image come. I could write about you: "She sat in the corner, she looked at me with such a face," then I'd imagine the face and direct it. Now I look at you and imagine first, and take notes from that. Most people think they work only when the camera is rolling, but that's not it. When the camera rolls, everything is done already. It's like life. Take this hotel room. When two newlyweds enter this room they know what they are going to do, they've written it before, in the elevator or on the street. And the real work's been done on the street or in the elevator. Here's the completion of the work: the camera's rolling. Cinematographers shoot a movie, and then for six months they don't touch a camera! What makes them think they're still working when they're not looking? Images are like life. And images can show you something in your life you don't want to see, which is probably why people react violently to *Hail Mary*. If you're jealous, you don't want to see the image of the other man or the other woman right away. Things like that. The image is something very strong when it comes at you. That's why movies are so popular. But it's not dangerous. A lot of people don't want to go to the doctor. They don't want to know what kind of disease they have, or how a disease might look. Maybe I can look because my father was a doctor. I was raised not to be afraid of certain categories of truth.

Godard/Sollers: The Interview (Extracts)

THE RELEASE OF *Hail Mary* triggered . . . the organization of an interview between [Philippe] Sollers and Godard, filmed by Jean-Paul Fargier, of which we reprint a few extracts here. . . . In this encounter between Sollers and Godard there is not, strictly speaking, a "dialogue." In the first part Sollers gives a masterly lecture on the Virgin. Subsequently, lunging into a critical analysis of Godard's movie, he begins to interview him. During the first part, Godard says virtually nothing. He listens, curious and attentive, and moves us with that sort of fragility of his. Then, he lets go and starts thinking out loud, his thoughts bordering on the monologue, and then Sollers remains shut out. We observe two radically different attitudes: on the one hand, Sollers: learned, brilliant, a master of derision; on the other, Godard: uncertain, an eternal victim, confiding his doubts. In each of his answers resonates a new question. Godard here shows himself for what he is: a poet, a jack-of-all-trades, an artist, and indubitably one of the greatest.

JACQUES KERMABON

Philippe Sollers: A very important aspect of your film is the hysteria: the clinical phenomenon of hysteria, in such a way that it appears in all its majesty. It has always been around, but here it appears with a new sound and in a new focus. There have been passions, convulsive passions, in connection with it, and in language, in an admirable way, for example, in Artaud. I find it absolutely striking that Jean-Luc Godard should film his Mary in bed, with undulating drapery effects, with a body that arches and even describes the classical hysterical arc. I don't know if you told her to make that arc, but that is what the hysterics of the Salpêtrière used to do.

Jean-Luc Godard: No, it was she. She said: "What if I did this once?"

P. S.: Terrific! That's called the hysteric arc, it's Joan of Arc, it's the rainbow. It is the position of unconscious pleasure, specifically not sexual. And you were filming it as though you were seeing with Charcot's eyes, with Freud at his side. Freud relates a remark Charcot made about the hysterics that he visited at the Salpêtrière. Charcot told him one day . . . : "You know, in any case, it is always the sexual thing." And Freud notes down somewhere: this is odd,

This interview was published in *Cinéma* 314 (February 1985): 33, consisting of extracts from a longer interview originally published in *Artpress* 88 (January 1985): 233–37. It appears here by permission of *Artpress*, translated by Pasquale G. Tatò.

he tells me that in private, why doesn't he say it publicly? Freud became himself the moment he thought that. . . .

J.-L. G.: I started making movies thinking that it meant "framing" something. I have tried it without success, and I have the feeling now that one doesn't frame like that any more [makes gesture], and that even those who did, like the Russians or the Germans, were not, in fact, framing . . . because they were looking for something else and the framing resulted from it. I have been affected by the framings of painters, in particular those of modern painters. In classical painting you see the framing right away: in Vermeer, in Velasquez, you feel that they did that, you believe that that was the essential part. But through modern painting I have discovered that Velasquez did not, in fact, frame. I see in Bonnard or in Matisse, even in flat tints or in découpages, that the framing comes later. Maybe it is presupposed, maybe there's an "Immaculate Conception" of the frame, but it comes later. The only "success," as when you win a card game, if you like, something the film's crew couldn't understand at all, even technically, is when there is no frame. I cannot explain it to a cameraman that there is no frame, that there is a point to be found.

P. S.: And how would you define that point?

J.-L. G.: The technical problem about this film, which, as always, echoes something else, was "to make that point." . . .

P. S.: The point then would be that one can actually see the hysteria?

J.-L. G.: Yes, there it was, it was the navel . . . in other words, Narcissus. . . .

P. S.: Yes, but also the hysteria in its manifestation of an absolute refusal of the touch. And what did you put there for language? You put Artaud. One hears Artaud, and one sees the effort at that moment —of his rejection, his exacerbated refusal of the body? . . .

J.-L. G.: I didn't perceive it like that. I was glad I had found a line from Artaud which helped me with the technicians. Because I would tell them: you guys, do you think the body has a soul? It's what they taught me at school and what my parents also taught me. Even though, at the same time (and I thank them for that) they raised me in such a way that I could later find other things than what they told me. There was a certain democracy in those great Protestant families that I come from and that left me the time to find, by myself, that in fact it is not the body that has a soul. And I found that line in Artaud, in which, by a simple play on words, he posits, like a theorem, a Euclidean postulate: "I want the soul to be body, so they won't be able to say that the body is soul, because it will be the soul which is body." I don't feel that as a rejection of the body.

P. S.: No, it's not a rejection of the body as such, but it is a proposition. . . .

J.-L. G.: You want to say that it is seeing things the way they are, well framed?

P. S.: That's it, the hedgehog in heaven [the hedgehog is described in Mary's soliloquy and shown later in the film].

J.-L. G.: The hedgehog, it was entirely by chance, but it fit well, because when you see it, it really has its head in its ass or its ass in its head. It's the only image of an ass that you can shoot. I think it's the first time someone has been able to film an ass.

Biographical Sketches and Filmographies

Anne-Marie Miéville

BORN IN Lausanne, Switzerland, on November 11, 1945, Anne-Marie Miéville has revealed few details about her life and given few interviews. She traveled to Paris in 1960 and tried a career as a singer, making two records. Unsuccessful, she returned home and collaborated on two short films with the Swiss filmmaker François Reusser, singing in one of them. It is not clear when she met Jean-Luc Godard. She worked as a set photographer for his film *Tout va bien* in 1972, and sharing a concern about the Palestinian cause, they codirected *Ici et ailleurs* in 1973. When Godard moved his Sonimage studio to Grenoble in the early 1970s, she was one of the backers. She lives in Rolle, Switzerland.

JOHN GIANVITO

Filmography

Films less than feature length are designated by (s).

1972	*Tout va bien* (set photographer only)
1973	*Ici et ailleurs* (codirector with Jean-Luc Godard)
1975	*Numéro deux* (coscreenwriter with Godard)
	Comment ça va? (coscreenwriter with Godard; actress)
1976	*Six fois deux* (codirector with Godard)
1978	*Papa comme maman* (s)
	France/tour/detour/deux/enfants (codirector with Godard)
1980	*Sauve qui peut (la vie)* (coscreenwriter with Jean-Claude Carrière, coeditor with Godard, set photographer)
	L'amour des femmes (coscreenwriter, set photography)
1981	*Passion* (set photographer only)
1982	*Scénario du film Passion* (credited as one of the collaborators)
1983	*Prénom: Carmen* (screenwriter)
	How Can I Love a Man (When I know he don't want me) (s)
1984	*Le livre de Marie* (s)
1985	*Détective* (cowrote scenario adaptation with Godard)
	Soft Talk on a Hard Subject between Two Friends, aka *Soft and Hard* (codirector with Godard)
1987	*Faire la fête* (s)
1988	*Mon cher sujet*
1989	*Le rapport Darty* (s, codirector with Godard)
1990	*Nouvelle vague* (art direction only)
	L'enfance de l'art (s, episode from the film *How Are the Kids?* codirector with Jean-Luc Godard)
1991	*Visages suisses* (s, episode in film of the same name, codirector with Godard)
	Mars et Venus (s)
	Contre l'oubli (s, episode in film of the same name, codirector with Godard)
1993	*Lou n'a pas dit non*

Jean-Luc Godard

JEAN-LUC GODARD was born on December 3, 1930, in Paris, the child of an upper-middle-class Protestant family. His father was a doctor; his mother was the daughter of a banker. Since their family home was in Switzerland, he became a Swiss citizen and was educated in Nyon. In 1947, he attended school in Paris, and from 1949 to 1951 he studied at the Sorbonne, receiving a certificate in ethnology.

During his student years in Paris, Godard became a devotee of Paris's numerous ciné clubs, particularly the Ciné-Club du Quartier Latin and the Cinémathèque française. He developed friendships with François Truffaut, Jacques Rivette, Claude Chabrol, Eric Rohmer, and André Bazin.

In the early 1950s, Godard traveled and supported himself with a variety of jobs, including construction work on a Swiss dam, the subject of his first short film, *Opération béton* (1954). He worked with Rivette and with Rohmer on an early short film by each filmmaker. He also began to write for *Cahiers du cinéma*, where he formulated his interest in cinema as a place to express ideas, concerns, and enthusiasms.

While working in the publicity department at the Paris offices of Twentieth Century–Fox in 1957, he met producer Georges de Beauregard, who agreed to finance Godard's first feature-length film. Released to great critical acclaim, winning Best Direction at the Berlin Film Festival in 1960, *Breathless (À bout de souffle)* established Godard as one of the foremost filmmakers of the *nouvelle vague* movement. From then on, Godard was a full-time filmmaker.

For Godard, along with others in France, 1968 was a year of political upheaval when his life and art were radicalized. From then to 1973, Godard produced nine films, alone or with Jean-Pierre Gorin, editor of the *Cahiers Marxistes-Leninistes*. He, Gorin, and others formed a filmmaking collective, the Dziga Vertov Group, inspired by the theory and practice of the famous Soviet filmmaker; the group lasted until 1972. But in 1971 he was seriously injured in a motorcycle accident with his editor, Christine Marsollier (he was a passenger), and was an invalid for almost two years.

Godard began experimenting with videotape and made a number of works for French television, usually in collaboration with Anne-Marie Miéville. However, with his film *Every Man for Himself (Sauve qui peut (la vie))* in 1980, Godard reentered the commercial mainstream. He followed this success with *Passion* in 1981 and *First Name: Carmen (Prénom: Carmen),* winner of the Golden Lion (the top prize) at the 1983 Venice Film Festival.

In the early 1960s, Godard set up his Sonimage studio in Paris, an experimental project partly financed by Gaumont. In the early 1970s, he moved Sonimage to Grenoble, financed by Gaumont, producer Jean-Pierre Rassam, and Godard and Anne-Marie Miéville. He began to call the company JLG Films in 1982; it is now located in Neuilly, a suburb of Paris. The company produced the two films discussed in this book.

Godard's published writings on film include *Godard on Godard* (1972; revised 1985, in French only) and *Introduction à une veritable histoire du cinéma* (1980).

A personal note: In 1961, Godard married actress Anna Karina; they were divorced in 1964. In 1967, he married actress Anne Wiazemsky, from whom he eventually was divorced. He lives in Rolle, Switzerland.

JOHN GIANVITO and MARYEL LOCKE

Filmography

The titles cited are film, video, or combinations of both, since Godard increasingly intermingles the two. Films less than feature length are designated by (s).

1954	*Opération béton* (s)
1955	*Une femme coquette* (s)
1957	*Tous les garçons s'appellent Patrick* (s)
1958	*Une histoire d'eau* (s, codirector with François Truffaut)
1959	*Charlotte et son Jules* (s)
	À bout de souffle (Breathless)
1960	*Le petit soldat*
1961	*Une femme est une femme*
	La paresse (s, *Sloth*, episode in *Les sept péchés capitaux* [*The Seven Deadly Sins*])
1962	*Vivre sa vie (My Life to Live)*
	Le nouveau monde (s, episode in *Rogopag*)
1963	*Les carabiniers*
	Le grand escroc (s, episode in *Les plus belles escroqueries du monde*)
	Le mépris (Contempt)
1964	*Bande à part (Band of Outsiders)*
	Montparnasse-Levallois (s, episode in *Paris vu par . . .*)
	Une femme mariée (A Married Woman, original title *La femme mariée*)
	Reportage sur Orly (s)
1965	*Alphaville, une étrange aventure de Lemmy Caution*
	Pierrot le fou
1966	*Masculin-feminin (Masculine-Feminine)*
	Made in USA
	Deux ou trois choses que je sais d'elle (Two or Three Things I Know about Her)
	Anticipation, ou l'Amour en l'an 2000 (s, episode in *Le plus vieux métier du monde* [*Love through the Ages*])
1967	*La Chinoise, ou plutôt à la chinoise*
	Caméra- oeil (s, episode in *Loin du Vietnam* [*Far from Vietnam*])
	L'aller et retour andate e ritorno des infants prodigues dei figli prodighi (s, episode in *Vangelo 70*, aka *La contestation*, aka *Amore e rabbia*)
	Week-end
1968	*Le gai savoir*
	Ciné-tracts (s, directed anonymously with several directors)
	Un film comme les autres (A Movie like the Others, direction credited to the Dziga Vertov Group)
	One Plus One (producer's version entitled *Sympathy for the Devil*)
	One American Movie/1 AM (film abandoned by Godard; footage later reedited and released in 1971 by D. A. Pennebaker as *One PM*, referred to

by some as One Parallel Movie or, perhaps more appropriately, One Pennebaker Movie)

1969   *British Sounds (See You at Mao)* (codirector with Jean-Henri Roger)
        Pravda (direction credited to the Dziga Vertov Group, Roger and Paul Burron)
        Vent d'est (Wind from the East, direction by Dziga Vertov group)
        Luttes en Italie (Struggle in Italy, direction by Dziga Vertov group)
        Communications (unfinished film begun in Québec)
1970   *Jusqu'à la victoire* (unfinished film by Dziga Vertov Group; much of this footage later reincorporated into the film *Ici et ailleurs*)
1971   *Vladimir et Rosa* (direction by Dziga Vertov Group)
1972   *Tout va bien* (codirector with Jean-Pierre Gorin)
        Letter to Jane (Investigation of a Still, codirector with Gorin)
1974   *Moi/Je* (uncompleted film)
        Ici et ailleurs (codirector with Anne-Marie Miéville)
1975   *Numéro deux*
        Comment ça va?
1976   *Six fois deux (Sur et sous la communication)* (codirector with Miéville)
1978   *France/tour/detour/deux/enfants* (codirector with Miéville)
1979   *Scénario vidéo de "Sauve qui peut (la vie)"*
1980   *Sauve qui peut (la vie) (Everyman for Himself)*
1981   *Passion*
        Changer d'image (Lettre à la bien aimée) (s, episode in *Changement à plus d'un titre*)
1982   *Scénario du film Passion*
        Lettre à Freddy Buache (s)
1983   *Prénom: Carmen (First Name: Carmen)*
        Petites notes à propos du film "Je vous salue, Marie" (s)
1984   *"Je vous salue, Marie" (Hail Mary)*
1985   *Détective*
        Soft Talk on a Hard Subject between Two Friends, aka *Soft and Hard* (codirector with Miéville)
1986   *Grandeur et décadence d'un petit commerce de cinéma*
        Meetin' W. A. (s)
1987   *Soigne ta droite, ou une place sur la terre comme au ciel*
        Enfin, il est en ma puissance!, aka *Armide* (s, episode in *Aria*)
        King Lear
1988   "Closed" Jeans commercials (multiple commercial spots for Marithe and Francois Girbaud)
        On s'est tous défilé (s)
        Puissance de la parole (s)
        Le dernier mot (s, episode in *Français vus par . . .*)
        Histoire(s) du cinéma (1A: "Toutes ces histoires"; 1B: "Une histoire seule")
1989   *Le rapport Darty* (s, codirector with Miéville)
1990   *Nouvelle vague (New Wave)*
        L'enfance de l'art (s, episode from the film *How Are the Kids?* codirector with Miéville)

1991   *Allemagne année 90 neuf zéro (Germany Year 90 Nine Zero)*
       Visages suisses (s, episode in film of the same name, codirector with Miéville)
       Contre l'oubli (s, episode in film of the same name, codirector with Miéville)
1993   *Hélas pour moi*

Shot Breakdown

Visual column by John Gianvito

Sound and subtitle column by Maryel Locke

IT IS A WELL-KNOWN aspect of the Godard method, virtually from the beginning of his career, that Godard directs his films without anything resembling a traditional full-length screenplay in hand. Instead, Godard directs each of his films through an involved process of improvisation and collaboration with his cast and crew. Working from notes, sketches, photographs, and other material, Godard habitually writes and rewrites the film throughout shooting. Less is known about Anne-Marie Miéville's approach. No formal screenplay of *Hail Mary* or *The Book of Mary* exists, to our knowledge, nor have we attempted in any way to recreate such a screenplay. Rather, what follows is a strict "shot breakdown" of both films in their final form.

A script is not a film, and this is even more the case for a shot breakdown. Whereas the intent of a screenplay is to offer an engaging, flowing narrative (as might be done even with Godard's unique elliptical narratives), this is not the case with a shot breakdown. Descriptions in a shot breakdown are intended to provide a streamlined synopsis of the primary visual ingredients—setting, movements, and behavior of the characters—with essential dialogue, narration, and sound information in each shot. (Not to be confused with a scene, a *shot* is defined here as each separate image from camera start to camera stop.) Inevitably, language remains a meager substitute for sights and sounds. At best, we hope to offer a skeleton key to the *experience* of witnessing *The Book of Mary* and *Hail Mary* in a theater as an aid to those interested in further understanding the content and structure of the films.

This shot breakdown is presented in two columns. On the left is the visual column, with a technical identification of the camera setup for each shot and a description of what is seen in the shot. On the right is the sound and subtitle column, with an indication in brackets of music or other sounds accompanying the shot. *The Book of Mary* comes first, followed by *Hail Mary*. The shots are numbered beginning with 1 in each film. There are 85 shots in *The Book of Mary* (28 minutes long) and 300 shots in *Hail Mary* (79 minutes long); the two films, linked under the title *Hail Mary* in catalogs and on commercial videocassette, are 107 minutes long.

Camera distance, placement, and movement will be indicated by the following abbreviations:

ECU Extreme close-up (a section of the face, as with a shot framed from forehead to chin or tighter, or section of a body or object)

CU   Close-up (full face or whole head, whole part of body or object)
MCU Medium close-up (a shot framing the shoulders and head of a character)
MS   Medium shot (waist-length shot of a character)
MLS Medium long shot (three-quarter-length shot, from knees to head)
LS   Long shot (ranging from the totality of a unified, room-size decor to a
       whole human figure)
ELS   Extreme long shot (remote distance; landscape or other large spatial shots;
       human figures subordinate to the total field)

We decided to use the English subtitles rather than a new translation of the French dialogue (see the French dialogue that follows) because the subtitles are what the English-speaking viewer sees on the screen. The translator for other material in our book examined the English subtitles and advised against a new translation, stating that he would have come up with much the same result. He considered these subtitles an excellent translation of the French dialogue in both content and style or register (in contrast, he felt, to the subtitles of many foreign films). We also knew that Godard cares greatly about his English subtitles. In a few cases we added words not in subtitles that the viewer would hear and understand, such as *Marie, Yes,* and *I love you,* putting them in brackets; in these instances, we felt that it helped the reader to understand the action.

A character speaking is identified by name. If the character moves offscreen during the same scene and still speaks, we use the term *(off)*. If this character reappears in the scene and speaks, we then use the term *(on)*. If a character on screen is not visibly speaking but is expressing an interior monologue, we use the term *(vo)* for voice-over. If a character is speaking but has not yet appeared on screen in the given shot or scene, we use the term *(vo)*.

All punctuation is as it appears in the subtitles. The subtitles in both films have italics when a character is reading from a book—with one exception in Godard when quotation marks are used (shot 36). Also, the Godard subtitles are in italics for a few of Mary's voice-over speeches.

Since sounds are important to both filmmakers, we have concentrated on indicating as many sounds as we could identify. As for the music, the filmmakers state the names of the composers but not the names of the compositions in the credits to each film. Miéville uses a movement from a Chopin piano concerto in one scene, and a movement from Mahler's Ninth Symphony in two other scenes—all of these when a record is being played on a record player. We designate these as such when they are first heard, afterward as [CHOPIN] and [MAHLER]. We identify additional music in one Miéville scene, which is from Godard's film *Contempt.*

Godard uses excerpts from numerous pieces by Bach, which we designate by sound or instrumentation such as [BACH—ORGAN]. Godard has stated that he chose his music chiefly for its sound quality when used in fragmentary form (see the Dieckmann interview in this book). Two cases where the title of the piece seem very pertinent to the meaning of the film are Godard's use of the familiar chorale "Jesu, Joy of Man's Desiring" (in a piano version) in a scene with Mary's child near the end of the film and the final chorus from the *St. Matthew Passion* at the end of the film. Godard also repeatedly uses the Dvořák Cello Concerto, which we identify on its first appearance and then designate as [DVOŘÁK]. In one scene, we hear a fragment of John Coltrane when Eva plays it on a record player.

Cast with Characters for Each Film
(not in the credits of the films)

The Book of Mary
The father ....Bruno Cremer
The mother ....Aurore Clément
Mary ....Rebecca Hampton
The traveler (Man) ....Copi
First little girl ....Valentine Mercier
Second little girl ....Cléa Rédalier

Hail Mary
Mary ....Myriem Roussel
Joseph..............................Thierry Rode
The angel (Gabriel) ....Philippe Lacoste
The little girl ....Manon Anderson
Juliette.............................Juliette Binoche
Jesus ....Malachi Jara Kohan
Arthur ....Dick
Professor ....Johann Leysen
Eva..................................Anne Gauthier

The Book of Mary

Visual	Sound and Subtitle
JLG | FILMS PEGASE | PRESENTENT [Note: Titles are presented as white letters against black.]	[BIRD CALLS; LAPPING WATER heard through titles]
LE LIVRE DE MARIE JLG FILMS 1984	THE BOOK OF MARY
AVEC BRUNO CREMER AURORE CLEMENT REBECCA HAMPTON COPI VALENTINE MERCIER CLEA REDALIER	
IMAGE JEAN-BERNARD MENOUD CAROLINE CHAMPETIER JACQUES FIRMANN IVAN NICLASS	
SON FRANÇOIS MUSY	
REGIE RAYNALD CALAGNI MARIE-CHRISTINE BARRIERE	Subtitles: A Whitlaw & W. Byron
MUSIQUES CHOPIN MAHLER	
LABORATOIRES SCHWARZ—BERNE LTC—PARIS	Subtitled by: CINETITRES—LTC
REALISATION ANNE-MARIE MIEVILLE	
1. **LS.** A body of water, a balcony railing in the foreground, a low mountain range on the horizon.	[BIRD CALLS, LAPPING WATER heard shots 1 through 22] **Father (vo):** What do you think? You'll escape routine if you're alone?

2. LS. Same as 1 with a brighter exposure.

Mother (vo): No, that's not it.

3. LS. Low angle. A mottled sky with tree branches in foreground.

Mother (vo): I just can't stand this deal,

4. MLS. The sun rises slightly from behind clouds.

Mother (vo): putting up with anything as long as we stay together.
Father (vo): You always come back to that.

5. LS. Same as 1 with different exposure.

Father (vo): Admit it: you're so . . . afraid of being abandoned,

6. LS. Same as 1 with different exposure.

Father (vo): you're fleeing . . . into loneliness.

7. MLS. A wooded shoreline.

Father (vo): You should know by now.

8. LS. An elegant doorframe seen through a thicket of branches.

Mother (vo): Since you're here,

9. MS. Low angle. A sun-dappled porch.

Mother (vo): for once, let's be serious.

10. MCU. A red rose in bloom.

Mother (vo): Seeing you is hardly a blessing now. Even for Mary.

11. MS. A vase filled with purple flowers next to a doll.

Mother (vo): It's no good.

12. CU. A bowl of yellow and green apples with purple flowers in the background.

Mother (vo): And I've had it. I can't work, I can't sleep.

13. MS. A bowl of apples upon a table, an empty chair behind.

Father (vo): I see: if we separate you'll sleep again?

14. MS. A lighted table lamp sits in front of a small picture, behind which is a vase of purple flowers.

Mother (vo): You see how brutal you are?

15. MCU. The lamp in front of the vase of flowers.

Father (vo): You're brutal too, in your way.

16. LS. A comfortably appointed living room.

Father (vo): You won't face up to things.

17. LS. A woman (the mother) sits in a chair, her head resting in her hand.

Mother: Listen, Paul, you've cheated on the contract from the start.

18. LS. Her back to the camera, the mother sits facing a man (the father) who stands looking out to a seafront balcony.

Mother: You can't brush that off. I think it takes constant inventiveness to succeed. In your line of work, you've lots of time for that.

19. LS. The mother, viewed from behind, sits talking as the father paces.

Mother: It doesn't interest you, that's all. So we play it safe and stay together. What's that do for the child?
Father: Loving's not investing.

20. LS. The mother sits as the father paces out of the room.

Father: You can save, too, not just give, or expect everything from one person.
Mother: The way . . .

21. LS. The living room with the dining room in the background.

Mother (off): . . . you've set things up, you could talk that way. You're never here. I spent much more time at home.

22. LS. Same as 18, the father paces as he speaks.

Mother: I put a lot in and get little back.
Father: We've been over this so often. What other way is there? [BIRDS, LAPPING WATER ENDS]

23. LS. The father stands opposite his wife with his back to the camera.

Father: Before, you . . .

24. LS. Same as 19.

Father: . . . didn't work, you took care of Mary. But now we're closer to an even footing.

25. LS. Same as 18. The mother stands up and moves around the room. The father sits while his wife settles into his former position overlooking the balcony.
[First apparent synchronized sound shot]

Mother: I don't agree. I'm still here serving, caring for things. That's a mother's job, not a woman's. I'm tired. Things have got to change for a while.
Father: You're so impatient.
Mother: Maybe. What I know now is . . . that I don't need to be dominated to feel understood. I no longer need to lose. [FOOTSTEPS]
Father: I don't see where that gets you, either.
Mother: I don't know. I want to see clearly.

BLACK

26. CU. A young girl (Mary) sits with eyes lowered. She glances back and forth as her parents speak.

Mother (vo): I wish you understood.
Father (vo): Understanding's scarce. Truth is often deadly. Your truths are fatal, so don't complain afterward.
Mother (vo): I'm not complaining.

Just trying to see clearly.
[SILVERWARE TOUCHING
DISHES BEGINS] Why is everyone
so scared . . .

27. CU. The father, wearing
sunglasses, faces the camera. As he
talks, he removes the glasses.

Mother (vo): of clarity?
Mary (off): Your eyes hurt?
Father: No, I'm all right. I don't
need your total sincerity. It's
comforting, but not interesting. Let's
not start again.

28. MS. Mary sits at the kitchen table
near her mother, across from her
father.

Mother: No, let's not! [BANGS
TABLE; SILVERWARE SOUNDS
END] But try to understand
sometimes. For 10 years we've copied.
Now I need to invent.
Father: No one's stopped you.
Anyway, women don't invent much.

29. CU. The father glances left.

Father: Even the soul was invented
by a man.

30. CU. The mother looks to her
husband, then to her daughter.

Mother: You're really encouraging.
Father (off): You don't need
encouragement now. We can see how
well you do on your own.
Mary (off): Good morning! We
continue with our operation. Now
we cut the eye in half. [KNIFE
TOUCHES DISH] It's black, if you
can see that.

31. MCU. Mary holds a nut between
her thumb and index finger.

Mary: Put this inside. It's the pupil.

32. CU. Mary's hands push the nut
down into the core of an apple that is
cut in half.

Mary (off): The pupil, seen from
outside, magnified, of course, is
brown. The eye is huge, but the
pupil takes up a lot of space. The rest
. . . is water.

33. MS. At the kitchen table, Mary
sits between her father and mother.

Mary: That's right, water. The pupil
floats like a baby in its mother's belly.
When you look at things, it's because
of the pupil, because it floats, and
when we move, as you see, it shifts.
Understand what I'm saying?
Mother: It's complicated. A bit
technical.

34. MS. Mary, seen from behind, sits opposite her parents.

Mary: Yes, it's mechanical and technical and surgical too. You operate once for this illness. If you do it twice, the patient dies. In any case,

35. CU. Mother.

Mary (off): the eye withers.

36. MS. Mary, viewed over the shoulder of her mother.

Mary: It's a very serious operation. Yes, I entirely agree there. You undergo it after you've almost been sick. Because this gentleman . . . you see his eye . . . has been completely . . . shaken, see? It's had a shock. [APPLE HITS DISH] This eye has been completely terrorized—so,—

37. ECU. The father. Mary kisses her father's cheek and leaves.

Mary (off): we can't do much for it. Well, that's all for this program. Good-bye. [DOOR OPENS AND CLOSES]
Father: Spoken to Mary?
Mother (off): Not yet, but I will, of course. And you'll have to tell her what keeps you so far from her, from me.
Father: You've thought of what it'll mean to her, shuttling between parents?
Mother (off): Stop talking as if it was all my doing.
Mary (vo): Silence, please.

BLACK

38. MS. Mary paces reading a book of Baudelaire. She looks up.

Mary: *My spirit with a heavy fear forebodes/*
In black battalions, stray ghosts ride/
Driving me on to moving roads/
closed in by bloodied skies on every side./
How strange and wicked was our act?/
Can you explain my trouble and my fright?
Silence! I said, silence!

39. MCU. Mary. She reads. She looks left.

Mary: Who can tell me . . . what Baudelaire meant to express in this poem? If you weren't asleep, that is. Get out your notebooks. I'll give you some dictation. Hurry! We have other things to do.

My spirit with a heavy fear forebodes . . ./ Heavy fear, black battalions, with two "t's," and "*stray ghosts . . .*" [DOOR KNOCKS] Silence!—Yes?—[DOOR OPENS; FOOTSTEPS]

Mother (off): Mary, I have something to tell you.

Mary: All right,

40. MS. Mary, viewed from behind. Her mother enters the frame and sits down. Mary turns toward her mother, then turns away.

Mary: go on. And make sure you've made no spelling errors. I have to talk to the principal.

Mother: I'm sure you know what it is. Dad's going to live elsewhere. Until winter, for example.

Mary: Right. To continue: *that seek to lead me on shifting ways . . .* [**Mother:** Mary!]

41. MS. The mother pulls her daughter to her. Mary pulls away and stands on her hands, her extended legs leaning against the wall.

Mother: You'll see Dad on weekends and holidays. It's not for long.

Mary: *Have we committed a strange act? Explain if . . .*

Mother: It's not that we don't love each other any more. On the contrary. But if he stays here, we'll quarrel. [MARY'S FEET BANG WALL]

42. MCU. Mary's hands and her mother's feet.

Mother: There's no cause to worry. I'd tell you if there were. Believe me. You can trust me. [DOORBELL]

BLACK

43. MS. The mother sits at a table repairing a lamp with a screwdriver.

[LOUD FOOTSTEPS through shot 45; TV PROGRAM: Dialogue and music from Godard's film, *CONTEMPT*]

Male TV Voice: *Why don't you want us to go to Capri?*

Female TV Voice: *Because you're an ass.* [TV: SLAP; GASP]

44. LS. Mary sits on the floor in front of a TV set, her mother sits at the kitchen table behind her. The father moves about the room.

Female TV Voice: *You scare me, Paul.*

Male TV Voice: *Don't just stand there, answer me!*

Father: I'll just take a few things. Won't be long. [PAPERS RUSTLE]

Female TV Voice: *I'm sorry.*

45. MS. Mary, seen from behind, watches TV. She glances left, then back to the TV, and sings.

[*CONTEMPT* THEME]
Father: I'm in a hurry, Mary. [Mary hums a BEETHOVEN THEME over *CONTEMPT* THEME]
Female TV Voice: *You go to Capri, Paul.*
Father (off): See you Saturday.

46. MS. Mary sits facing the TV and sings. The camera zooms in and pans right, following Mary as she stands and walks out of the room.

Father (off): —OK?—
[FOOTSTEPS; DOOR CLOSES; MARY HUMS; FOOTSTEPS; *CONTEMPT* THEME ENDS]

BLACK

47. LS. High angle. Mary glides into her mother's arms in a bathtub. Like a cat, she licks her mother's shoulders.

[BATHTUB WATER SLOSHES]

48. MCU. Mary and her mother embracing in the tub. Mary moves away out of the frame as her mother sits back.

[WATER SLOSHES; FAINT BUZZING through shot 51]
Mary: Tell me . . . about when I was little.
Mother: Again!
Mary: Go ahead.
Mother: You seem especially fond of hearing that. You're right. It's the strongest memory of love. [BIRDS] It's hard to recover that strength

49. MS. Mary sits back in the tub.

Mother (off): without going backward. [BIRDS]

50. MS. The mother seated in the tub.

[FAINT BIRDS]

51. MS. Mary, same as 49. In the foreground, her mother climbs out of the tub.

[WATER SLOSHES; BIRDS]
Mother (off): You just have to be able to give and accept. I'll prepare something to eat. See you downstairs. Dry your hair well. [FOOTSTEPS]

BLACK

52. LS. Two young girls walk up a path, toward the camera.

[OUTDOOR SOUNDS; LAUGHTER; BIRDS; FOOTSTEPS]

53. LS. Mary walks outside up a flight of stone steps.

[FOOTSTEPS; BIRDS]

54. LS. High angle. Mary enters from the right and joins the two girls.

First Girl: —Hi!—What's up? [FAINT TRAFFIC, BIRDS to shot 57]

55. MS. The three girls talk.

Mary: I'm taking a train.
Second Girl: Where're you going?
Mary: To see my father.
Second Girl: Doesn't he live here?
Mary: Not right now.

56. MCU. The two girls talk to Mary. One girl walks off left. The other girl snatches a stuffed animal from Mary and holds it.

First Girl: Your folks divorced?
Mary: No, they're not.
Second Girl: That your bear?
First Girl: Glad my folks aren't divorced. You have no luck.

57. MS. Mary takes back her animal and hurries away from the girls.

Mary: That's enough. [BIRDS; FOOTSTEPS; TRAIN RUMBLE STARTS]

58. LS. The interior of a moving train. Mary enters the car and walks forward. She looks left as someone grabs her arm.

[LOUD TRAIN RUMBLE]
Man (off): Hi, Mimi.

59. MS. Mary sits next to an older man who steadies her as she sits.

[LOUD TRAIN RUMBLE]
Mary: My name's not Mimi, it's Mary.
Man: Where're you going?
Mary: To see my father.
Man: That's right, he's gone away. It's good for him a little . . .
Mary: It's no big deal.
Man: Of course not. And you can travel with your bear, so it's no trouble.
Mary: It's not a bear. It's a panther.
Man: Certainly. You're right. I'm a dumbbell about animals . . . I don't know.
Mary: Where's you going? [RUMBLE ENDS]
Man: Passing the time. I'm on relief. I'm not working these days. I stay at home. I've a lot of housework, I like my place to be clean, you see.
Mary: Get bored?
Man: Not at all. Because . . . I study my own case. And I have my afternoons programmed. I go out . . .

on my bike, my moped, whatever you want to call it. It takes me everywhere. [TRAIN RUMBLE] I get back at 7 or 9 in the evening. If it's nice out, I take my time,

60. CU. Mary reads her book of Baudelaire.

Man (off): I stop where I please.
Mary: *Forever damned be the feckless dreamer/*
who, in his stupidity, first strove

61. LS. Mary sits on a bench at the train platform anxiously looking around. Her father arrives from up a stairwell behind her. Mary sees him and hurries toward him. They embrace and depart together.

Mary (vo): *enamored of an insoluable and sterile problem,/*
to mix honesty with love.
[WARNING CHIMES; LOUDSPEAKER ANNOUNCEMENT; TRAIN STATION NOISE]

BLACK

62. MS. Viewed from the back, Mary and her father sit before a desk table.

[PAPERS RUSTLE]
Father: Have you studied triangles?
Mary: We've just started. I have to know the 4 types for Monday.
Father: Know what a jagged line is?
Mary: One that changes direction.
Father: Yes, but how?
Mary: By forming angles.
Father: And an angle?
Mary: It's when the lines close.
Father: And when they meet?
Mary: That's the apex.

63. MS. Mary and her father. They alternately form the shapes of angles with their hands. The father then opens a notebook.

Father: Also called an intersection.
Mary: An angle's like this.
Father: Like this, too.
Mary: No, it's like this.
Father: To get that, you first need this. [PAPERS RUSTLE] All right. There are 4 kinds of triangles. The right-angle triangle. It looks like this.

64. CU. The father, his nose prominent.

Father: The side opposite the right angle is the hypotenuse. The equilateral triangle has 3 equal sides. The isosceles triangle . . . You listening, Mary?

65. CU. The father's hands as he draws triangles on notebook paper.

Father (off): The isosceles has 2 equal sides, and the scalene has 3 unequal sides.

66. MCU. High angle. Upon an open notebook, the father draws triangles; Mary begins to draw a triangle, then stops and lays her hand flat upon the page. Her father plays with her fingers.

Father (off): Draw them. Helps you to remember them. [TAPS ON NOTEBOOK]

67. MS. Mary and her father. Her father smiles at her.

Father: Are you hungry?
Mary: Terribly. [CHOPIN PIANO CONCERTO]

68. MCU. The father sits listening to music and staring off. Mary enters behind him and offers a bite of her apple; he bites into the apple.

[CHOPIN]
Mary: Want a bite? [BITES APPLE] That the concerto I liked so much? [BIRDS]
Father: That's the one. Don't recognize it?
Mary: Oh, yes.

69. MS. Mary sits down on her father's lap.

[CHOPIN; BIRDS]
Mary: No, not really, in fact. Sounds like talk, don't you think, people in a discussion.
Father: Agreeing or disagreeing?
Mary: A bit of both. Changes of mood, icy, exasperated, I demand, fire, fire, careful, error, error, horror, suffering . . .
Father: Hey. Calm down. There's a Mahler Symphony I can't find. Ask Mom for it next time.
Mary: —OK.—

70. LS. The father packs Mary's bag. Mary walks on and off screen carrying items to be packed. She picks up her stuffed panther and sits pensively.

Father: Bring your pajamas, too. [CHOPIN ENDS; BIRDS; FOOTSTEPS] Don't forget your toothbrush again. You've got to go now. It's time. You ready? [TRAFFIC NOISE]

71. LS. Mary and her father exit building, step out onto the sidewalk, and walk off.

[TRAFFIC; DOOR CLOSES]

72. LS. Viewed from behind, Mary comes to a halt while her father continues walking. He turns around, removes his sunglasses, and walks back to her. They embrace and walk off together, turning a corner out of sight.

[TRAFFIC; BIRDS]

73. LS. From inside the living room, Mary steps into the dining room (in the background), sets down her bag, and takes an apple. She returns to the living room and begins to eat it. She plays a record and moves in rhythm to the music.

[FOOTSTEPS; DROPS BAG; BITES APPLE; FOOTSTEPS; MAHLER SYMPHONY]

74. LS. Mary dances out onto the terrace, then back inside.

[MAHLER; DANCING FOOTSTEPS]

75. LS. Mary falls onto a cushioned footstool. She strikes it with her fists, rolls over with it, then rolls herself over backward. She claws rhythmically at the carpet.

[MAHLER; THUMPS FOOTSTOOL]

76. MS. Mary spreads her arms out in front of her, as if swimming with great effort.

[MAHLER]

77. MS. Mary swings punches into the air.

[MAHLER]

78. MCU. Mary punches the air.

[MAHLER]

79. MS. Mary's punches turn into a dance. She runs in a circle, then falls to the floor immobile.

[MAHLER; FOOTSTEPS; THUMP TO FLOOR]

80. MCU. High angle. Mary's head, facedown on the floor. Her mother's hands enter the frame and turn her over. The camera tilts up as the mother pulls Mary up to embrace her.

[DOOR SLIDES; MAHLER; FOOTSTEPS]
[**Mother:** Mary. Oh, la.]
Mother (vo): Are you dead or just tired?
Mary: Dead. [MAHLER ENDS]
Mother (vo): But everything that happens should interest you. You're so curious. You surprise me.
Mary: It's not like before.
Mother: Nothing can stay the same. It becomes . . . [MAHLER]

81. CU (two-shot). Mary rests her head on her mother's shoulder.

[MAHLER]
Mother: . . . it becomes different. When a thing stops moving, it's dead. You must have confidence.
Mary: Sure, still, it's not like before.
Mother: In French, Mary is "Marie." Know what it makes?
Mary: What?

BLACK

82. LS. Mary, with her back to the camera, sits in the kitchen. Opposite her can be seen the open doorway in the background where a man stands waiting. Her mother enters and walks over to Mary, leans down, and writes a note.

Mother: A - I - M - E - R -: to love.
Mary: Ah, yes. [MAHLER ENDS]

[PITCHER SET ON TABLE; FOOTSTEPS]
Mary: You're beautiful! Your dress is beautiful.
Man: We'll be late. We must be going.
Mary: The hairdo becomes you.
Mother: Think so? It's not my favorite.
Mary: You're darling, really.
Mother: I'll leave you the number.

83. MS. Mary sits at the table, a soft-boiled egg before her. To the right stands her mother. Her mother pulls out a mirror from her purse and examines her makeup. Looking up off screen, Mary's mother proceeds to kiss her good-bye, then walks off. Using her knife as a baton, Mary conducts in rhythm with the music she is humming.

[TRAFFIC]
Mother: If something comes up, call. I won't be home late.
Mary: Don't forget tomorrow. I get to go out.
Mother: I haven't forgotten. [MAN'S VOICE; CHAIR SCRAPES] I've got to go, dear. Don't watch TV too late.
Mother (off): I'll kiss you when I come in. [FOOTSTEPS; DOOR SLAMS; MARY HUMS]

84. MS. Mary continues to use her knife as a baton. Setting the knife down, she studies the egg.

[FAINT STREET NOISES; MARY LOUDLY SINGS BEETHOVEN THEME]
Mary: It would be killing the unification of Europe in the egg. This business must be smothered, in the egg. Can't make an omelet without breaking eggs. —So . . .— I don't know.

85. CU. The egg. Holding the egg steady with one hand, Mary cracks off the top of the egg with the knife.

Mary (off): Get lost! It's the only way. [TWO CRACKS ON EGGSHELL; TOP OF EGGSHELL FALLS ON TABLE]

Hail Mary

(Intertitle 1:) EN CE TEMPS LA [Note: Titles and Intertitles are presented as white letters against black]

AT THAT TIME

1. LS. Light rain falls across windswept grassy reeds on a country slope.	[THUNDERSTORM; RAIN]
SARA PEGASE ⎪ FILMS JLG PRESENTENT	[BACH—CELLO AND HARPSICHORD; BIRD CALLS]
2. MS. The surface of a body of water is disturbed by the splash of an object just out of frame, causing the reflected sunlight to break into myriad patterns of light.	[ROCK SPLASHES IN WATER; BIRD CALLS; BACH—SAME]
"JE VOUS SALUE, MARIE" ©COPYRIGHT JLG FILMS 1984	HAIL MARY [BIRD CALLS; BACH—SAME]
3. MS. Same as 2 (variation).	[ROCK SPLASHES IN WATER; BIRD CALLS; BACH —SAME]
AVEC MYRIEM ROUSSEL THIERRY RODE PHILIPPE LACOSTE MANON ANDERSEN MALACHI JARA KOHAN JULIETTE BINOCHE DICK	[BIRD CALLS; BACH—SAME]
4. MS. Same as 2 (variation).	[ROCK SPLASHES; BIRD CALLS; BACH—SAME]
PHOTOGRAPHIE JEAN-BERNARD MENOUD JACQUES FIRMANN SON FRANÇOIS MUSY REGIE PHILIPPE MALIGNON FRANÇOIS PELLISSIER	[BACH—SAME]
5. MS. Same as 2 (variation).	[ROCK SPLASHES; BIRD CALLS; BACH—SAME]
REALISATION JEAN-LUC GODARD	[BIRDS; BACH—SAME]
6. MS. Same as 2 except the water surface is very violently disturbed at first, then calms.	[ROCK SPLASHES; BACH FADES; SPLASHES]

7. MS. Seen in profile, a man (Joseph) sits eating and drinking inside a café. Opposite him across the table can be seen the hands of a woman (Juliette).

[BACH ENDS; RESTAURANT NOISE]
Juliette (vo): Out of my mouth is shit.
Joseph: Stop talking.
Juliette: (vo): Stop eating.

(Intertitle 2:) EN CE TEMPS LA

AT THAT TIME [SILENCE]
Juliette (vo): With you, silence can be unbearable.

8. MS. Juliette sits across from Joseph, who continues to eat.

[BACH—ORGAN; RESTAURANT NOISE]
Juliette: We can get married, if you like. I'm not afraid. Maybe that could help us. [BACH ENDS; RESTAURANT NOISE]
Juliette: I wonder . . .
Joseph: What?
Juliette: All women want something unique. [BACH —ORGAN]
Joseph: Can't you see I'm not listening? You know, men think they enter a woman.

9. LS. Along the left sideline, women basketball players sit on a bench observing the game to the right. They are wearing blue and white costumes.

[NOISE OF PLAYERS AND SPECTATORS AT BASKETBALL GAME IN GYM]

(Intertitle 3:) EN CE TEMPS LA

AT THAT TIME [SILENCE; RESTAURANT NOISE]
Juliette (off): How are you doing with Mary?
[GYM NOISE]

10. MLS. Basketball players seated on the bench. The coach leans forward and cues player number 10 (Mary) to warm up. Mary gracefully exercises from side to side behind the bench.

[BACH—PIANO; GYM NOISE; WHISTLE]
Joseph (off): That's my business.

11. LS. The two opposing teams compete on the court. A basket is scored.

[BACH—PIANO; GYM NOISE]

12. MCU. Mary, attentively observing game.

[BACH—PIANO; GYM NOISE]
Coach (vo): Listen Mary, when there's a break-out, move fast.

Mary (vo): *I wondered if some event would happen in my life.* [WHISTLE]

13. LS. A basket is scored at the far end of the court. As the teams advance toward the camera, time-out is called.

[BACH—PIANO; GYM NOISE; BACH ENDS; WHISTLE]

14. MS. After the coach signals time out, Mary rises from bench to substitute for a player.

[GYM NOISE]

15. LS. Full moon (small) in the upper right corner of the frame.

[BACH—PIANO; GYM NOISE]

16. MS. Mary, in profile, shoots the basketball.

[BACH—PIANO]
Mary (vo): *I've had only the shadow of love.*

17. MS. Full moon (large).

[BACH—PIANO]
Mary (vo): *—yes,—in fact, the shadow of a shadow, like the reflection of a water-lily in a pond,* [BACH ENDS] *not quiet, but shaken by ripples in the water,* [BASKETBALL BOUNCES] *so that even the reflection is deformed and not yours . . .* [WHISTLE]

18. MS. A young blond woman (Eva) examines a Rubik's cube in front of a window.

[Mary finishes while the professor speaks; STREET NOISE; CLASSROOM VOICES]
Professor (vo): So the sun, visible at last, began to shine on the primeval oceans and then, it's said, life appeared [BACH —ORGAN] entirely by chance. There was hydrogen, nitrogen . . .

(Intertitle 4:) EN CE TEMPS LA

AT THAT TIME
Professor (vo): What if it wasn't chance? [BACH ENDS; VOICES; DOOR SLAMS; FOOTSTEPS]

19. CU. Eva.

[CLASSROOM NOISE]
Eva: 100 times that of the universe?
Professor (vo): What does that mean? That there was never time, chance had no time. Since life hadn't time to appear . . .
Man (whispers, vo): On earth!
[NOISE ENDS]

20. CU. Male student.

Professor (vo): . . . then it came from elsewhere, from space. [BACH—CHORAL] We wonder what an extra-terrestrial looks like. Go to a mirror and look at yourself. [BACH ENDS] It's just a hypothesis, but . . .

21. MS. The professor stands before a chart in a classroom. He points to it and paces in front of it. The red "dip" in the center of the scientific graph somewhat resembles a pair of red lips.

[FAINT STREET NOISE]
Professor: Look at this dip. It can only be explained . . . by something in this cloud intercepting light . . . at a specific wavelength. There is a bacteria, of a very common sort, that absorbs light on 3.4 microns. That's its signature. Any body, inert or alive, leaves its special mark on the electric field. In my opinion, this establishes [TAPS ON BLACKBOARD] a very strong presumption that life exists in space. We're from there. [BACH—CHORAL]

22. CU. The back of a student's (Pascal's) head, his blond hair wildly sprouting outward.

[BACH—CHORAL; FAINT STREET NOISE]
Professor (off): We are extra-terrestrials. We weren't born in an amino-acid soup, suddenly, by chance. No deal. [BACH ENDS] The figures say "no."
Pascal: What if it wasn't chance?
Professor (off): Exactly. The astonishing truth is that life was willed, desired, [BACH—CHORAL] anticipated, organized, programmed by a determined intelligence. Eve, stand behind Pascal.
Eva (off): My name's Eva. [BACH ENDS]
Professor (off): Yes, stand behind Pascal and cover his eyes.

23. CU. Pascal. He holds up the cube as Eva's hands cover his eyes. The professor passes in the background.

[FAINT STREET NOISE]
Professor (off): They say it would take 1.35 trillion years . . . to find the solution blindfolded, but [RUBIK'S CUBE CLICKS] if there's someone beside you who can see, and says no

to every wrong move, and yes to every move toward a solution, at the rate of one move per second, how long's needed?
Pascal: 2 minutes.
Professor (off): From 1.35 trillion years to 2 minutes.

24. ECU (two-shot). Eva, covering Pascal's eyes, looks down (offscreen) at the twisting Rubik's cube.

[STREET NOISE; RUBIK'S CUBE CLICKS]
Professor (vo): That's what happened. Memory!
Eva: Yes . . . yes . . . yes . . . yes . . . —No!—[BACH—ORGAN]

25. ECU. Two hands twist the Rubik's cube until it is solved.

[Eva (off): yes . . . yes . . . no, no . . . yes . . .] [BACH—ORGAN; RUBIK'S CUBE]

26. MCU. The darkly silhouetted face of the professor in front of a window.

[Eva (off): yes . . . yes . . . yes . . . yes . . .] [BACH—ORGAN; RUBIK'S CUBE ENDS]

27. CU. The silhouetted face of the professor.

[BACH—ORGAN]
Pascal (off): Were you exiled for these ideas?
Professor: These . . . and others. See you Monday.
Pascal (off): Is the law of falling bodies because life fell from the sky?
Professor: Yes. [BACH ENDS] Goodbye.
Eva (off): Well!
Pascal (off): Coming?
Eva (off): Like a drink at my place one evening? [CLASSROOM NOISE]

28. CU. Eva, in profile, the lower half of her face visible in reflection against the classroom window.

Professor (off): That's another story. [LAUGHTER; CLASSROOM NOISE; DVOŘÁK —CELLO CONCERTO (further mention of "Dvořák" will refer to this composition)]

29. LS. Low angle. Through a silhouetted forest the lights of an airplane can be seen. Camera tilts up as the airplane advances and soars overhead.

[WIND; AIRPLANE TAKEOFF; DVOŘÁK]

30. MCU. Mary stands reflected before a bathroom mirror brushing her hair. A bare light bulb is over the mirror. She pauses and looks skyward in startled reaction.

[DVOŘÁK; AIRPLANE OVERHEAD]

31. LS. Low angle. Camera tilts following the plane as it moves down and out of sight behind electrical wires.

[DVOŘÁK; AIRPLANE; DVOŘÁK ENDS]

32. MS. An extremely distant jet plane travels left to right across the sky, its path cutting straight through a large setting sun.

[AIRPLANE; WIND; DVOŘÁK]

33. CU. A young girl looks expectantly out a sliding glass door.

[DVOŘÁK]

34. LS. Inside an airport terminal, a man (Gabriel) and the young girl cross to the right, stop, and kneel down in order to tie his shoe.

Girl: Your shoe! [DVOŘÁK ENDS; AIRPORT TERMINAL NOISE]

35. MS. The laces of Gabriel's red, white, and blue saddle shoe are carefully tied by the girl's right hand and his left hand.

[CHIMES]

36. MCU. Inside a taxi, Joseph sits reading aloud from a book; his dog sits beside him.

[AIRPORT TRAFFIC]
Joseph: "The question is if this creature [TAXI ENGINE] called man ever existed. [AIRPORT LOUDSPEAKER] Legendary man is a figment of the popular imagination . . ."

37. LS. Walking hurriedly through an airport corridor, Gabriel bumps an unidentified man, kicking his briefcase across the floor. The man grabs Gabriel, but Gabriel shrugs him aside and walks away. The young girl runs back to the man, hits him, then runs after Gabriel.

[ANGRY VOICES; MAN COMPLAINS]

38. MS. At night, seated in his taxi, Joseph feeds his dog while continuing to read his book aloud. Gabriel and the young girl climb into the backseat.

[COMPLAINTS; PEOPLE ENTER TAXI; AIRPLANE OVERHEAD]
Gabriel: While there are Bourbons in Spain there'll be no peace.
Girl: That's not your line, Uncle Gabriel!
Gabriel: Right!

39. CU. Joseph reacts to money being handed to him.

Gabriel (off): Straight ahead.
Joseph: Where's that? [AIRPORT LOUDSPEAKER; AIRPLANE; TAXI ENGINE]
Gabriel (off): Here's $500.

40. LS. The taxi pulls away through an evening rain.

[TAXI DRIVES]

41. LS. Forward-traveling shot on a roadway at night as the lights of oncoming traffic speed past.

[TAXI DRIVES; DVOŘÁK]
Gabriel (off): It's closed.

42. LS. Forward-traveling shot. On a roadway at night, an occasional vehicle passes by in the oncoming lane.

[DVOŘÁK ENDS; AIRPLANE]
Girl (off): How about there?
Gabriel (off): No, there should be a house alongside.
Joseph (off): What are you looking for?

43. LS. Same as 42. A gas station comes into view across the street.

STREET NOISE]
Girl (off): Here!
Gabriel (off): Stop at this station.

44. LS. The taxi pulls into the gas station alongside the pumps. Gabriel and the girl get out. Joseph attempts to get out but is pushed back into the taxi by Gabriel. Gabriel and the young girl walk off left. Joseph and his dog exit from the taxi.

[STREET NOISE]
[**Joseph (off):** No, no.]
Gabriel (off): Here's $500, [DVOŘÁK PHRASE] for God's sake. [TAXI BRAKES SQUEAL; DOOR CLOSES; DVOŘÁK PHRASE]
Gabriel: We'll be back!
[AIRPLANE]

45. CU. Mary pulls on a sweater, looks off right. Red and blue flowers are reflected on a window in the foreground.

[DVOŘÁK]
Gabriel (off): You've a daughter, Mary?
Father (off): What's it about?
Joseph (off): Mary . . .
Gabriel (off): She's here!

46. MS. Viewed from behind, a man (Mary's father) is seated inside the gas station. Gabriel and the young girl face him, the girl rising up between them. Gabriel and the girl exit.

[DVOŘÁK]
Girl: For God's sake!
Father: Mary, help!

47. LS. Joseph stands outside with his dog. Gabriel and the young girl enter from the left. Joseph shoves Gabriel. Mary enters from the

[SHOUTS; TRAFFIC; DVOŘÁK ENDS]
[**Girl:** Mary.]
[**Gabriel:** Mary.]

background; she shoves Joseph away and starts to put the dog in the taxi.

48. MS. Holding the passenger door open, Mary allows the dog to climb inside. Joseph walks around to the other side, closely followed by Mary's father, who threatens Joseph with a wrench. Joseph enters the driver's seat as the father circles around the taxi and exits right. Mary speaks to Joseph, then slams the passenger door shut. She confronts Gabriel (offscreen), then bows her head.

[TAXI DOOR SLAMS]
Mary: Why're you here? We said Saturday. Don't, Dad, it's Joseph.
Joseph: They brought me here.
[DVOŘÁK PHRASE]
Mary: I'm sick of your tricks. Forget it! [WIND] OK, what is it?
Gabriel (off): It's you, Mary.
[WIND; RAIN; TRAFFIC]

49. LS. A traffic light, on the left of the frame, changes from yellow to red. A small crescent moon is seen at lower right.

[DVOŘÁK; TRAFFIC; TAXI DOORS SLAM]

50. MCU. Viewed from behind, Joseph sits at at the wheel of the taxi. He turns, his face moving from shadow into light as he looks off in the direction of the camera.

[DVOŘÁK; TAXI DISPATCHER ON RADIO; TRAFFIC]
Mary (off): What do you want?

51. MCU. Mary looks plaintively skyward, lowers her eyes, then looks off left.

[DVOŘÁK ENDS; TRAFFIC]
Mary: What do you want?
Gabriel (off): And you, my lady? Your fiancé?
Joseph (off): What's it to you?
Gabriel (off): We couldn't care less. But you're going to have a child.
Mary: By whom?
Gabriel (whispers, off): You'll have a baby.
Mary: I sleep with no one.
Joseph (off): Mary, shit,

52. MS. Gabriel leans on the roof of the taxi. He counts out money and hands it offscreen. He lights a cigarette.

[TRAFFIC]
Joseph (off): who are these people?
Gabriel: Go on! Straight ahead! Here's $500.
Mary (off): By whom?
Gabriel: It won't be his. Never!
Mary (off): By whom?
Gabriel: Don't play innocent!
Mary (off): By whom?
Girl (off): Mary,

53. CU. The young girl.

[TRAFFIC]
Girl: Be pure, be rough. Follow Thy way.
Mary (off): What? My way! but the voice or the word?

54. CU. Mary, in left profile.

[TRAFFIC]
Girl: Don't be silly! **(off):** I know where you're going and soon you will too. [DVOŘÁK]

55. LS. Gabriel climbs into the back of the taxi which then pulls away. Mary chases after the departing taxi, stops, and slumps to the ground; rises, and skips back in the direction of the station. A sign, *bonne route*, is visible on the right.

[DVOŘÁK; TAXI ENGINE]
Girl: Don't forget!
Gabriel: Don't forget, what goes in, goes out. [DOORS SLAM; DVOŘÁK ENDS] **(off):** And what goes out, goes in! [DVOŘÁK]

56. ELS. Five people walk along a rocky coastal abutment, some throwing stones into the water.

[DVOŘÁK ENDS; STONES SPLASH IN WATER]
Eva: I'm tired. Shall we stop?

57. LS. Viewed through branches in the foreground, the five people join two others and settle on the shore.

[FOOTSTEPS ON SAND]
Professor (vo): *We each go on* [DVOŘÁK PHRASE] *and each of us attains what he can reach.*
Eva: Hölderlin . . . his last work.
Male Student: Those ants are strictly the invisible man.

58. MLS. The professor, Eva, and a female student sit on the beach while a young man explores the wooded background. Another student joins the seated group.

Second Male Student: I swear it was here! [BIRDS; MOTOR BOAT]
Eva: You never find ants near water.
Male Student: Wrong. Some ants seek gold.
Eva: I read "Scientific American" too.
Professor: What about these ants?

59. MS. A male and female student sit on the beach. The woman lights a cigarette.

Male Student: Oliver found an anthill. He rigged wiring to warm the ants in winter. [BIRDS] He wanted to keep them awake

60. MS. Eva, tossing a pebble in her hands.

Male Student (off): in winter, hoping they'd use that leisure time, to invent things. [BIRDS]

61. MS. The professor and the female student with a cigarette.

Professor: —What?
Male Student (off): —Music, maybe. [DVOŘÁK]

62. MS. A woman, viewed from the waist down, wearing only a striped shirt, irons a jersey with the number 10 on it.

[DVOŘÁK]

63. MCU. Mary, ironing, turns her head sharply after repeated car honks.

[DVOŘÁK PHRASE]
Mary: There's no escape.
[DVOŘÁK; CAR HORN]

64. LS. High angle. In daylight, Joseph stands alongside his parked taxi honking the horn. He puts his jacket in the rear trunk, honks again, then runs off to the right up a flight of steps.

[STREET NOISE; CAR HORN; DVOŘÁK]

65. CU. Low angle. Joseph, the sun behind him, speaks and looks downward.

[DVOŘÁK]
Joseph: What is this? Miracles don't exist. [DVOŘÁK ENDS] Kiss me. What is all this? [AIRPLANE]

66. MS. Mary, viewed from her waist to her knees, wears panties and a striped shirt. She caresses her rounded stomach, her hand coming to rest on her pubic mound.

Mary: There's no escape, for us. [SILENCE]

(Intertitle 5:) EN CE TEMPS LA

[BIRDS]
Professor (vo): Let's go on with our story.

67. MS. The professor is seated on the beach, Eva is in CU in foreground.

Professor: Imagine . . . our descendants in 8 million years, 100 million. Their wisdom and knowledge are unimaginable today. They suddenly notice that the supposedly fixed balance of the universe is subtly changing. [BIRDS]

68. LS. Viewed from below, two large-winged birds encircle each other's path against a blue sky.

[DVOŘÁK]

69. LS into MS. Mary and Joseph descend the steps outside her house, Mary bouncing a basketball. She heads toward the taxi in foreground. Joseph follows, then grabs her. Mary

[DVOŘÁK]
Professor (vo): Won't our descendants try to preserve life? [DVOŘÁK ENDS]
Joseph: Kiss me. [DOG BARKS]

pulls away. Joseph then knocks the ball from her hand and pushes her onto the taxi's hood.

70. **MS.** Joseph has Mary pinned on the taxi hood. He attempts to kiss her. She turns her head aside. The bright sun reflects on the hood. The wind blows strong. Joseph moves off her.

71. **LS.** The sun, largely obscured by dark moving clouds.

72. **MS.** Joseph again pins Mary onto the taxi hood.

(Intertitle 6:) EN CE TEMPS LA

73. **CU.** The professor.

74. **CU.** Sunlight reflected on rippling water.

75. **LS.** The sun seen cradled amidst the branches of silhouetted trees.

76. **CU.** Eva, looking upward.

77. **LS.** An orange sky and the last yellow glow of the sun behind a silhouetted horizon.

78. **CU.** Gently moving patterns of sunlight on water.

79. **MCU.** The professor's writing pad. He circles the word *DIEU* on his pad.

80. **CU.** Eva.

Mary: I kiss you, I do.
Joseph: Just once, Mary.
Mary: You should trust me.
[BASKETBALL BOUNCES]
[DVOŘÁK; STREET NOISE; BIRDS]

[STONES SPLASH IN WATER; BIRDS]
Professor (vo): A prior intelligence programmed life. It struggled to exist

Professor (vo): in a pitiless universe. [WATER SPLASHES] It preserved life.

Male Student (vo): How'd you think of it? [BIRDS]

Professor: Because of computers. When I consider it . . . that computer intelligence stuns me.
[LAPPING WATER; BIRDS; PEN SCRATCHES]

Professor (off): If our distant descendants [LAPPING WATER]

[FAINT TRAFFIC]

Professor (off): tried to encode [LAPPING WATER; PEN SCRATCHES] life as they know it

Professor (off): in a message of magnesium, or Bohr, or God knows what, [LAPPING WATER; PEN SCRATCHES through shot 80]

Professor: wouldn't they try to transmit the secret . . . of Creation?

Eva: Maybe the message has always been clear.
Professor (off): Yes, that Voice deep in our consciences whispers, [BIRDS] if we listen: you're born of

something, somewhere else, in
Heaven. Seek and you will find more

81. LS. In silhouette, the teacher and
students walk one by one through
the woods, right to left.

Professor: than you dream of.
[AIRPLANE]

82. LS. Inside a deserted basketball
court, the far wall of windows reveal
someone walking past outside.

[DVOŘÁK]
Juliette (off): Come to

83. MS. Viewed from behind, Joseph
is seated inside a building. Juliette
walks past, pauses to pet Joseph's
dog, then exits right.

[DVOŘÁK; FOOTSTEPS]
Juliette: see the princess? You can't
fall any lower.
Joseph: Who asked you?
Juliette: Do I tell him to come?
Joseph: Leave me alone.

84. CU. The dog turns his head.

[DVOŘÁK ENDS; BASKETBALL
BOUNCES]
[**Joseph (off):** Mary.]

85. CU. Joseph, wearing sunglasses.

[GYM NOISES]
Joseph: Why not tell the truth?
Mary (vo): I am telling it. Maybe the
words come out wrong, or it's my
voice, but it's the truth.
Joseph: Be simpler if you said you've
seen other men.

86. CU. Mary, in right profile, looks
down.

[DVOŘÁK]
Mary: I sleep with no one.
Joseph (off): So where's the child
from? [DVOŘÁK ENDS]

87. MCU. The dog.

[DVOŘÁK; GYM NOISE]
Joseph (off): Where'll it come from?
[DVOŘÁK ENDS]

88. MS. Mary sits near Joseph, the
stairwell behind him. He strikes the
basketball out of her hands. She
responds and looks at him directly.

Joseph: Answer me! [BASKETBALL
BOUNCES] . . . Look at me!
Mary: I'm looking at you.

89. LS. Dark clouds obscure the sun.

Joseph (off): Child must come from
somewhere. For 2 years now I can't
touch you. Why?

90. MLS. Mary stands in the
foreground holding a basketball as
Joseph walks toward her. Juliette rises
from a seated position in
background, passes between them,

[DVOŘÁK]
Joseph: Kiss me.
Mary: I don't know, Joseph . . .
Joseph: By God! It's incredible!
[BASKETBALL BOUNCES]

then exits left. Mary puts her hand to Joseph's heart, then walks off left.

91. LS. Women's basketball practice. Mary runs for a lay-up shot.

92. LS. During a basketball game, Mary is fouled as she attempts a shot.

93. MS. High angle. Seated before an open window, Mary strokes a child's head, then reads her open book.

94. CU. Mary looks off, smiling slightly.

95. MS. A man rests his hand against his mouth as he speaks.

96. MS. A doctor writes and talks as he sits at his desk. Mary sits opposite him, her back to the camera. The doctor folds his hands upon his desk and looks directly at Mary. A nurse crosses through the background. Mary exits. The doctor answers the phone.

Juliette: Call, or stop by the theater. [DVOŘÁK ENDS]
Joseph: Please kiss me.
Mary: Not that way. I do kiss you, really. [BASKETBALL BOUNCES]
Joseph: You must be sleeping around. It's the only answer. Guys with big cocks!

[DVOŘÁK MIXES WITH BACH— CHORAL; BOTH END]

[BASKETBALL GAME; WHISTLE]

Joseph (off): We're through, Mary. Ciao! [PATIENTS' VOICES IN DOCTOR'S WAITING ROOM]

First Man (vo): Hi! You here too?
Second Man (vo): I keep dreaming. Can't sleep. It wears me out. Last night, before I went home, I dreamed I had to paint the whole building. I thought: that'll take time.

Second Man (vo): That'll take time. I couldn't sleep.
First Man: Must be a reason. You should make notes.
Second Man (vo): Yes, but I can't write, so I draw.
First Man: If it's a picture, you can't forget. [DOOR CLOSES]
Second Man (vo): I must learn to write

Second Man (vo): if I want to forget.
First Man (vo): That's it.
Doctor: Your Dad well?
Mary: Yes, thanks.
Doctor: Still pumping gas?
Mary: He wants out.
Doctor: You getting married soon? Broken up with Joseph? He seemed serious. What's wrong, Mary?
Mary: I've got a pain! In the belly.
Doctor: We'll have a look. Take her blood pressure, Esther. [PHONE

97. MS. Mary, wearing an undershirt, sits in profile. The doctor and nurse cross in the foreground. The doctor examines Mary's pulse and her throat. He exits from the frame.

RINGS] Go next door and undress. Be right there.

[BACH—HARPSICHORD AND STRINGS]

Doctor (on phone, off): If you put on weight, you'll be fine. [BACH ENDS]

Mary: Does the soul have a body? [FAINT TRAFFIC]

Doctor: What do you mean, young lady, the body has a soul.

Mary: I thought it was the opposite. [BACH—SAME] Doctor! [BACH ENDS]

98. LS. Her back to the camera, Mary sits upright in her underwear on the examination table. She slides left, drawing her legs up onto the table.

Mary: I must be pregnant.

Doctor: When was your last period? Take off your panties and lie down there. [BACH—SAME]

Mary: It's no use. [BACH ENDS]

99. MS. The doctor washes his hands in a sink. He turns his head around as he talks to Mary.

[TAP WATER SPLASHES]

Mary (off): What? I didn't hear you.

Doctor: I've always wondered what we know about a woman, and I found that all you can know is what a man already knew. There's a mystery there.

100. CU. Mary is leaning forward, her cheek upon her leg; she rubs a scar on her knee. The doctor crosses in front of her and places his hand on her knee. She lifts her head.

Doctor (off): Do you want this child? [BACH PHRASE—SAME] Was it with Joseph?

Mary: It wasn't with any body.

Doctor (off): Some song and dance! Lie down.

Mary: It's no song and dance. I'm happy.

Doctor (off): Now tell about your period. I must examine you, if you say it hurts.

101. MS. The doctor stands before Mary, partially obstructed by the back of her head. He strokes her hair lightly.

Mary: It came normally, very intense.

Doctor: When?

Mary: Friday.

Doctor: Then quit being stupid. It's nothing.

Mary: See for yourself! I haven't slept with anyone. I touch no one. No one caresses me. I want you to

102. **MCU.** Mary's knees. She lies backward and slips off her panties. The doctor opens her legs and, in profile, he gazes down, examining her.

see if my baby's already there. [BACH PHRASE —SAME]
Doctor: You're hiding . . .

Doctor (off): . . . something from us.
Mary: I'm not. I tell you. You see? I'm going to have a baby and I've slept with no man. [BACH PHRASE —SAME] Joseph won't believe it. You tell him.
Doctor: Lie still!
Mary: Will you hurt me?
Doctor: Don't be afraid. I was there when you were born.
Mary: Being a virgin should mean being available, or free, not being hurt. Well,

103. **MS.** The doctor bends forward, his hand on Mary's knee. He turns right, then slowly straightens up, rising out of the frame. Mary sits up and cradles her knees. He places his hand on her shoulder.

Mary: do you believe me? [BACH PHRASE—SAME]
Doctor: It's true that it's true.
Mary: Tell Joseph.
Doctor: Esther!
Mary: May I get dressed?

104. **MCU.** Joseph, in sunglasses, stands alongside his cab, the taxi sign opposite him. Behind him, Eva and the professor walk up into the middle of the frame, kiss, then advance toward Joseph.

Joseph: It must be mine! [TRAFFIC]

105. **MS.** Joseph, sitting on the front fender of his cab, hops down and closes the rear door of the cab after the professor and Eva have entered. Joseph then stares forward in the direction of the camera.

[TRAFFIC]
Joseph: Where to now?
Eva: Paradise villa, Hermance road.
Joseph: I quit work at 5 p.m.
Eva: Sure, that's OK.
Professor: Is it in France? [DVOŘÁK]
Eva: It's very close. You'll see, it's as pretty as Czechoslovakia.

[DVOŘÁK]

106. **MS.** Mary, naked, about to climb into the tub, looks upward and closes bathroom door.

107. **MS.** Joseph starts to climb into the taxi, then gets back out and stares fixedly off left, ignoring the shoulder taps of Eva.

[TRAFFIC; DVOŘÁK]

108. LS. Gabriel and the young girl, holding hands, stand in front of the cab, a river behind them.

[TRAFFIC; DVOŘÁK]

109. LS. Joseph walks in front of his taxi to the river's edge, looks left and right, but there is no one else in view. As the taxi horn honks, he hurries back.

[DVOŘÁK; CAR HORN; WATER SPLASHES]

110. LS. High angle. Mary kneels in a shallow tub of water, washing herself.

[WATER SPLASHES]
Mary (vo): *Yet I rejoiced in giving my body to the eyes . . . of Him who has become my Master forever, and glanced*

111. LS. An occasional solitary bird flies before a golden sunset.

Mary (vo): *at this wondrous being. For in truth, He was that, then and always, not for His looks nor for what He did, but in the silent power of what He was, the power gathered up in Him, vast as a mountain on the sky that you can't measure or name,* [DVOŘÁK PHRASE; BIRDS] *but only feel.*

112. MS. Mary talks on the phone while eating an apple.

[BIRDS]
Mary: Tonight? No, I've a practice session.
JOSEPH (on phone, vo): OK, I'll go jump in the lake!
Mary: Jump in the lake? Ophelia's no role for you. [BITES APPLE]
Joseph (vo): What are you talking about?
Mary: "To be or not to be . . ." Don't know it?
Joseph (vo): I had to quit school when I was 12.
Mary: Sorry. I must go.
Joseph (vo): OK, I'll go jump in the lake!
Mary: No. Stop it!

113. LS. A lake and shoreline are foregrounded by willow branches.

[DVOŘÁK]

114. LS. Eva slides open a glass door and enters an elegant living room.

[DVOŘÁK ENDS]

115. MS. At night in a telephone booth, Joseph talks on the phone,

[DVOŘÁK; BANGS ON PHONE]

then angrily slams the side of the phone itself with his hand.

116. MS. A bright sun glows in an orange sky. A bird flies left.

117. Eva and the professor stand before a living-room picture window looking out at a lake bathed in a very bluish dusky light. Eva walks off left, followed by the professor.

[DVOŘÁK ENDS]

Eva: What's on your mind?
[SLIDING DOOR CLOSES]
Professor: Night changes its own look and meaning.
Eva: Heidegger. "3 lectures in the . . .
Professor: Bavarian Academy."
Eva: Winter of '59.
Professor: —Yes.— [TABLE CLOCK CHIMES HOUR; CLOCK TICKS]
Eva (off): Know why he wasn't shot? As soon as we talk . . . politics, you clam up.

118. LS. Eva and the professor enter dining room, the professor then exiting to the left, Eva advancing toward the table. A black maid adjusts the place setting and walks off right. Eva eventually selects an apple from a fruit bowl.

[CLOCK TICKS]
Professor (off): I think politics today . . . must be the voice of horror.
Eva: The voice, but the way or the word?
Professor (off): The voice of horror of which nothing can be said.
[WIND] Can I put this on?
Eva: What is it?
Professor (off): You can't find that in Prague.

119. CU. Eva bites into an apple.

[AMPLIFIED SOUND: EVA BITES APPLE; CLOCK TICKS]

120. MS. The professor leans back in a chair and lights a cigarette. Eva enters the frame holding an apple and sits upon the arm of his chair. The professor caresses her.

[CLOCK TICKS]
Eva: You OK?
Professor: A smoke, a sax solo, that's all a man wants.
Eva: I often wonder that in music . . .
Professor: What? [EXHALES SMOKE]
Eva: We marvel at a new phrase, but, really, there could be nothing.
[BITES APPLE; WIND] This is the time.
Professor: And the place.
[COLTRANE—JAZZ PIANO; PHONE RINGS]

121. MLS. In the foreground, a cigarette burns in an ash tray. After a moment, Eva enters from left in the nude and answers the phone in the background. After hanging up, she walks to the foreground, takes a puff on the cigarette, then walks off left.

Eva: —Yes.— No, not tonight. [WIND; COLTRANE—JAZZ SAX] **Mary (vo):** *I think the spirit acts on the body, breathes through it, veils it to make it fairer than it is. For what is flesh . . .*

122. CU. Mary reads. Her father walks off left, momentarily obscuring her.

Mary (vo): *. . . alone?* [COLTRANE ENDS; DOOR OPENS] **Father (vo):** I have business. I'll be in late. Write down the pump figures. **Mary:** Yes, Dad. *What is flesh, . . . alone?* [DOOR CLOSES] *You may see it and feel only disgust. You may see it only in the gutter, drunken, or in the coffin, dead. The world's as full . . . of flesh as a grocer's counter is of candles at the start of winter. But not until you've brought a candle home and lit it can it give you comfort.* [TRAFFIC]

123. LS. Outside the gas station, Mary's father lights a cigarette. While Mary checks the figures on the gas pumps, her father walks off left, coat in hand.

[TRAFFIC; DVOŘÁK; DOOR CLOSES]

124. LS. In the foreground a taxi sits, its yellow *Taxi* sign prominent. In the background, Mary finishes jotting down numbers and skips into the gas station. As snow descends, the station lights are turned off, leaving only the *Taxi* sign visible.

[DVOŘÁK; DOOR CLOSES]

125. ELS. From out of a black sky, clouds slide past to reveal a white quarter moon.

[DVOŘÁK ENDS; BANGS; TRAFFIC]

126. MCU. Juliette stands in left profile. In soft focus in the background, Joseph stands beneath fluorescent lights. He advances and circles around Juliette. He rests his head and hand upon her shoulder.

[TRAFFIC; BANGS] **Juliette:** Come on . . . Don't you like my body? **Joseph:** That's not it. **Juliette:** Then what? It's because of her. **Joseph:** I don't know. It's making me sick. I don't know. **Juliette:** I know, it's her. It always is . . . I'm a real woman, too.

127. ELS. A quarter moon is slowly obscured by a moving cloud.

128. LS. As he speaks and strolls along the sidewalk, Joseph sees the young girl inside a clothing store. She immediately runs as Joseph darts inside after her.

129. MS. As Gabriel stands alongside a suit rack, the young girl hands him a jacket. Joseph steps up to Gabriel and touches his shoulder. Gabriel tries on the jacket. Juliette walks into the background.

130. CU. Juliette.

131. MS. Seated in front of a clothing rack, the young girl begins to read from a notepad.

132. CU. Joseph, in right profile. Gabriel's hand swats Joseph on the back of the head. He removes Joseph's glasses and waves his hand in front of Joseph's face.

Joseph: I'd like to love you, but I don't know how.
Juliette: Let's go home.

Juliette (off): Come on. [DVOŘÁK; TRAFFIC]

Joseph: I'm coming. [TRAFFIC; DVOŘÁK ENDS]

[CARS GOING BY punctuate shots 129 through 134]
Girl: You're complicating things, don't you think? What?
Joseph: If God exists, nothing's . . .

Joseph (off): . . . allowed.
Gabriel (off): What are you doing with that tramp?
Girl (off): No, Uncle Gabriel. Not like that!
Gabriel (off): When he's around, I forget my lines! It's awful. He's a real nothing. Got the list?

Joseph (off): What list?
Girl: —He wants to know everything. [PAGES RUSTLE] Like everyone! He doesn't even know how to walk his dog.
Gabriel (whispers, off): Like everyone.
Girl: He's scared of the hole.
Gabriel (whispers, off): Like everyone.
Girl: He has no taste in ties.
Gabriel (whispers, off): Like everyone.
Joseph (off): Zero equals zero.
Girl: He lacks trust.

Gabriel (whispers, off): That's no fault. **(full voice):** What's the common denominator between zero and Mary?
Mary's body! Answer, nitwit!

133. MS. Sitting and reading from her notepad, the young girl looks over to Joseph, who is offscreen.

Joseph: Dunno!
Girl (off): He wears blind man's glasses, the dolt.
Gabriel (off): Try and follow the movement . . . Not with your hand, your eyes!
Joseph (off): She'll make a fool of me!
Gabriel (off): Look at me in the eyes.
Joseph (off): If some guy's knocked her up . . .
Gabriel (off): We're not "some guy"!
Joseph (off): I don't get it. [SLAP]
Girl: Have trust.

134. MCU. Gabriel, viewed over Joseph's shoulder. Gabriel slaps Joseph in the face, then turns away.

Gabriel: Trust!
Joseph: I've none left. [SLAP]
Gabriel: And love, you jerk!
Joseph: Love . . . [DVOŘÁK]

135. CU. The young girl looks up and, glancing offscreen left, moves her lips. [While there is no live sound, one can visibly read her lips mouthing the words "Oui, l'amour, c'est . . ."]

[DVOŘÁK]

136. MS. Sunlight reflects across a rippling ocean.

[DVOŘÁK]

137. MCU. An orange-yellow sun with very slight cloud cover.

[DVOŘÁK]

138. MS. Seen through a front store window, Mary approaches and begins to touch, then sets aside a tube of lipstick on a display counter. She shakes her head no. Holding Julien Green's book *St. Francis of Assisi* under her arm, she exits.

[DVOŘÁK ENDS; STREET NOISE; CUSTOMER'S VOICE; STORE DOORBELL]

139. MS. Joseph sits in bed reading the book, *Demain les chiens.* Mary enters frame and hands him her book on St. Francis.

[STREET NOISE]
Mary (off): I've come. **(on):** What's wrong? Your eyes again?
Joseph: What's the book?
Mary: It's for you.
Joseph: *Into the maze of life goes the dashing young man. The best horse, the finest armor and clothes, to be knight, Lord, a Great Prince, he wants it all. But Someone . . .*

169. LS. A diffused sun, an occasional bird flying.

Joseph (vo): *located farther in space.* [DVOŘÁK] *It is only, he said, a legendary deformation of Horla's idea of the world*

170. CU. The dog, Arthur.

[DVOŘÁK]
Joseph (vo): *whose dogs knew of it since ancient times* . . . Go, Arthur. [DVOŘÁK ENDS]

171. MS. Viewed from the back, Joseph sits in his taxi adjusting his tie, the gas station in background.

[TRAFFIC]
Joseph: The time has come. I'll go see the boss lady. This time I think we've won. [BACH—CHORAL]

172. LS. Mary moves away from the window and begins to undress until she wears only an undershirt.

[BACH—ORGAN ENDS; DOG BARKS]
Mary: I no longer wish to understand. [KNOCKS] Does it matter what I am or am not? [KNOCKS]

173. CU. Mary suddenly looks up sternly.

Mary: No, not already!

174. MS. Joseph stands by a partially open door in Mary's room. A polaroid of Mary holding a basketball is pinned to a basketball poster on the door. Joseph slowly enters, closes the door, and walks forward.

[DOG BARKS; DOOR CLOSES]

175. MLS. Mary sits on the bed. Joseph sits down beside her and gently touches her shoulder, a basketball behind him on the bed.

Mary: We can't escape one another anymore than . . . we can escape him. [TRAFFIC; BIRDS]

176. MS. High angle. Joseph gently glides his hand down Mary's arm. She pushes him away and looks plaintively skyward, clenching her fists.

[TRAFFIC; DVOŘÁK PHRASE]

177. LS. High angle. Leaning forward, Mary drops to the floor and begins pounding it with her fists. She breathes deeply and begins to stand up.

[BANGS ON FLOOR]
Joseph: Mary, what are you doing? [DVOŘÁK; BIRDS; LABORED BREATHING] Stop it!

178. CU. Joseph. Mary's hand touches the top of his head. He raises

[TRAFFIC; BIRDS]
Mary (off): Tell me you love me.

his hand up and begins repeatedly to reach out to touch Mary, who is offscreen.

179. MCU. Joseph's hand is on Mary's stomach. She pushes it away. Joseph reaches forward to touch her. She stops his hand. As he touches her again, a man's hand enters from the left, pushing Joseph's hand away.

180. ECU. Mary, her mouth agape.

181. LS. High angle. Mary, in the foreground, moves aside, revealing Gabriel holding Joseph by the throat on the bed. Mary drops to her knees beside them. Gabriel releases Joseph, then shoves him to the floor.

182. MS. A field of blooming wildflowers.

183. MCU. Mary.

184. MS. Joseph rises from the floor and sits on the bed. Mary steps up to him and gently strokes his hair. The back of a chair in the foreground visually separates them. Joseph reaches out suddenly to touch Mary's belly. Mary shouts, "No!," and he withdraws his hand. Slowly he reaches out again, gently pressing his palm against her stomach. She approves. He withdraws his hand. He repeats the action a second and a third time.

185. MCU. Mary's protruding abdomen is revealed as she lifts her shirt. The flat of Joseph's palm repeatedly touches her abdomen gently, then withdraws. She turns aside in profile.

Joseph: I love you. [DOG WHIMPERS]

[**Mary:** No. No.]
[**Joseph:** I love you.]
[**Mary:** No. [DOG BARKS]]
[**Joseph:** Mary, I love you.]
[**Mary:** No, no, no, no.]
[DVOŘÁK]]

[DVOŘÁK]

[DVOŘÁK ENDS]
Joseph: But why? Why?
Gabriel: Because! [DVOŘÁK] Because it's Law!

[DVOŘÁK]

[DVOŘÁK ENDS; TRAFFIC]
Gabriel (off): Got it?
Joseph (off): Yes . . . I'll sacrifice myself.
Gabriel (off): Asshole! [SLAP] First, a hole isn't a hole. Second: Taboo wipes out sacrifice. [TRAFFIC]
Joseph (off): But why?

Gabriel (off): Because that's the rule! [FOOTSTEPS]
Mary: I love you.
[**Joseph:** Mary.]
[**Mary:** No! [CHURCH BELLS RING HOUR] Yes.]
Joseph: Is that, I love you? [DVOŘÁK] Is that it? That?
[**Mary:** Yes.]
[**Joseph:** I love you.]
[**Mary:** Yes.]

[DVOŘÁK; BACH—ORGAN CHORD]

186. **LS.** Camera zooms in, tilts down. Delicate gray and rose-tinted clouds against a fading bluish sky.

[BACH—ORGAN CHORD; DVOŘÁK]
Mary (vo): *Suddenly a light shone in my heart, warm and gentle as a glowing fire . . . What, on earth, or even heaven, beats knowing you please the One you love, and Who is your master?*

187. **MCU.** Reddish green plants, with blue flowers in lower right foreground.

[DVOŘÁK]
Mary (vo): *I remember what He said about sin, as we watched the dragonflies.*

188. **LS.** A verdant tree-crested meadow with blooming red flowers. In the distance a train moves by.

[DVOŘÁK ENDS]
Mary (vo): *If you thought of it rightly, it just wasn't there.*

189. **LS.** A meadow of bright yellow flowers, crested by three blooming trees.

[RUSHING WATER]
Mary (vo): We're speaking

190. **MS.** A field of bright yellow flowers.

Mary (vo): His Word. [WATER ENDS] How else can we be close . . .

191. **CU.** Joseph. Mary's hand touches his head.

Mary (vo): . . . to His Word than by speaking it?

192. **MS.** Mary dresses while Joseph sits on the bed. She seats herself at her desk upon which rests a vase of flowers. She touches and smells one.

[**Joseph:** Mary. [CHAIR SCRAPES; FAINT BIRDS]]
Mary: Yes? What?

193. **ECU.** The stamen and pistil inside a deep red and yellow tulip.

Mary (vo): We're speaking, and we're speaking of the Word.

194. **ECU.** The inside of a red tulip, revealing the stamen and pistil.

Mary (vo): What we're speaking of, the Word, is always ahead of us. [DVOŘÁK]

195. **ECU.** The interior of an orangish-red tulip, revealing the stamen and pistil.

[DVOŘÁK]

196. **MS.** Mary pirouettes, then sits down next to Joseph. She lays her head on his shoulder. He gently strokes her hair.

[DVOŘÁK ENDS]
Mary: Then you won't leave me?
[BIRDS]
Joseph: I'll stay. I'll never touch you. [DVOŘÁK] I'll stay.

197. **CU.** A clock face with a sweeping red second hand, moves to 12:31.

[DVOŘÁK ENDS; FAINT TRAIN NOISE]

198. MCU. Viewed through the open window of an automobile driver's seat, Eva sobs while a man wearing a wristwatch strokes the back of her head.

[SOBS]
Professor (vo): Don't believe [STREET NOISE] the dollar'll drop. Don't believe vacation will be fun. **(on):** You can believe rain falls downward. It's a law of nature.
Eva: The world's too sad!
Professor: It isn't sad. It's big! I must go.
Eva: Don't I count for you? [TRAIN GOES BY]

199. MS. The professor exits the car and stands between the car in the foreground and a speeding railway train in the background. Eva exits car in foreground.

[TRAIN LOUDLY GOES BY]
Professor: My wife and son count too. Now that I've a visa I must go see what's going on, no? Understand?

200. MS. The professor opens the rear passenger door. Eva grabs him by his lapels and shakes him. He releases her grip. She turns aside, then turns back around to slap him.

[TRAINS GOING BY OVERWHELM VOICES]
Eva: Tell how much do your wife and son count?
Professor: I don't get it.

201. CU. The professor looks on as Eva, back to the camera, follows through with the slap. She then caresses his cheek. He kisses her hand. She moves away, returns into the frame, then exits the frame again.

[FAINT TRAINS]
Eva: Bastard! [SLAP] I'm sorry. You say your wife's in jail, and you sleep with me.
Professor: Please, Eve.
Eva: Eva. It's all over with Eve. Go on, beat it, since it's what you want. [FOOTSTEPS] Give me back my 32,000 francs.
Professor: I'll send it to you.
Eva: You really are a nothing.

202. LS. Eva stands by her car as the professor removes his suitcase and walks away. He stops for a moment to talk with two men, shakes their hands, then continues off. Eva gets into the car, closes the open passenger door, then rests her head upon the car horn as another train roars past.

[TRAIN GOES BY; CAR DOORS SLAM; PROLONGED HONKING; TRAIN GOES BY]

203. LS. Low angle. In the upper right corner of the frame, a small half-moon. In the lower right corner, an illuminated train crosses diagonally through the frame.

Mary (vo): What makes a soul is its pain. [TRAIN ENDS] He'll be the first to hear my pain for them.

204. ECU. With eyes closed, Mary rests, her face in partial shadow. She opens her eyes.

Mary (vo): And he told me: Daughter, I'm suffocating to see you suffocate. God's a creep, a coward who won't fight, who counts . . . [CHURCH BELLS RING]

205. MS. Mary lies facedown atop her bed, wearing only an undershirt.

[CHURCH BELLS RING]
Mary (vo): . . . on ass alone, that is, on a quiet heart, for existence, an excess of ingress.

206. LS. Low angle. Mary lies faceup on her bed, her feet in the foreground.

Mary (vo): I want no carnal joy; I don't [BELLS RING HOUR] want to wear out my heart in one go, or my soul, in one go. Even pain won't get me in one go, and I won't . . .

207. LS. A light blue and orange sky permeated by heavy gray clouds.

Mary (vo): . . . disappear into it. It will disappear with me. [DVOŘÁK]

208. LS. At night, the taxi stops at a red light.

[MOTORBIKE; TRAFFIC; CAR HORN; RAIN; THUNDER]

209. LS. The full moon in upper right frame.

[TRAFFIC]
Mary (vo): It will always be [MOTORBIKE; THUNDER] horrible . . .

210. ECU. Mary, lying flat in bed, looks upward and speaks. A deep shadow covers her mouth and cheek.

Mary (vo): . . . for me to be the Master, but, there'll be no more sexuality in me. [THUNDER] I'll know the true smile of the soul,

211. MS. Trees and tall reedy grass in the countryside.

Mary (vo): not from outside . . . [THUNDER]

212. ECU. Same as 210.

Mary (vo): but from inside.

213. LS. In daylight, Mary lies in her underwear on her bed.

Mary (vo): Like a pain that's always deserved. [THUNDER; BIRDS]

214. MS. A summer meadow in half shadow.

[BIRDS]

215. MS. Mary writhes in bed.

[THUNDER; BIRDS]

216. MS. Wildflowers stirred by the wind.

[THUNDER; BIRDS]

217. MCU. Mary's hand, resting on her naked lower abdomen, forms into a fist.

[BIRDS]

218. LS. High angle. On her bed, Mary tosses off her sheet revealing

Mary (vo): It's not a matter of experience but of total disgust, total

her naked chest. She arches her body, turning in different directions.

219. MS. Same as 1. Camera zooms in at end of shot.

220. CU. Mary's fingers press against her pubic hair.

221. MCU. Mary lies awake in bed at night, her face diagonally dissected by a deep shadow.

222. MS. Blowing, rainswept reeds.

223. LS. The sun low in an orange cloud-dappled sky.

224. LS. A lake and tree-lined ridge against an orange sky. A bird in flight.

225. LS. A bird crosses a blue-gray sky.

226. MS. The sun in an orange sky.

227. LS. In an orange sky, the sun is hidden beneath a bank of clouds.

228. LS. Sunlight reflected on horizontal bands of rippling water.

229. MS. The sun on the left of the frame, dark clouds on the right.

230. MS. Thick weedy grass.

231. MS. A hedgehog.

232. CU. The hedgehog rolled up in a ball.

233. MS. The hedgehog.

---

hatred, and not of morality or dignity. [THUNDER]

[BIRD CALLS; RAIN; THUNDER]
Mary (vo): The Father . . .

Mary (vo): and Mother must fuck to death over my body. Then Lucifer will die, and we'll see . . . We'll see who's [THUNDER] weariest, him . . .

Mary (vo): . . . or me. [WIND]

Mary (vo): Earth and sex are in us. [WIND] Outside there are only stars.

[WIND; BIRDS]

Mary (vo): Wanting isn't expanding by force. [BIRDS]

[WIND]
Mary (vo): It's recoiling into oneself . . .

[WIND]
Mary (vo): . . . from level . . .

[WIND]
Mary (vo): to level, for eternity.

[WIND]

Mary (vo): You don't need a mouthhole to eat with . . . [BIRDS]

Mary (vo): and an asshole [CRICKETS] to swallow infinity. Your ass must go

[CRICKETS]
Mary (vo): . . . in your head, and so descend

[CRICKETS]
Mary (vo): . . . to ass level, then go left . . .

Mary (vo): or right to rise higher.

234. LS. A radiant sun emerging from behind a white cloud in a blue sky.

[BACH—FLUTE]

235. LS. In daylight, Mary lies in bed. Her stomach rises and falls beneath the sheet covering her.

Mary (vo): God is a vampire who suffered me in him . . . because I suffered and He didn't, and He profited from my pain. [TRAFFIC; BACH—VIOLIN]

236. LS. People walk along a city sidewalk. A man hands money to a man in a car.

[BACH ENDS]

237. LS. At night, Mary lies naked on her bed. Her abdomen rises and falls as she breathes, her feet in foreground.

Mary (vo): Mary is a body fallen from a soul. I am a soul imprisoned by a body. My soul makes me sick at heart, and it's my cunt . . . I'm a woman . . . though I don't beget my man through my cunt. [BIRDS] I am joy. I am she who is joy, and need no longer fight it, or be tempted, but to gain an added joy. [BIRDS]

238. CU. Mary's hand rests on her swollen abdomen, which rises and falls as she breathes, her appendectomy scar visible.

[HEAVY BREATHING; DVOŘÁK PHRASE]

239. MCU. Same as 221. Mary smiles slightly.

Mary (vo): I am not resigned. Resignation is sad. How can one be resigned to God's will? [WIND] Are we resigned to being loved? This seemed clear to me. Too clear. [WIND; BIRDS]

240. MS. Full moon.

[BIRDS; SPECTATORS' CHEERS]

241. LS. Joseph and a pregnant Mary sit upon gymnasium bleachers with other spectators, looking off right. Mary wears a scarlet and pink coat.

[CHEERS; BACH—VIOLIN]

(Intertitle 9:) EN CE TEMPS LA

AT THAT TIME
[BACH—VIOLIN; CHEERS]

242. LS. Momentarily obscured by a figure in the extreme foreground, Mary and Joseph sit in the crowded bleachers looking off right.

[BACH—VIOLIN]

243. LS. Full moon in the upper right frame.

[BACH—VIOLIN; CHEERS; WHISTLE; HORN BLASTS]

244. LS. Women basketball players during a game. A player lunges for a ball.

[BACH—VIOLIN]

245. LS. Same as 242.

[BACH ENDS; CHEERS]

246. LS. Players running down court passing basketball.

[CHEERS]

247. LS. Same as 242. As Mary watches the game, Joseph puts on his glasses and begins to read a book.

[CHEERS]

248. LS. Players during the game. The number 10 is worn.

[BACH—VIOLIN; CHEERS]

249. MS. Full moon.

[BACH—VIOLIN]

250. LS. Referee and players during the game. Mary and Joseph in the background.

[BACH—VIOLIN]

251. MCU. Juliette sits among her teammates upon the bench.

[BACH—VIOLIN]

252. LS. Players during a game.

[CHEERS]

253. MS. Full moon.

[BACH—VIOLIN; CHEERS]

254. LS. Same as 242. Mary watches as Joseph continues to read his book.

[BACH—VIOLIN; CHEERS]

255. LS. Players during a game. A player shoots the ball.

[BACH—VIOLIN]

256. MS. Full moon.

[BACH—VIOLIN]

257. MCU. A large illuminated white globe fills the left foreground. Slowly, Mary walks up into the frame and carefully sits down next to the light. She is breathing heavily. Joseph comes and sits beside her. He looks at her. She looks up toward the sky.

[GYM NOISE; CRICKETS; DISTANT CHEERS; FOOTSTEPS; HEAVY BREATHING; WHISTLE; DOG BARKS; WIND]

258. LS. The full moon in the upper left corner, the white globe in the lower foreground.

[BACH—VIOLIN; WIND]

259. LS. Rolling blue-green waves on an expansive horizon.

[BACH—VIOLIN; WIND]

260. LS. Swelling waves rolling to shore.

[BACH—VIOLIN; WIND]

261. **LS.** The gas station covered in snow. On the roof above the pumps, the word *self* is visible, the rest of the sign covered by snow.

[BACH—VIOLIN]

262. **LS.** A slow camera tilt follows a low airplane at night, seen through silhouetted trees.

[BACH—VIOLIN; AIRPLANE]

263. **MS.** Through the windshield of a moving car during a snowy night, a snowplow ahead is visible, its lights flashing.

[BACH—VIOLIN; CRIES OF A BABY; BACH ENDS]

(Intertitle 10:) EN CE TEMPS LA

AT THAT TIME
[BACH—VIOLIN]

264. **MCU.** A cow licks her newborn calf.

[COW LICKS AND MOOS]

265. **MS.** A young child stands in a barn, near a cow.

Joseph (vo): Oh, Mary, what a strange road . . .

266. **MCU.** Two rabbits.

Joseph (vo): I had to take to reach you.

267. **MS.** Trees with pink blossoms in full bloom.

Mary (off): Now what's wrong?

268. **CU.** Slight pan right. Two horses—one turns its head to the right.

[HORSES WHINNY]

269. **LS.** A tree with pink blossoms in full bloom.

Father (vo): Here they are!
[RUSHING BROOK]

270. **MS.** Seated inside a car, Mary hands her baby out to her father. In the background, Joseph and a woman stand on the opposite side of the car. Mary's father hands the baby back to Mary.

[RUSHING BROOK]
Mary: Do you believe it now?
Father: Will he call Joseph "Dad"? What'll you do? Tell him later that's not his father?
Mary: That's life.

271. **MCU.** A donkey being held by its bridle.

[RUSHING BROOK]
Joseph (off): I came about the station. [CHICKENS CLUCK]
Father (off): We'll talk about it.
Joseph (off): I figured it out. I can pay it back in 2 years.

272. **MCU.** Inside the car, the baby wriggles in Mary's lap.

[BACH—CHORAL]

273. MCU. The donkey, held in a bridle, stares into the camera.

[BACH—CHORAL]
Father (off): Sure!
Joseph (off): —No.—
Mary (off): Dad! Joseph!
Woman (off): Thanks, Mary.
[BABY CRIES; BACH — CHORAL; CAR DOOR SLAMS]
For every woman.

274. LS. In front of a country house, Mary and a pregnant woman slowly stroll, each taking a turn holding the baby.

[BACH ENDS; BABY CRIES; RUSHING BROOK]

275. LS. Trees with pink blossoms in bloom. A bird soars up through frame.

[BACH—PIANO]

276. MS. In an indoor swimming pool, Mary, with baby in arms, bursts forth from beneath the water's surface.

[WATER SPLASHES; BACH — PIANO]

277. MS. In an orange-gray sky, the sun, half enveloped in clouds, arches up.

[BACH—PIANO]

278. MS. In the pool, Mary holds her baby afloat on his back while he paddles and splashes the water with his feet and arms.

[BACH ENDS; WATER SPLASHES; BABY CRIES]

279. MLS. A field of bright yellow flowers.

[BACH—PIANO; BABY CRIES]

280. LS. Mary and baby in the pool. While the baby splashes to stay afloat, Joseph joins them.

[BACH ENDS; BABY CRIES; SILENCE]
Mary (vo): How did He look? What was He like? There are no looks . . . in love, no outward seeming.

281. MS. Low angle. The sun radiates through yellow flowers in bloom.

Mary (vo): No likeness. Only our hearts will tremble in the light.

282. ELS. High angle. Four small boys are seen in a forest glade. Two are playing with a ball. One boy (Jesus) comes over to speak to them and leads them away. The fourth boy runs to follow along.

[DISTANT TRAFFIC; BIRDS; OUTDOOR RUSTLE]
Mary (vo): I can't describe Him as He stood there, but I can tell you how the women looked on seeing Him. [CHILDREN'S SHOUTS; BALL KICKED]

Jesus: Come with me. Come with me. What's your name?
Fabian: Fabian.
Jesus: Now your name's Peter. And what's your name?
Florent: Florent.
Jesus: Now your name's James.
Fourth Boy: What's my name?

283. **MS.** In a kitchen, Mary stands behind Joseph, who sits at a table opposite young Jesus, his back to the camera. Mary pours coffee for them. She holds out her nightgown as her son ducks under it.

Joseph: Where's my coffee? I'm late. [BREAKFAST CLATTER]
Jesus: Where's my coffee! Where's my coffee!
Mary: Junior'd better be nice this morning. Or we won't play whale tonight.
Jesus: Please, Mom,

284. **MS.** Mary, in her nightgown, looks down toward Jesus, who is under her nightgown.

Jesus (off): let's play whale! What's that called?
Mary: The hedgehog, or the lawn.
Jesus (off): What's that called?
Mary: Bells.
Jesus: What's that called?
Mary: Loaves . . . bread . . .
Joseph (off): He's too old to see you naked now. [HITS TABLE]
Mary: *Quia respexit*, Joseph.

285. **MS.** Seated at the kitchen table, Jesus drinks from his cup while Mary strokes his hair.

Joseph (off): Some day, you know, [BACH—CONTRALTO WITH CHORAL] he who is your father may forget you. Then you'll regret I'm not around.

286. **MS.** Jesus stands alongside the car and reaching into the passenger window he hands Mary a bouquet of white flowers as she hands him his blue sweater. Joseph sits behind the wheel.

[BACH—ORCHESTRA]
Mary: Look at me!

287. **CU.** Jesus viewed from inside the car.

Jesus: I am He who is.
[BACH ENDS]
Joseph (off): Quit clowning! Get in! [THUNDER]

288. **MS.** The car is parked alongside a patch of trees. Jesus runs away from the car into the background and

Jesus (off): I must tend to my Father's affairs. [THUNDER]
Joseph: By God, we'll see about that!

offscreen left as Joseph gets out of the car and begins to chase after him. Mary gets out. Joseph stops and returns to the car.

289. LS. A sunny tree-ridged meadow.

290. MS. The legs of a woman in white high-heel shoes stroll across a painted intersection. She carries a red shopping bag. Following her can be seen the legs of a man wearing red, white, and blue saddle shoes.

291. MS. The same two pairs of legs as those in 290 stroll past painted arrows on a roadway surface.

292. MS. The feet of the woman in white heels and other pedestrians' feet, including the man in saddle shoes, are viewed crossing a roadway crosswalk.

293. MS. Dressed in white, Mary steps up to her car in the foreground, as Gabriel, wearing his saddle shoes, arrives alongside, his car in the background. He calls out. As Mary puts her shopping bag in her car and climbs in, Gabriel stands by his open car door and honks his horn to get her attention. Looking over, Mary gets out of her car.

294. MS. Gabriel stands by his car and raises his arm in salute.

295. MS. Mary stands alongside her car, but Gabriel and his car have now disappeared. She looks around, looks up to the sky, then gets back into her car.

296. MCU. Facing left and seated inside her car, Mary lights and smokes a cigarette.

297. CU. A very faint smile comes and goes upon Mary's face. She smokes her cigarette. She rests her

Mary: Stop it! [THUNDER] He'll be back. [BACH —ORCHESTRA]
Joseph: When? [BACH ENDS]
Mary: At Easter,

Mary: or Trinity Sunday. [CAR DOOR SLAMS; CAR STARTS]

[TRAFFIC; FOOTSTEPS]

[TRAFFIC; FOOTSTEPS]

[TRAFFIC; FOOTSTEPS]

Gabriel: Madam! [HONKS HORN] Hey, Madam.
Mary: What is it?

Gabriel: Nothing. Hail, Mary! [TRAFFIC; BELLS RING; BIRDS]

[BELLS: BIRDS; TRAFFIC]

[BELLS; BACH—CHORAL; BIRDS]

[BACH—CHORAL; BIRDS; AIRPLANE]

	Le Père	Tu es toujours tellement impatiente.
	La Mère	Peut-être.
		Ce que je sais maintenant, Paul,
		c'est que j'ai plus besoin d'être maîtrisée pour me sentir comprise,
		j'ai plus besoin de perdre.
	Le Père	Je vois pas ce que tu vas gagner non plus avec ça.
	La Mère	Je sais pas.
		J'ai envie de voir clair.
26.		J'aurais bien aimé que tu comprennes.
	Le Père	Y a pénurie de compréhension.
		La vérité apporte souvent la mort et tes vérités sont fatales,
		ne viens pas t'en plaindre ensuite.
	La Mère	Je ne me plains pas. Je cherche seulement à voir clair,
		et je ne vois pas pourquoi tout le monde a si peur
27.		de la clarté.
	Marie	T'as mal aux yeux?
	Le Père	Mais non, ça va.
		Ta sincérité absolue ne m'intéresse pas.
		C'est réconfortant humainement, mais c'est pas intéressant.
		On va pas recommencer.
28.	**La Mère**	Non, on va pas recommencer.
		Mais tu pourrais t'intéresser à comprendre quelquefois.
		Pendant dix ans on a fait de la copie,
		maintenant j'ai besoin d'inventer.
	Le Père	Mais personne t'a empêchée d'inventer.
		De toute façon les femmes inventent peu.

29.		Même l'âme, c'est un homme qui l'a inventée.
30.	**La Mère**	C'est fou ce que tu es encourageant.
	Le Père	Ah ben maintenant, tu te passes d'encouragements.
		Tu nous montres comme tu te débrouilles bien toute seule.
	Marie	Bonjour. Voilà la suite de notre opération.
		Alors, maintenant, nous coupons l'oeil en deux.
		Voyez, l'oeil est noirci, si vous pouvez le constater.
31.		Je mets ceci à l'intérieur, qui est la pupille.
32.		La pupille, vue de l'extérieur, grossie évidemment,
		est marron.
		L'oeil est énorme,
		mais la pupille prend beaucoup de place,
		et le reste, c'est de l'eau.
33.		C'est de l'eau, oui,
		voyez, la pupille flotte comme un bébé dans le ventre de sa mère.
		Quand on regarde quelque chose, c'est à cause de la pupille,
		parce qu'elle flotte,
		et quand on bouge,
		voyez, elle se déplace.
		Vous comprenez ce que je vous dis?
	La Mère	C'est assez compliqué, c'est technique un peu.
34.	**Marie**	Oui, oui, c'est en même temps mécanique et en même temps technique,
		et en même temps chirurgique.
		C'est une seule opération pour ce genre de maladie.
		Si on en fait deux, à la deuxième, il meurt l'individu.
		De toute façon

35.		l'oeil se fane après.
36.		C'est une opération vraiment très grave,
		oui, ça je suis entièrement d'accord.
		C'est une opération qu'on subit après qu'on ait eu presque une maladie.
		Parce que ce monsieur-là, voyez, l'oeil de ce monsieur,
		eh bien il a été complètement bouleversé, voyez,
		il a eu un choc,
		il a été complètement terrorisé cet oeil,
		alors,
37.		on ne pourra pas tellement le ravoir.
		Voilà. Nous rendons l'antenne,
		au revoir.
	Le Père	Tu as parlé à Marie?
	La Mère	Pas encore,
		mais je lui parlerai bien sûr.
		Il faudra que tu lui dises aussi ce qui te retient loin d'elle,
		de moi.
	Le Père	Mais tu as pensé à ce que ça représentera pour elle,
		ce trafic d'un parent à l'autre?
	La Mère	Arrête d'en parler comme si tout ça venait de moi seulement.
	Marie	Un peu de silence.
38.		"Je sens fondre sur moi de lourdes épouvantes
		et de noirs bataillons de fantômes épars
		qui veulent me conduire en des routes mouvantes
		qu'un horizon sanglant ferme de toutes parts.
		Avons-nous donc commis une action étrange?
		Explique si tu peux mon trouble et mon effroi."
		Silence.
		J'ai dit silence.

39.

Est-ce que quelqu'un peut me dire

ce que Baudelaire a voulu exprimer en écrivant ces vers?

Si bien sûr, vous n'avez pas trop dormi.

Bon, sortez vos cahiers, je vais vous dicter quelques phrases.

Allez, vite, vite, nous n'avons pas que ça à faire.

"Je sens fondre sur moi de lourdes épouvantes,

de lourdes épouvantes,

et de noirs bataillons,

—avec deux l—

de fantômes épars."

Silence.

Oui?

La Mère   Marie, il faut que je te dise quelque chose.

Marie   Bon,

40.

continuez. Et vérifiez si vous n'avez pas fait de fautes d'orthographe.

Il faut que je parle avec la directrice.

La Mère   Tu sais sûrement ce que je vais te dire.

Papa va aller habiter ailleurs. Pas pour longtemps.

Jusqu'à l'hiver par exemple.

Marie   Bon, je reprends.

... "qui veulent me conduire en des routes mouvantes..."

La Mère   Marie,

41.

tu verras papa les week-ends, les jours de congé,

de toute façon c'est pas pour longtemps.

Marie   "Avons-nous donc commis une action étrange? Explique si..."

La Mère   Tu sais, Marie, c'est pas qu'on s'aime plus.

Au contraire.

Mais c'est mieux que de rester là à se disputer.

42.		Marie, il n'y a pas de raison de t'inquiéter. Je te le dirais sinon.
		Crois-moi, tu peux me faire confiance.
43.	**TV**	Pourquoi est-ce que tu ne veux pas qu'on aille à Capri?
		Parce que tu es un âne.
44.		Tu me fais peur, Paul,
		d'ailleurs, c'est pas la première fois.
	Le Père	Je suis venu un peu plus tôt que prévu. Tu veux que je t'aide?
	TV	Tu n'avais qu'à me répondre. Pourquoi est-ce que tu ne réponds pas au lieu de rester les bras en bas?
	La Mère	Non, non, ça va.
	TV	Tu as l'air... Pourquoi est-ce que...
	Le Père	J'ai deux ou trois choses à prendre. Ca sera pas long.
	TV	Je te demande pardon.
45.	**Le Père**	Je suis pressé là, Marie.
	TV	Vas-y toi, Paul, à Capri.
	Le Père	Je t'attends samedi au train,
46.		d'accord?
	TV	Pourquoi, il t'a dit quelque chose?
		Absolument pas.
47.	**No Dialogue**	
48.	**Marie**	Tu me racontes...
		quand j'étais petite.
	La Mère	Encore!
	Marie	Allez.
	La Mère	Il me semble que tu aimes particulièrement entendre ça.
		Tu as raison.
		C'est le plus fort souvenir d'amour.

		Ce qui est difficile, c'est de retrouver cette force
49.		sans revenir en arrière.
50.	**No Dialogue**	
51.		En fait, il suffit de savoir donner et recevoir.
		Bon, je vais faire à manger, je t'attends en bas.
		Allez, sèche bien tes cheveux, Marie.
52.–53.	**No Dialogue**	
54.	**Fille 1**	Hé, Marie!
		Salut.
	Fille 2	Salut.
	Marie	Salut.
	Fille 1	Tu fais quoi?
55.	**Marie**	Je vais à la gare.
	Fille 2	Mais tu vas où?
	Marie	Ben, voir mon père.
	Fille 2	Mais il habite pas ici?
	Marie	Non, pas pour le moment.
56.	**Fille 1**	Ils sont divorcés tes parents?
	Marie	Mais non, ils sont pas divorcés.
	Fille 2	C'est ton ours?
	Marie	Oui.
	Fille 1	En tout cas, je suis bien contente que mes parents soient pas divorcés.
		T'as vraiment pas de chance.
57.	**Marie**	Bon, ça suffit là.
58.	**Copi**	Salut Mimi.
59.	**Marie**	Je m'appelle pas Mimi, je m'appelle Marie.
	Copi	Tu vas où Mimi?
	Marie	Je vais voir mon père.
	Copi	Oh c'est bien.
		Ah c'est vrai, il est plus là.
		Mais ça lui fait du bien tu sais, un peu...

Marie	Bon, on va pas en faire un drame.
Copi	On ben sûrement pas.
Copi	De toute façon comme ça, toi, tu peux naviguer avec ton petit ours, comme ça c'est pas gênant.
Marie	C'est pas un ours, c'est une panthère.
Copi	Ah c'est ça, oui. T'as raison.
	Moi je suis très peu connaisseur de bêtes. Je sais pas.
Marie	Et toi, tu vas où?
Copi	Ben moi, je me distrais comme ça. Je suis à l'assurance, tu vois.
	Je travaille pas ces temps.
	Je reste à la maison, j'ai tellement de ménage à faire, etc.,
	parce que j'aime bien que chez moi, c'est pas mal propre, tu vois.
Marie	Tu t'ennuies pas?
Copi	Non, je m'ennuie pas du tout. Parce que
	j'étudie mon cas en même temps comme ça.
	Et puis, j'ai mon programme pour la sortie de l'après-midi.
	Avec ma petite bicyclette, vélomoteur, comme tu veux l'appeler, puis voilà.
	Y me ramène partout,
	puis j'arrive peut-être à sept heures, à neuf heures, le soir,
	s'il fait beau, je suis pas pressé pour rentrer.

60.   Je m'arrête dans tous les coins, hé.

Marie	Maudit soit à jamais le rêveur inutile
	qui voulut le premier, dans sa stupidité

61.

	s'éprenant d'un problème insoluble et stérile,
	aux choses de l'amour, mêler l'honnêteté.
Haut-Parleur	Sur voie 4, train direct pour Nyon, Morges, Lausanne,

Berne, Olten, Lucerne et Chiasso,

en voiture s'il vous plaît.

62.   **Le Père**   Vous avez déjà un peu appris les triangles?

Marie   Non, on a juste commencé.

Là, je dois apprendre les quatre triangles pour lundi.

Le Père   Tu te souviens ce que c'est une ligne brisée?

Marie   C'est une ligne qui change de direction.

Le Père   Oui, mais comment?

Marie   En faisant des angles.

Le Père   Et un angle?

Marie   C'est quand les lignes se ferment.

Le Père   Et quand elles se rencontrent?

Marie   C'est le sommet.

63.   **Le Père**   Ca s'appelle aussi l'intersection.

Marie   C'est comme ça un angle.

Le Père   Oui, mais aussi comme ça.

Marie   Ah non, comme ça.

Le Père   Pour qu'il y ait ça, faut d'abord qu'il y ait ça.

Bon, alors,

il y a quatre sortes de triangles.

Le triangle rectangle,

c'est celui qui a un angle droit,

64.   et son côté opposé à l'angle droit s'appelle l'hypoténuse.

Le triangle équilatéral,

c'est celui qui a trois côtés égaux.

Le triangle isocèle,

tu m'écoutes Marie?

65.   Le triangle isocèle a deux côtés égaux,

et le scalène a trois côtés inégaux.

66.   Essaie de dessiner aussi, tu t'en souviendras mieux.

67.		T'as faim, Marie?
	Marie	Oui, énorme.
68.	Marie	T'en veux?
		C'est celui-là que j'aimais bien de concerto?
	Le Père	Oui, c'est celui-là.
		Tu le reconnais pas?
	Marie	Ah oui.
69.		Non, pas tellement, en fait.
		On dirait des phrases, tu trouves pas?
		Des gens qui s'expliquent.
	Le Père	Qui se disputent ou qui s'entendent?
	Marie	Un peu les deux.
		Saute d'humeur, glacial, exaspéré,
		j'exige,
		feu, feu, attention, erreur, horreur, souffrance...
	Le Père	Ho, ho, calme-toi.
		Il y a une symphonie de Mahler que je retrouve pas.
		Tu demanderas à ta mère de te la donner la prochaine fois.
	Marie	D'accord.
70.	Le Père	Marie,
		ramène aussi ton pyjama.
		Et n'oublie pas ta brosse à dents, cette fois.
		Allez, faut y aller maintenant. C'est l'heure.
		T'es prête?
71.–79.	**No Dialogue**	
80.	La Mère	Marie...
		Marie.
	La Mère	Hou la...
	La Mère	Eh bien Marie,
		est-ce que tu es morte ou est-ce que tu es simplement fatiguée?

La Mère	Hou hou...
Marie	Morte.
La Mère	Mais tout ce qui arrive, ça devrait t'intéresser, toi qui es si curieuse.
	Tu m'étonnes.
Marie	C'est plus comme avant.
La Mère	Mais rien ne peut rester comme avant.
	Ca devient,
	ça devient,

81.

	ça devient autrement.
	Tu vois bien, quand plus rien ne bouge,
	c'est que c'est mort.
	Il faut de la confiance, Marie.
Marie	Oui, mais quand même, c'est plus comme avant.
La Mère	Est-ce que tu as remarqué ce qu'il y a dans ton nom, Marie?
Marie	Quoi?
La Mère	Il y a aimer.
Marie	Ah oui.

82. **Marie**   Oh, t'es belle. Elle est belle ta robe.

L'Ami	J'ai peur qu'on soit en retard, faut y aller.
Marie	Ca te va bien cette coiffure.
La Mère	Tu trouves? C'est pas vraiment comme ça que je me préfère.
Marie	Ah si, t'es chou vraiment.
La Mère	Bon, je te laisse le numéro, Marie.

83.

	S'il y a quelque chose, tu appelles, de toute façon je ne rentre pas tard.
Marie	Demain, c'est moi qui sors, t'as pas oublié?
La Mère	Oh non, Marie, j'ai pas oublié.
L'Ami	Bon, faut y aller, là.
La Mère	Bon, faut que j'y aille, ma chérie.
	Pas trop longtemps, la télé, hein?
	Je viens t'embrasser quand je rentre.

	La Mère (suite)	A tout à l'heure.
84.	**Marie**	Ce serait tuer dans l'oeuf l'organisation de l'Europe.
		Il faut absolument étouffer cette affaire,
		dans l'oeuf.
		D'ailleurs on ne fait pas d'omelette sans casser des oeufs.
		Alors,
		je sais pas, moi.
85.		Va te faire cuire un oeuf,
		ça me paraît la seule solution.
	Carton	EN CE TEMPS-LA
1.–2.	**No Dialogue**	

Je vous salue, Marie

3.–6.	**No Dialogue**	
7.	**Juliette**	Tout ce qui sort de ma bouche, ça devient de la merde.
	Joseph	Arrête-toi de parler, c'est simple.
	Juliette	Arrête-toi, toi aussi, de manger.
	Carton	EN CE TEMPS-LA
	Juliette	Avec toi, des fois, je supporte mal le silence.
8.		On peut se marier si tu veux.
		J'ai pas peur.
		Peut-être que ça pourra nous aider.
		Je me demande...
	Joseph	Quoi?
	Juliette	Toutes les femmes désirent quelque chose qui soit unique au monde.
	Joseph	Tu vois pas que je t'écoute pas.
		Tu sais,
		les hommes croient qu'ils entrent dans une femme.

9.	**No Dialogue**	
	Carton	EN CE TEMPS-LA
	Juliette	Où t'en es avec Marie?
10.	**Joseph**	C'est mes affaires.
11.	**No Dialogue**	
12.	**Entraineur**	Ecoute Marie,
		chaque fois qu'il y a un passage, tu n'hésites pas,
		il faut absolument l'empêcher de passer,
		c'est tout.
	Marie	Je me demandais si quelque événement allait survenir dans ma vie,
13.–15.	**No Dialogue**	
16.		de l'amour, je n'avais que l'ombre,
17.		oui,
		et même l'ombre d'une ombre,
		comme lorsqu'on aperçoit dans l'étang le reflet d'un nénuphar,
		non pas tranquille, mais agité par les rides de l'eau,
		si bien que ce reflet tout déformé vous échappe en partie,
		cependant
18.	**ensemble**	(le monde en était pour moi renouvelé.
	Professeur	(Et que le soleil enfin visible
		se mette à briller sur les océans primitifs,
		alors, la vie apparut, dit-on,
		tout à fait par hasard,
		il y avait de l'hydrogène, de l'azote.
	Carton	EN CE TEMPS-LA
	Élève	Et s'il n'y avait pas de hasard?

19.	Eva	Cent fois celle de l'univers?
	Professeur	Ca signifie quoi?
		Qu'il n'y a jamais eu le temps,
		le hasard n'a pas eu le temps,
		puisque la vie n'a pas eu le temps d'apparaître,
	Voix	sur la terre,
20.	Professeur	c'est parce qu'elle est venue d'ailleurs,
		de l'espace,
		on se demande à quoi peut bien ressembler un extra-terrestre,
		prenez un miroir et regardez-vous,
		okay,
		c'est juste une hypothèse, mais
21.		regardez ce creux,
		ça s'explique seulement
		si quelque chose dans ce nuage intercepte la lumière
		à une longueur d'onde bien précise.
		Or, il y a une bactérie,
		d'une sorte très répandue,
		qui absorbe la lumière sur trois, quatre microns,
		c'est sa signature,
		tout corps, inerte ou vivant,
		laisse sa marque particulière dans le champ électrique,
		à mon avis,
		il y a là
		une très forte présomption
		que la vie existe dans l'espace,
		on vient de là
22.		nous sommes tous des extra-terrestres,
		on n'est pas né dans une soupe d'amino-acides,
		brusquement, par hasard,
		rien à faire,
		les chiffres sont contre.

	Élève	Et s'il n'y avait pas de hasard?
	Professeur	Exactement,
		c'est l'invraisemblable vérité,
		la vie a été voulue,
		désirée,
		prévue,
		ordonnée
		programmée par une intelligence résolue.
		Eve, mettez-vous derrière Pascal.
	Eva	Eva, monsieur, Eva.
	Professeur	Oui, mettez-vous derrière Pascal, et rendez-le aveugle.
23.		On a dit qu'il faudra mille trois cent cinquante milliards d'années
		pour trouver la solution les yeux bandés, mais
		s'il y a quelqu'un à côté de vous qui voit clair,
		et qui vous dit non à chaque mouvement qui est faux,
		et oui à chaque mouvement qui vous rapproche de la solution,
		à raison d'un geste par seconde,
		il faudra combien?
	Élève	Deux minutes.
	Professeur	De mille trois cent cinquante milliards d'années à deux minutes,
24.		c'est ce qui s'est passé,
		il y a de la mémoire.
	Eva	oui, oui,
		oui, oui,
		non,
25.		oui, oui,
		non,
26.		oui, oui, oui,
		oui, oui, oui,
		non.

27.	Élève	C'est pour ces idées qu'on vous a chassé ou autre chose?
	Professeur	Ca, et autre chose,
		au revoir, à lundi.
	Élève	La loi de la chute des corps, c'est parce que la vie est tombée du ciel?
	Professeur	Oui, au revoir.
	Eva	Alors.
	Élève	Tu viens?
	Eva	Vous viendrez un soir boire un verre à la maison?
28.	Professeur	Ca, c'est un autre scénario.
29.–33.	No Dialogue	
34.	Petite Fille	Ton soulier, ton soulier.
35.	No Dialogue	
36.	Joseph	C'est de savoir si cette créature appelée l'homme a jamais existé,
		l'homme tel qu'il apparaît dans la légende n'est qu'une création de l'imagination populaire.
37.	No Dialogue	
38.	L'Ange	Tant qu'il restera des Bourbons en Espagne, on ne sera pas tranquille.
	Petite Fille	Mais non, oncle Gabriel, c'est pas ça le texte.
	L'Ange	Ah oui,
39.		tout droit.
	Joseph	C'est où, tout droit.
	L'Ange	Voilà cinq cents dollars, et pas de commentaire mon vieux.
40.	No Dialogue	
41.		Non, d'ailleurs, c'est fermé.
42.	Petite Fille	Et là?
	L'Ange	Non, je ne crois pas, il doit y avoir une maison à côté.

	Joseph	Qu'est-ce que vous cherchez?
43.	**Petite Fille**	Ici, ici.
	L'Ange	Arrêtez-vous à cette station.
44.	**Joseph**	Non, non.
	L'Ange	Voilà cinq cents dollars, vous obéissez nom de Dieu.
		On revient,
45.		vous avez pas une fille qui s'appelle Marie?
	Le Père	Qu'est-ce que vous lui voulez?
	Joseph	Marie, Marie.
	L'Ange	Elle est là, nom de Dieu.
46.	**Petite Fille**	Nom de Dieu.
	Père	Marie, au secours, Marie.
47.	**Petite Fille**	Marie.
	L'Ange	Marie.
48.	**Marie**	Qu'est-ce que tu fais là, on avait dit samedi.
	Joseph	C'est pas moi, c'est eux.
	Marie	Non, laisse, papa, c'est Joseph.
	Joseph	C'est pas moi, je te dis, c'est eux.
	Marie	J'en ai marre de tes trucs, tu sais,
		laisse,
		bon, alors, qu'est-ce qu'il y a?
	L'Ange	Il y a toi, Marie.
	Joseph	T'as raison, elle est folle.
	Petite Fille	Il y a toi, Marie.
	Marie	Qu'est-ce que vous voulez?
	L'Ange	Et toi?
	Petite Fille	Et toi?
49.	**No Dialogue**	
50.	**Marie**	Qu'est-ce que vous voulez?
51.		Qu'est-ce que vous voulez?
	L'Ange	Et vous, ma demoiselle?
		C'est ta fiancée?

	Joseph	Qu'est-ce que ça peut vous faire?
	L'Ange	On s'en fiche. Mais tu vas avoir un enfant.
	Marie	De qui?
	L'Ange	Tu vas avoir un enfant.
	Marie	Je couche avec personne.
	Joseph	Marie, merde,
52.		c'est quoi ces gens?
	L'Ange	Allez. Tout droit, voilà cinq cents dollars.
	Marie	De qui?
	L'Ange	Et il ne sera pas de lui, jamais.
	Marie	De qui?
	L'Ange	Ne fais pas l'innocente.
	Marie	De qui?
	Petite Fille	Marie,
53.		sois pure, sois dure, ne cherche que ta voie.
	Marie	Ma voie,
		mon chemin ou le son de ma voix?
54.	Petite Fille	Ne fais pas l'imbécile,
		j'ai ta parole et tu trouveras bientôt la tienne,
		n'oublie pas.
55.	L'Ange	N'oublie pas, ce qui entre sort,
		et ce qui sort, entre.
56.	Eva	Je suis fatiguée, on s'arrête.
57.	Professeur	Chacun va,
		et chacun parvient jusqu'au lieu où il peut atteindre.
	Eva	Hölderlin, c'est le dernier vers qu'il a écrit.
	Élève	Le dernier ver de terre.
	Eva	Ah, c'est drôle.
	Élève	En tout cas, ces fournis, c'est l'homme invisible.
58.	Élève	Non, je vous jure que c'était là.
	Eva	Mais il n'y a jamais de fourmis au bord de l'eau.

	Élève	C'est faux, il y a des fourmis qui sont chercheuses d'or.
	Eva	Oui, oui, moi aussi j'ai lu l'American Scientific.
	Professeur	C'est quoi ces fourmis?
59.	Élève	Olivier avait trouvé une fourmilière,
		et il avait bricolé une installation électrique pour leur tenir chaud l'hiver.
	Élève	La théorie, c'est que si on empêchait les fourmis de dormir
60.		en hiver,
		on pourrait peut-être transformer leur temps de sommeil en temps de loisir,
		sûrement qu'elles inventeraient des choses.
61.	Professeur	Quoi?
	Élève	J'avais pensé à de la musique?
62.	No Dialogue	
63.	Marie	On n'échappera pas.
64.	No Dialogue	
65.	Joseph	Qu'est-ce que t'inventes, il y a pas de miracles,
		embrasse-moi,
		qu'est-ce que t'inventes, qu'est-ce que t'inventes?
66.	Marie	On n'échappera pas,
		l'un à l'autre.
	Carton	EN CE TEMPS-LA
	Professeur	Si on continuait notre scénario,
67.		imaginez
		nos descendants dans huit millions d'années, ou cent millions,
		ils sont d'une sagesse et d'une science inconcevables aujourd'hui,
		ils s'aperçoivent un jour,

que les grands équilibres de l'univers qui semblaient immuables

sont en train de se modifier, subtilement,

68. **No Dialogue**

69. est-ce que nos lointains descendants

n'essaieraient pas malgré tout de sauver la vie?

Joseph	Embrasse-moi.
Marie	Je t'embrasse, moi.
Joseph	Une seule fois, Marie.
Marie	Il y a qu'à avoir confiance.

70. **No Dialogue**

71. **Professeur** — Une intelligence antérieure a programmé la vie,

c'était une créature qui luttait pour l'existence

72. dans un univers impitoyable,

elle a sauvé la vie.

Carton — EN CE TEMPS-LA

Élève — Comment vous y avez pensé?

73. **Professeur** — A cause des ordinateurs,

quand j'y repense,

l'énorme puissance de calcul de cette intelligence me bouleverse complètement,

74. **No Dialogue**

75. si nos descendants lointains

76. **No Dialogue**

77. décidaient de coder

à leur tour la vie,

78. dans un message de magnésium,

bore,

Dieu sait quoi,

79. est-ce qu'ils ne tenteraient pas de transmettre le secret

	Insert	DIEU
		de l'origine.
80.	**Eva**	Mais peut-être que nous savons lire le message depuis toujours.
	Professeur	Oui, cette voix tout au fond de la conscience,
		qui souffle aux plus attentifs,
		tu es né de quelque chose, ailleurs, dans le ciel,
		cherche, et tu trouveras bien plus
81.		que tu n'imagines.
82.	**Juliette**	T'es venu voir la princesse?
83.		En tout cas, tu peux pas tomber plus bas.
	Joseph	Je t'ai rien demandé.
	Juliette	Tu veux que je lui dise de venir?
	Joseph	Fous-moi la paix.
84.		Marie,
85.		à quoi ça t'avance de pas dire la vérité?
	Marie	Je te la dis,
		peut-être que les mots sortent mal,
		ou ma voix,
		mais je la dis.
	Joseph	Pourquoi tu dis pas que t'as rencontré d'autres hommes, ça simplifierait?
86.	**Marie**	Je couche avec personne.
	Joseph	D'où il viendra cet enfant, alors?
87.		D'où il viendra cet enfant, alors?
88.		Réponds, alors,
		regarde-moi.
	Marie	Je te regarde.
89.	**Joseph**	Il vient bien de quelque part cet enfant.
		Pourquoi depuis deux ans je peux jamais te toucher?

90.		Embrasse-moi.
	Marie	Mais je sais pas, Joseph.
	Joseph	C'est pas vrai, nom de Dieu, mais c'est pas vrai.
	Juliette	Téléphone, si tu veux, ou passe un soir au cinéma.
	Joseph	Embrasse-moi, je t'en supplie, Marie.
	Marie	Pas comme ça,
		je t'embrasse, moi, c'est vrai.
	Joseph	Je suis sûr que tu couches avec des autres, c'est impossible autrement,
		j'espère qu'ils ont des grosses queues au moins,
91.–92.	**No Dialogue**	
93.		c'est fini, Marie, tchao.
94.	**Client**	Salut, t'es là aussi?
	Client	J'arrête pas de rêver, ça me fatigue, je dors plus,
		cette nuit, avant de rentrer chez moi,
		j'ai rêvé que j'étais obligé de repeindre toute la façade de l'immeuble,
		je me suis dit: ça va prendre du temps, mon vieux,
95.		ça va prendre du temps, j'ai pas dormi.
	Client	Il y a sûrement une explication, faut noter des fois.
	Client	Oui, mais tu vois, je sais pas écrire, alors je dessine.
	Client	Oui, mais alors, c'est parce que c'est des images que tu n'oublies pas.
	Client	Faut que j'apprenne à écrire alors,
96.		si je veux oublier.
	Client	Tout à fait.
	Docteur	Ton père va bien?
	Marie	Oui, merci.
	Docteur	Toujours dans l'essence?
	Marie	Non, non, il veut quitter.
	Docteur	Et ce mariage, ça approche?
		C'est fini, Joseph,

		il avait l'air sérieux.
		Esther, la chemise de Madame Malignon.
		Alors, qu'est-ce qui ne vas pas, Marie?
	Marie	J'ai mal,
		dans le ventre.
	Docteur	Bien, on va voir ça,
		vous lui prendrez la tension, Esther,
		toi passe à côté, enlève ta robe, j'arrive.
97.		Oui,
		non,
		non, non et non,
		il faudra grossir,
		et tout ira bien, tu verras.
	Marie	Est-ce que l'âme a un corps?
	Docteur	Qu'est-ce que tu racontes, ma fille, c'est le corps qui a une âme.
	Marie	Je vais être bien triste, je croyais le contraire,
		docteur.
98.	**Marie**	Docteur, je dois avoir un enfant.
	Docteur	Tu as eu tes règles quand?
		Allez, enlève ta culotte et étends-toi là.
	Marie	Mais ça va servir à rien,
99.		quoi?
		Qu'est-ce que vous dites? J'ai pas entendu.
	Docteur	Je disais que je me suis toujours demandé ce qu'on savait d'une femme,
		et j'ai découvert qu'on ne peut en savoir
		que ce qu'un homme en a déjà su,
		il y a là un mystère.
100.		Tu le veux cet enfant?
		C'est avec Joseph?

	Marie	C'est avec personne.
	Docteur	Qu'est-ce que tu chantes, allez, étends-toi.
	Marie	Je chante pas, je suis joyeuse.
	Docteur	Pourquoi tu me dis pas pour tes règles?
		Il faut bien que je t'examine puisque tu me dis que tu as mal.
101.	Marie	Elles sont venues normalement, même plus forte que d'habitude.
	Docteur	Quand?
	Marie	Vendredi.
	Docteur	Mais alors arrête de faire l'imbécile, il va rien y avoir.
	Marie	Ben allez-y, regardez, je dors avec personne,
		je touche personne,
		personne ne me caresse,
		mais je viens pour que vous regardiez si mon enfant est déjà là.
	Docteur	Tu nous caches
102.		quelque chose, Marie.
	Marie	Rien, je vous dis,
		voyez,
		voyez, je vais avoir un enfant et je n'ai connu aucun homme.
		Joseph ne le croit pas,
		dites-lui que c'est vrai.
	Docteur	Ne remue pas sans arrêt, petite.
	Marie	Vous allez me faire mal?
	Docteur	T'as pas à avoir peur,
		c'était moi qui étais déjà là à ta naissance.
	Marie	Etre vierge, ça devrait être...
		être disponible,
		ou libre,
		pas faire mal,
		alors,
103.		vous me croyez?
		alors, vous le croyez?

	Docteur	C'est vrai que c'est vrai.
	Marie	Vous le direz à Joseph.
	Docteur	Esther.
		Je peux me rehabiller?
104.	Joseph	Il faut qu'il soit de moi.
105.	Joseph	Où on va maintenant?
	Eva	Villa Paradis, sur la route d'Hermance.
	Joseph	Vous savez, je termine à dix-sept heures.
	Eva	Oui, oui, ça va, ça va.
	Professeur	C'est en France?
	Eva	Tout près, vous verrez,
		c'est aussi beau que la Tchécoslovaquie,
		alors,
		alors,
		alors.
106.–109.	No Dialogue	
110.	Marie	Et cependant, j'éprouvais une sorte de joie à offrir ainsi mon corps
		au regard de celui qui était devenu mon maître pour toujours,
		en glissant un regard
111.		vers cet être merveilleux,
		car en vérité, alors comme aujourd'hui, il l'était,
		non par son aspect ni par ses actes,
		mais par cette force muette qu'il recélait,
		cette puissance concentrée aussi formidable qu'une grande montagne élevée vers le ciel,
		et qu'on ne pouvait ni mesurer, ni décrire,
		mais simplement, sentir.
112.		Ce soir,
		non j'ai l'entraînement, tu sais bien.
	Joseph	Bon, très bien, je vais me jeter au lac.
	Marie	Oh, te jeter au lac,
		mais Ophélie, c'est pas un rôle pour toi.

	Joseph	De quoi tu parles, je comprends pas.
	Marie	Etre ou ne pas être, t'as pas appris ça à l'école?
	Joseph	Je suis pas comme toi, j'ai dû arrêter l'école à douze ans.
	Marie	Excuse-moi,
		bon, je te laisse.
	Joseph	Bon, très bien, je vais me jeter dans le lac.
	Marie	Non, arrête.
113.–116.	**No Dialogue**	
117.	**Eva**	Johannes.
	Professeur	Oui.
	Eva	Andréa?
		A quoi vous pensez?
	Professeur	Le soir, il change sa propre figure et son propre sens.
	Eva	Heidegger, trois conférences à...
	Professeur	Bayerische Akademie.
	Eva	Hiver 59.
	Professeur	Oui.
	Eva	Vous savez pourquoi il n'a pas été fusillé?
		J'ai déjà remarqué que dès qu'on parle
		de politique, vous restez silencieux,
		ça va, ça va, Andréa, laissez-nous,
		c'est vrai, non?
118.	**Professeur**	Vous savez, il me semble que la politique aujourd'hui
		ne peut être que la voix de l'horreur.
	Eva	La voix, mais le chemin ou la parole?
	Professeur	La parole de l'horreur, dont rien ne peut être dit,
		je peux mettre ça?

	Eva	C'est quoi?
	Professeur	Impossible de trouver ça à Prague, vous savez.
119.	**No Dialogue**	
120.	**Eva**	Ca va?
	Professeur	Une cigarette, un air de saxo, c'est tout ce que l'homme désire.
	Eva	Avec la musique, je me demande souvent...
	Professeur	Quoi?
	Eva	On s'émerveille qu'une nouvelle phrase arrive, mais,
		après tout, il pourrait ne rien y avoir,
		le moment est venu.
	Professeur	Et l'endroit aussi.
121.	**Eva**	Oui,
		non, pas ce soir,
		pas ce soir.
	Marie	Je crois que l'esprit agit sur le corps, le transfigure,
		le couvre d'un voile qui le fait apparaître plus beau qu'il n'est.
		Qu'est-ce donc que la chair
122.		par elle-même?
	Pere	Je vais à mes affaires, je rentre tard, n'oublie pas de relever les compteurs.
	Marie	Oui, papa.
		Qu'est-ce donc que la chair
		par elle-même,
		on peut la regarder et n'en éprouver que du dégoût,
		on peut la voir ivre dans le ruisseau,
		ou morte dans le cercueil,
		car le monde est plein de chair
		comme le comptoir de l'épicier est plein de chandelles au début de l'hiver,
		mais ce n'est qu'après en avoir apporté une chez vous,

		et l'avoir allumée,
		qu'elle peut vous offrir un réconfort.
123.–125.	**No Dialogue**	
126.	**Juliette**	Allez, viens,
		mon corps te plaît pas?
	Joseph	C'est pas ça.
	Juliette	C'est quoi?
		Joseph,
		c'est elle.
	Joseph	Je sais pas,
		ça me rend malade, je sais pas.
	Juliette	Je sais, je sais, c'est elle,
		toujours.
	Joseph	Non.
	Juliette	Moi aussi je suis une vraie femme.
	Joseph	Oui,
		je voudrais t'aimer mais je sais pas.
	Juliette	Allez, viens, on rentre,
127.		viens.
128.	**Joseph**	Oui, je viens.
129.	**Petite Fille**	Vous en faites des histoires,
		vous trouvez pas, un peu.
	Joseph	Si Dieu existe, alors rien n'est permis.
	Petite Fille	Quoi?
	Joseph	Si Dieu existe, alors rien
130.		n'est permis.
	Juliette	Tu viens, nom de Dieu, ou quoi?
	L'Ange	Qu'est-ce que tu fabriques avec cette pouffiasse?
	Petite Fille	Mais non, oncle Gabriel, pas comme ça.
	L'Ange	Oui, mais dès qu'il est là, j'oublie mon texte, c'est terrible.
		C'est vraiment un zéro, ce type, t'as la liste?

131.	Joseph	La liste de quoi?
	Petite Fille	Il veut tout comprendre.
	L'Ange	Comme les autres.
	Petite Fille	Il sait même pas tenir son chien en laisse.
	L'Ange	Comme les autres.
	Petite Fille	Il a peur du trou.
	L'Ange	Comme les autres.
	Petite Fille	Il choisit mal ses cravates.
	L'Ange	Comme les autres.
	Joseph	Oui, zéro égale zéro.
	Petite Fille	Il oublie la confiance.
132.	L'Ange	C'est pas un défaut, mon vieux,
		quel point commun il y a entre zéro et Marie?
		le corps de Marie.
		Réponds, espèce de nullard.
	Joseph	Je vois pas.
	Petite Fille	Il porte des lunettes d'aveugle, cet imbécile.
	L'Ange	Essaie de suivre le mouvement,
		pas avec la main, avec les yeux, espèce d'enfoiré.
	Petite Fille	Il faut protéger Marie.
133.	Joseph	Si je reste avec elle, on trouvera que je suis ridicule.
	L'Ange	Il regarde pas en face.
	Joseph	Si quelqu'un d'autre lui a fait un enfant.
	L'Ange	On n'est pas quelqu'un d'autre.
	Joseph	Je comprends pas.
	Petite Fille	Il faut avoir confiance,
134.		la confiance.
	Joseph	J'en ai plus.
	L'Ange	Et l'amour espèce de taré.
	Joseph	L'amour.
	Juliette	Moi, je me tire, tchao.
135.–138.	No Dialogue	
139.	Insert	DEMAIN LES CHIENS. (Titre de livre)
	Marie	Je suis venue.
		Qu'est-ce que tu as? C'est encore tes yeux?

Joseph		C'est quoi encore ce livre?
Marie		C'est pour toi.
Joseph		Dans le labyrinthe de la vie, ce jeune ambitieux s'élance,
		le meilleur cheval, la plus riche armure, les plus beaux vêtements,
		être Chevalier, Seigneur, Grand Prince, il veut tout.
		mais quelqu'un
140.		est caché qui l'attend, sans arme, sans titre, sans orgueil, Dieu,
		je te remercie.
Marie		Tu le veux pas.
Joseph		Je préfère mon livre.
Marie		C'était pour changer.
Joseph		Je veux pas.
Marie		Il est drôle, pour la pluie, il disait: soeur pluie,
		et pour le feu: frère feu.
Joseph		Et le corps?
		Pour le corps?
Marie		Le corps,
		le corps,
		le corps: frère âne.
141.	**Joseph**	Pourquoi mon corps te dégoûte, et ne dis pas: je t'embrasse, moi.
	Marie	Non, j'ai peur aussi,
142.		tout ça n'arrive pas tous les jours,
		alors, j'ai peur, un peu,
		faut être deux,
		pourquoi tu crois pas que l'esprit agit sur le corps?
	Joseph	Je crois le contraire.
	Marie	Ca me fait peur.
143.	**Joseph**	Dis-moi que tu m'aimes pas, au moins,
		je supporte pas ce silence.

144.	**Marie**	Frère silence,
		je vois bien que tu m'aimes, mais il faudra autre chose.
	Joseph	Ca t'est bien égal qu'on se voie plus, que je sois malade, que je sois mort.
	Marie	Est-ce que je suis vivante?
		Peut-être que je peux te faire que du mal.
	Joseph	Je comprends pas,
		je comprends pas,
		Marie.
	Marie	C'est un grand secret,
		c'est un grand secret.
145.	**Joseph**	Mon amour.
	Marie	On ne sait pas le dire,
		tellement grand,
		que tout est consommé,
		et tu m'abandonneras.
	Joseph	En tout cas, il faut que je sache.
	Marie	Tu veux savoir quoi?
		La main de Dieu est sur moi, et tu ne peux m'en défendre.
146.	**Joseph**	Qu'est-ce qu'on fait?
	Marie	Je dois rentrer.
	Joseph	C'était pas la peine de venir.
	Marie	C'est pas ton corps,
		ce qui me dégoûterait c'est que tu ne me croies pas.
	Joseph	Pourquoi j'ai pas le droit de vouloir aussi que cet enfant soit de moi?
		Si tu me disais avec qui t'es allée,
		c'est vrai, je m'en fiche, j'accepte, si tu restes avec moi,
147.		si je reste avec toi, si je dors avec toi, si je me réveille avec toi.

	Marie	Et Juliette alors?
	Joseph	Mais je l'aime pas, c'est toi.
	Marie	Très bien,
		regarde,
		donne-moi ta main,
		oh, nom de Dieu,
148.		voilà, touche.
		Tu vois bien que je couche avec personne,
		mais j'aurai quand même un enfant, et si tu ne le crois pas, ça n'ira pas.
	Joseph	Alors, je ne serai que ton ombre.
149.	Marie	Mais l'ombre de Dieu, tout homme ne l'est-il pas?
		Pour une femme qui aime son homme,
150.		je veux que l'âme soit corps,
		et on ne pourra pas dire que le corps est âme, puisque c'est l'âme qui sera corps,
151.		qu'il me soit fait selon votre Parole.
152.–155.	**No Dialogue**	
156.	Joseph	Oui, elle est mariée.
	Homme	Alors, je m'excuse, au revoir Madame.
	Marie	Madame.
	Joseph	Qui c'est?
157.		J'ai reçu ta lettre,
		je pensais pas que le basket c'était ça,
		la fatigue, la victoire,
		la fatigue,
		mais qu'est-ce que tu voulais dire?
		Faudra autre chose,
		tu disais que tu voyais bien que je t'aimais.
	Marie	Oui,
		je le vois.

158.	**Joseph**	Mais tu disais qu'il faudra autre chose.
	Marie	Tu trouveras.
		Qu'est-ce que tu fais toute la journée maintenant?
		Parle-moi.
	Joseph	C'est invraisemblable, il vient jamais,
		ça fait quatre jours que j'attends,
		j'ai réparé le moteur, j'ai installé le téléphone, la vidéo,
		tout marche,
		le matin il me téléphone d'être prêt,
		et le soir arrive, il est pas venu,
		sont étranges,
		les gens riches.
	Carton	EN CE TEMPS-LA
159.	**Marie**	C'est lequel?
	Joseph	Le gros blanc, là-bas.
	Carton	EN CE TEMPS-LA
	Marie	Je peux aller le voir?
160.	**Joseph**	Oui,
		puisqu'on se marie, je pourrai te regarder toute nue,
		une fois,
		je regarderai seulement.
	Marie	Oui,
		tu regarderas.
161.		Il y a longtemps que je ne sais plus ce que c'est
162.		qu'une conversation ordinaire,
		et pourtant la nature l'emporte,
		je voudrais parler comme tout le monde,

parce qu'en dépit des apparences je souffre, comme tout le monde,

et même un peu plus.

Marie   Par force, on tirera de moi ce que je n'ai pas le courage de donner,

163.   vous serez chaste avec moi,

vous ne voudrez pas prendre celui qui, lui, ne vous a jamais pris,

être chaste, c'est connaître toutes les possibilités

164.   sans s'y perdre.

Joseph   C'est là une entreprise impossible,

165.   il faudrait admettre, pour qu'un pareil voyage fût réalisable,

que les étoiles que nous voyons la nuit

166.   sont des vastes mondes situés à de grandes distances du nôtre,

et nul n'ignore, bien entendu,

que les étoiles ne sont que des lumières accrochées au ciel,

167.   dont la plupart sont très, très près de nous,

pour nous, c'est peut-être

168.   la meilleure explication de l'origine

de cette idée d'un autre monde

169.   situé plus loin dans l'espace,

ce n'est, dit-il,

qu'une déformation légendaire de la notion de monde de Horla

170.   dont les chiens connaissent l'existence depuis la lointaine Antiquité,

allez, Arthur,

171.   le moment est venu,

je vais voir la patronne,

je crois qu'on a gagné, cette fois.

172.   **Marie**   Je n'ai plus envie d'y voir clair,

qu'est-ce que ça fait ce que je suis ou ne suis pas,

173.		oh non, pas déjà,
174.	**No Dialogue**	
175.		nous n'échapperons pas plus les uns aux autres que nous ne lui échappons.
176.	**No Dialogue**	
177.	**Joseph**	Marie, qu'est-ce que tu fais? Marie, arrête.
178.	**Marie**	Joseph, Joseph, Joseph, dis-moi que tu m'aimes.
	Joseph	Je t'aime.
179.	**Marie**	Non.
	Joseph	Je t'aime.
	Marie	Non, non.
	Joseph	Je t'aime.
	Marie	Mais non.
	Joseph	Mais Marie, je t'aime.
	Marie	Non, non, non, non.
180.	**No Dialogue**	
181.	**Joseph**	Mais pourquoi? Pourquoi?
	L'Ange	Parce que, parce que c'est la loi,
182.	**No Dialogue**	
183.		alors, t'as compris?
	Joseph	Oui, je me sacrifierai.
	L'Ange	Espèce de trou du cul, d'abord un trou n'est pas un trou, et ensuite: le tabou épargne le sacrifice.

	Joseph	Mais pourquoi?
184.	L'Ange	Parce que c'est la règle.
	Marie	Joseph,
		je t'aime.
	Joseph	Marie.
	Marie	Non,
		oui.
	Joseph	C'est ça, je t'aime?
	Marie	Oui.
	Joseph	C'est ça?
		ça?
	Marie	Oui.
	Joseph	Je t'aime.
	Marie	Oui.
185.	No Dialogue	
186.	Marie	Dans mon coeur naissait une clarté
		chaude et douce comme un feu rayonnant,
		qu'y a-t-il sur la terre ou même au ciel
		qui vaille la certitude de plaire au regard de celui qu'on aime,
		et qui est votre maître,
187.		je me souvenais de ce qu'il avait dit au sujet du péché
		pendant que nous contemplions les libellules,
188.		c'est que si on le considérait de la bonne manière, il n'existait pas,
		il disparaissait, comme l'enveloppe des libellules
		quand elles luttent pour leur liberté.
189.	Marie	Nous parlons
190.		Sa Parole.
	Joseph	Marie.
	Marie	Comment pouvons-nous être autrement proches

191.		de Sa Parole qu'en la parlant.
192.	**Joseph**	Marie.
	Marie	Oui, quoi?
193.		Nous parlons,
		et nous parlons de la Parole,
194.		cela, de quoi nous parlons, la Parole, est toujours déjà en avance sur nous.
195.	**No Dialogue**	
196.	**Joseph**	Alors, tu ne m'abandonneras pas?
		Je resterai,
		je ne te toucherai jamais,
		je resterai.
197.	**No Dialogue**	
198.	**Professeur**	Que le dollar baisse, faut pas le croire,
		que les vacances seront agréables, faut pas le croire,
		que la pluie tombe de haut en bas, ça tu peux le croire,
		c'est une loi de la nature.
	Eva	Le monde est trop triste.
	Professeur	Il n'est pas triste, il est grand,
		je dois m'en aller.
	Eva	Alors, je compte pas pour toi, hein?
199.	**Professeur**	Mais mon fils et ma femme comptent aussi,
		maintenant que j'ai un visa, il faut que j'aille là-bas voir ce qui se passe, non,
		tu comprends?
200.	**Eva**	Ta femme et ton fils, ils comptent jusqu'à combien?
	Professeur	Je comprends pas.
201.	**Eva**	Salaud,
		je m'excuse.
	Professeur	Ça va.
	Eva	Tu me racontes que ta femme est en prison, et pendant ce temps, tu couches avec moi.

	Professeur	Eve, je t'en prie.
	Eva	Eva,
		Eve c'est fini,
		allez, fiche le camp puisque
		c'est ça que tu veux,
		d'abord rends-moi les trente-deux mille francs.
	Professeur	Oui, je les renverrai.
	Eva	T'es vraiment un pauvre type.
202.	**No Dialogue**	
203.	**Marie**	Ce qui fait une âme, c'est sa douleur,
		il sera le premier de ceux qui ont emporté ma douleur pour eux,
204.		et il m'a dit:
		ma fille, j'étouffe de vous voir étouffer,
		—Dieu est un con et un lâche, qui ne veut pas se battre, et ne compte
205.		que sur le cul,
		c'est-à-dire sur le repos du coeur pour être,
		et qu'il faut pousser à bout pour passer,
206.		—Je ne veux pas de la jouissance,
		parce que je ne veux pas m'épuiser le coeur en une fois, pour être,
		ni l'âme en une fois,
		même la douleur ne m'aura pas en une fois,
207.		et je ne disparaîtrai
		pas dedans,
		mais elle disparaîtra avec moi,
208.	**No Dialogue**	
209.		—ce sera toujours épouvantable et terrible
210.		pour moi d'être le maître,
		mais il n'y aura plus de sexualité en moi,
		je connaîtrai le sourire vrai de l'âme,

211.		non à l'extérieur,
212.		mais à l'intérieur,
213.		comme une douleur qui chaque fois se méritera,
214.–217.	**No Dialogue**	
218.		—ce n'est pas une affaire d'expérience, mais de dégoût de tout et de haine pour tout,
		et non de morale ou de dignité,
219.		—il faut que le père
220.		et la mère se baisent sur mon corps, à mort,
		alors Lucifer mourra,
		et on verra,
		on verra qui sera le plus fatigué,
		de lui
221.		ou de moi,
222.		—la terre et le sexe sont en nous,
		dehors, il n'y a que des étoiles,
223.	**No Dialogue**	
224.		—vouloir, n'est pas s'étendre par la force,
225.		mais se renverser, de plus en plus en soi,
226.		d'étage
227.		en étage, pour l'éternité,
228.	**No Dialogue**	
229.		—on m'a pas besoin d'un trou de bouche pour manger,
230.		et d'un trou de cul pour avaler de l'infini,
		il faut prendre le cul
231.		dans sa tête,
		puis avec le cul dans la tête, descendre
232.		au niveau du cul,
		et s'en aller, à gauche,
233.		oui à droite, pour monter plus loin,
234.	**No Dialogue**	
235.		Dieu est un vampire qui a voulu me souffrir en lui

parce que je souffrais, et qu'il ne souffrait pas,

et que ma douleur lui profitait,

236. **No Dialogue**

237.

—Marie est un corps tombé de l'âme,

moi, je suis une âme prisonnière d'un corps,

mon âme me fait mal au coeur, et c'est mon con,

je suis une femme,

bien que je n'engendre pas mon homme par mon con,

—je suis la joie,

celle qui est la joie et n'a plus à lutter contre elle,

ni être tentée,

mais à gagner une joie de plus,

238. **No Dialogue**

239.

—je ne suis pas résignée, la résignation est triste,

comment se résigner à la volonté de Dieu,

est-ce qu'on se résigne à être aimée?

cela me paraissait clair,

trop clair.

240.–241. **No Dialogue**

Cartons   EN CE TEMPS-LA

242.–263. **No Dialogue**

EN CE TEMPS-LA

264. **No Dialogue**

265. **Joseph**   Oh Marie, quel drôle de chemin

266.   j'ai dû faire pour arriver jusqu'à toi.

267. **Marie**   Qu'est-ce qu'il y a encore?

268. **No Dialogue**

269. **Pere**   Les voilà.

270. **Marie**   Tu y crois maintenant?

Pere   Alors, à Joseph, il va lui dire papa?

Comment tu vas faire,

		plus tard, tu vas lui dire que c'est pas son père?
	Marie	C'est la vie.
	Pere	Joseph.
271.	Joseph	Je suis venu vous parler de la station.
	Pere	On va voir ça.
	Joseph	J'ai calculé, je peux la rembourser en deux ans.
272.	No Dialogue	
273.	Pere	Mais oui.
	Joseph	Non.
	Marie	Papa, Joseph.
	Femme	Je te remercie, Marie.
	Marie	Ah oui, pourquoi?
	Femme	Pour toutes les femmes. (pas très audible)
274.–279.	No Dialogue	
280.	Marie	Comment était-il, à qui ressemblait-il?
		Dans l'amour, on ne voit rien,
		ni regard, ni trait,
281.		ni ressemblance,
		non, nos coeurs trembleront seulement dans la lumière,
282.		je ne pourrai jamais vous le décrire tel qu'il était là,
		mais je puis vous dire ce que firent toutes les femmes en l'apercevant.
	Enfant	Viens avec moi,
		venez avec moi,
		comment tu t'appelles?
	Autre Enfant	Fabien.
	Enfant	Maintenant tu t'appelleras Pierre, et toi, comment tu t'appelles?
	Autre Enfant	Florent.
	Enfant	Maintenant tu t'appelleras Jacques.
	Autre Enfant	Et moi, comment je m'appelles?
283.	Joseph	Alors, ça vient ce café, je suis pressé.
	Enfant	Alors ça vient ce café, alors ça vient ce café, alors ça vient ce café?

	Marie	Non, les petits garçons sont gentils, ce matin, sinon ce soir on jouera pas à la baleine.
	Enfant	Si, si, maman,
284.		à la baleine,
		ça, ça s'appelle comment?
	Marie	Le hérisson, ou la prairie.
	Enfant	Ca, ça s'appelle comment?
	Marie	Les cloches.
	Enfant	Ca, ça s'appelle comment?
	Marie	Les miches, ou le pain.
	Joseph	Il faut arrêter de te montrer toute nue avec lui maintenant.
	Marie	Quia respexit, Joseph.
285.	Joseph	Un jour, tu sais,
		peut-être que celui qui es ton père t'abandonnera,
		alors tu regretteras que je sois pas là.
286.	Marie	Regarde-moi.
287.	Enfant	Je suis celui qui est.
	Joseph	Allez, pas d'histoires, monte derrière.
288.	Enfant	Non,
		il faut que je m'occupe des affaires de mon père.
	Joseph	Nom de Dieu, on va voir ça.
	Marie	Non, arrête.
		il reviendra.
	Joseph	Quand?
	Marie	A Pâques,
289.		ou à la Trinité.
290.–292.	No Dialogue	
293.	L'Ange	Madame,
		hé Madame.

	Marie	Oui, quoi?
294.	**L'Ange**	Rien, je vous salue, Marie.
295.–297.	**No Dialogue**	
298.	**Marie**	Moi, je suis de la Vierge,
		et je n'ai pas voulu de cet être,
299.		j'ai marqué l'âme qui m'a aidée, c'est tout.
300.	**No Dialogue**	

Index